The War on the Poor

THE WAR
ON THE POOR

CLARENCE B. CARSON

ARLINGTON HOUSE   NEW ROCHELLE, N.Y.

Contents

Preface

There is a sense in which the work which follows is autobiographical. That is a peculiar remark to make about a book which deals primarily with the economic history of the United States in the last several decades. Yet, it is so. I first began to become aware of things going on beyond family and friends in the midst of the Great Depression. (Indeed, one of the early adult remarks I remember that puzzled me had to do with banks closing. What could that mean? I had no idea, for the only bank I knew about was the ditch bank along the side of the road.) I grew up on a farm, and very early began to hear talk of various government programs. Though I did not evaluate the information at the time, I was vaguely aware that farming became less and less profitable in the course of the 1930's. People were leaving the farms to go to work in factories. Some farmers went deeper and deeper into debt year after year.

Here was an enigma. The government seemed to make ever greater efforts to help farmers. But the more they "helped," the more difficult it became to continue farming. Farmers even advanced theories to explain this untoward development. Those in governmental power meant well, they said, but the aid was short-circuited along the way. For many years, the facts which went to make-up the enigma lay dormant. I studied history, taught it, and began to write it. I became interested in economics, and eventually was assigned the task of teaching the economic history of the United States. I puzzled at the enigma until I began to get an inkling of the explanation. The government was, however unwittingly, making a kind of war on farmers with its programs. That is the biographical germ of the idea. The extension of it into all sorts of other areas of economic activity follows from an awareness of the nature of government activity and economic principles.

Yet, there is a sense in which what follows is only very partially my work. I have relied heavily upon the researches and interpretation of a host of scholars and commentators. It is doubtful that any one man could perform the immense amount of research which goes to support the conclusions of this book in a life time. Certainly, I have not done so. Many others had done it for me. I have given them credit in footnotes and will not repeat the information here. Without the work of many others, this one of synthesis would not have been done. What I have not credited are those works and those people from whom I have learned what of economic principles I know. I would like to single out Leonard Read's Foundation for Economic Education for the contribution it has made to my understanding. Moreover, portions of Chapter III were taken from *The Flight From Reality*, published serially in their journal, *The Freeman* (October 1964 through November 1966). Also, my colleague, Dr. Hans Sennholz has perservered over the years in instructing me in economic matters, and I availed myself from time to time of his learning in dealing with points taken up in the book.

There are some more particular obligations, too, which I made in preparing this work. Miss Jane Rees provided much assistance with her researches in newspapers and periodicals. Misses Nancy Ollinger and Sandra Birnley undertook the unenviable task of rendering my scratches on typescript into beautifully typed manuscripts. Messrs. Timothy Wheeler and Llewellyn Rockwell of Arlington House have assisted materially both by their generous approval of what was submitted and by making the work a congruous whole editorially.

Let me hasten to add that none of these people is responsible for any errors which may appear herein. Those are mine alone. Nor should their assistance be construed as approval of the interpretations made in the book. That burden is mine.

My wife, Myrtice Sears Carson, should be given much credit for the work ever having been done. Not only did she bear gracefully the inconveniences which attend living with one who writes, but she read copy faithfully through several typescripts, and insisted that what was written be made to make sense.

CLARENCE B. CARSON
Grove City, Pennsylvania
January, 1969

The War on the Poor

CHAPTER I

The Poor: Victims of Good Intentions

O N March 16, 1964, President Lyndon B. Johnson sent a special message to Congress asking for a declaration of war: a declaration of War on Poverty. The phrase cropped up early in his message:

> We have come a long way toward this goal.
> We still have a long way to go.
> The distance which remains is the measure of the great unfinished work of our society.
> To finish that work I have called for a national war on poverty. Our objective: total victory.

He claimed that such a conflict had been going on for a long time in American history, going back perhaps as far as the founding of the nation. His program, he would have us believe, would be part and parcel of an age long effort to extend opportunity in America. As he said,

> The war on poverty is a further step in that pursuit.[1]

[1] *Public Papers of the Presidents of the United States: Lyndon B. Johnson, 1963-64*, I (Washington: U. S. Government Printing Office, 1965), 376.

These and other prefatory remarks were followed by descriptions of particular proposals for the conflict ahead. His concluding remarks are particularly interesting, for they describe the struggle in the conventional terms of war:

> It will . . . give us the chance to test our weapons, to try our energy and ideas and imagination for the many battles yet to come. As conditions change, and as experience illuminates our difficulties, we will be prepared to modify our strategy.
>
> And this program is much more than a beginning.
>
> Rather it is a commitment. It is a total commitment by this President, and this congress, and this nation, to pursue victory over the most ancient of mankind's enemies.
>
> On many historic occasions the President has requested from Congress the authority to move against forces which were endangering the well-being of our country.
>
> This is such an occasion.
>
> On similar occasions in the past we have often been called upon to wage war against foreign enemies which threatened our freedom. Today we are asked to declare war on a domestic enemy which threatens the strength of our nation and the welfare of our people.[2]

The goal of War on Poverty is, we are told, the Great Society. The course of the war has not been smooth, and one wonders if it has brought us closer to that goal. Every skirmish, not to mention the major battles, has been greeted by startling revelations, examples of malfeasance, allegations of corruption, charges of misuse of funds, and so on. The Job Corps has been charged with coddling delinquents and with expenditures out of all proportion to accomplishments. Poverty funds have been the object of unseemly and acrimonious debates between new organizations and old party leaders at the local level. Poverty workers have engaged in the most blatant agitation and participated in street demonstrations. So many are the problems and so flagrant some of the abuses that critics are having a field day. Nor is the criticism partisan only; some members of the President's own party appear near

[2] *Ibid.*, p. 380.

revolt. After more than two years of helping to get the President's programs through Congress, Senator Abraham A. Ribicoff, a Democrat and, in general, an advocate of ubiquitous government, characterized the Johnson administration in these harsh words: "It's frozen, afraid of new ideas, unwilling to admit some of its programs won't work."[3]

Much, if not all, such criticism is superficial, however. At most, it rarely goes beyond the assertion that "some" of the programs "won't work." Criticism is usually along one or more of three lines: one, that the government is trying to do too many things too fast, that there are too many programs too hastily conceived; two, that the programs need to be more carefully administered; and three, that not nearly enough money is being spent to attain the objects sought. On the last point, one publication reports that in 1966 Martin Luther King called for an expenditure of $10 billion by the Federal government to wipe out poverty, Bayard Rustin for $185 billion, and Michael Harrington, official prophet of the poverty war, for a cool one trillion dollars.[4] So long as the examination of the programs is superficial, or piecemeal, it is all too easy to turn the criticisms to arguments for larger expenditures.

What follows is intended as an examination of the effects of such programs over a short span of history. It will not be concerned with abuses and corruption except as they inhere in the nature of the programs themselves. It will start with the basic premises on which the programs are founded and examine the results in the light of the claims. There will be no gratuitous assumptions that if the programs were better administered, more cautiously undertaken, or more heavily financed that they would achieve their objects. Each of these assumptions must be discounted before any useful examination can be made of results. Otherwise, this bias—for that is what such assumptions add up to—can be continued from now until doomsday without ever having been brought to ac-

---

[3] Washington *Post* (December 3, 1966), section A, p. 4.
[4] *National Review Bulletin*, vol. 18, no. 5 (Dec. 20, 1966), p. 3.

count. Undoubtedly, the War on Poverty could be better administered, could be more cautiously undertaken, and could be more sumptuously financed. These will remain as possibilities as long as there are such programs administered by human beings from the limited wealth on this planet. But if we await perfection in these matters before evaluating the programs they will remain forever unevaluated.

The following premises will serve as bases for evaluation. First of all, the War on Poverty is not new. The rhetoricians of President Johnson have produced the phrase to describe programs similar in kind and with the same end in view to others that have been around for quite a while. Franklin D. Roosevelt began his own "war on poverty" in his Second Inaugural Address delivered in January of 1937, and in this he only made more explicit what had underlain earlier action. He said, in part:

> . . . In this nation I see tens of millions of its citizens—a substantial part of its whole population—who at this very moment are denied the greater part of what the very lowest standards of today call the necessities of life.
>
> I see millions of families trying to live on incomes so meager that the pall of family disaster hangs over them day by day.
>
> I see millions whose daily lives in city and on farm continue under conditions labeled indecent by a so-called polite society half a century ago.
>
> I see millions denied education, recreation, and the opportunity to better their lot and the lot of their children.
>
> I see millions lacking the means to buy the products of farm and factory and by their poverty denying work and productiveness of many other millions.
>
> I see one-third of a nation ill-housed, ill-clad, ill-nourished.
>
> It is not in despair that I paint you that picture. I paint it for you in hope—because the Nation, seeing and understanding the injustice in it, proposes to paint it out.[5]

[5] Franklin D. Roosevelt, *Nothing to Fear*, Ben D. Zevin, ed. (New York: Popular Library, 1961), p. 105.

In short, Roosevelt saw poverty widespread in the land and proposed governmental programs to remove it. The antecedents of the War on Poverty go back much beyond the New Deal, but the story of that can wait. The point here is that about the only thing new about the War on Poverty is the phrase itself. (Such programs have been around quite long enough for the results to have been in—long since.)

Secondly, the purpose of the War on Poverty has been to help the poor. Many other motives may indeed have been at work—for example, politicians desiring to be re-elected—, but for purposes of evaluating results the impact of the programs on the poor will be the sole, or major, consideration.

Thirdly, it is alleged that the poor can be helped by positive government action. This claim has been used to advance hundreds of programs and even now feeds the fires that produce the bureaucratic energy behind the multiplying programs of the War on Poverty. According to the claims, government can produce full employment, raise incomes, manipulate the currency, establish minimum wages, shorten hours of work, restrict agricultural production, provide social security—all this, and much more, to the great advantage particularly of the poor.

Fourthly, politicians who advance such programs are frequently described as pragmatic. That is, they are supposed to test their programs by their workability. The programs themselves are alleged to be experiments, and, like any other experiment, their results are expected to lead to proof or disproof of the hypothesis. The method is useful; it is one of the means for testing a thing. It is certainly appropriate, too, that government programs which parade as being pragmatic should be tested by their workability—that is, by the extent to which they produce the results sought or not.

These, then, are the premises upon which the examination of poverty programs will proceed: that present programs are extensions or additions to those of a similar nature that have been going on for quite some time; that the purpose of the

War on Poverty has been and is to help the poor; that those who have advanced such programs have done so on the assumption that government can intervene in the economy in ways to aid the poor generally; and that the programs should be tested by whether they achieve the results sought or not.

Much of the body of this work will be devoted to examination and accounts of particular programs, but some introduction to what will be encountered is in order. In the main, what will be encountered—what this writer has encountered in his research—is a set of contradictions; contradictions between stated purposes and end results, contradictions between prognoses and the fate of the patients, contradictions between expectations and fulfillments. A few preliminary examples will serve to introduce the phenomena.

ITEM:

A large portion of the people of the world live in more or less abject poverty. Leaving out of account those under Communism, poverty is so widespread as to be virtually universal in India, in Pakistan, in the Moslem countries of the Near East, in most of Africa, and in nearly all the countries of Latin America. One third (or is it one half?) of the world's people are said to go to bed hungry at night. For years now the leaders in American government have professed their concern for the poor, not only in the United States but also around the world. The War on Poverty, as Johnson describes it, is to be worldwide.

Yet here is the contradiction. Despite the need for food in so many places in the world, millions upon millions of acres of arable land lie idle in America. Nor is this something separate from government policy. The United States government has deliberately produced much of this by crop restrictions over many years, and more recently by actually paying farmers to take their lands out of cultivation. Government price supports have priced many American goods out of the world market, and surpluses accumulate of products that can nowhere find buyers. Does concern for the world's poor express itself in such action?

ITEM:

Everybody likes a sale. Shoppers flock in great numbers to reputable stores when they are having sales. Sometimes stores will announce very great reductions on a limited number of valuable items. It is not unheard of in such circumstances for some people to stay in line all night to be the first in the store when it opens in the morning. A sale is a reduction in price, if it is as advertised. To say that everybody likes a sale is tantamount to saying that everyone likes a decline in prices. There is no mystery about this: lower prices mean that people can purchase more goods than they otherwise could with the funds they have available. They mean that the purchasing power of one's assets is increased proportionately.

Yet—and herein lies the contradiction—those in the government have for years conspired to raise prices. They have inflated the currency, mainly by way of the Federal Reserve system. They have restricted agricultural production, used price supports, established minimum wages, supported union monopolies, established prices as in transportation—all of which have had the impact of raising prices or, on occasion, maintaining them at artificially high levels. These policies weigh particularly heavily on the poor who have the most limited assets and may be expected to suffer the most from any rise in prices. With such friends in high places, the poor could hardly endure enemies!

price increase

ITEM:

Farm programs have been undertaken for the supposed purpose of rescuing the small farmer, for helping the poor to stay on the land, for balancing the rural and urban population of the country, and particularly to aid the rural poor. Let Franklin D. Roosevelt describe the purpose in the words which he used in his first inaugural address in 1933:

Hand in hand with this [putting people to work] we must frankly recognize the overbalance of population in our industrial centers and, by engaging on a national scale in a redistribution, endeavor to provide a better use of the land for those best fitted for the land. The task can be helped by definite efforts to raise the values of agricultural products and with this the power to purchase the output of our cities. . . . It can be helped by insistence that the Federal, State, and local Governments act forthwith on the demand that their [farms and homes] cost be drastically reduced. . . . It can be helped by national planning for and supervision of all forms of transportation and of communications and other utilities which have a definitely public character.[6]

Numerous farm programs have been enacted over the years with the supposed purpose of achieving the above ends. Acreage has been restricted, prices supported, loans made, arid lands irrigated, transportation of agricultural products controlled, and so on.

The results have been quite otherwise than predicted, quite often the diametric opposite. If the population was overbalanced in industrial centers in 1933, one wonders how it would be described in 1968: Under the ministrations that have followed government intervention rural population has declined precipitately. In 1933, according to one writer, there were about 32 million people living on farms, a figure that had not changed much since 1910, amounting to about one fourth of the population of the United States in 1933. "By 1940 farm population had dropped to 30 million, or 23 per cent of all Americans. In the 1950 census only 23 million persons were counted on farms, and they amounted to just 15 per cent of the total population; and by 1961 the number had declined to less than 15 million, a mere 8 per cent of the total population of the United States."[7]

What of the poor farmers who were supposed to be helped?

[6] *Ibid.*, p. 28.
[7] Julius Duscha, *Taxpayer's Hayride* (Boston: Little, Brown and Co., 1964), p. 67.

Have they been? If a consensus were taken of those who have studied the problem recently, the conclusion would probably be that they have not been. Regarding who gets the subsidies that are paid out, a recent writer says:

> In the 1960's the commercial sector of the farm economy in which nearly all of the $5 billion in subsidies were being poured each year constituted a highly specialized and heavily capitalized but sharply declining number of Americans—the two million plus farmers who were growing 85 per cent of all the food and fiber.
>
> The other 1.6 million farms . . . were receiving few of the subsidy benefits.[8]

In short, the small farmer, far from being rescued, is swiftly ceasing to exist. How this has come about cannot here be suggested, but there is a relationship between the programs and rural poverty.

ITEM:

According to union lore, labor unions are supposed to be instruments in the class struggle against employers and management. They are supposed to balance the power of wealth in the hands of employers with their own power of numbers. The United States government has for a long time lent its weight to union organizations, by exempting them from anti-trust prosecution, by setting up a National Labor Relations Board, by the promotion of arbitration, and in other ways. This was done on the assumption that government was aiding the underdog against the power of wealth.

Yet anyone who has witnessed a violent strike should have seen the contradiction. In this case, almost all eyes appear to be blinded by ideology. The violence is not usually perpetrated against owners and managers. It is not their houses that are bombed, their automobiles that paint is thrown upon, they who are shot at, or they who are assaulted at the gates.

[8] *Ibid.*, p. 68.

Instead, it is other workers, or would-be workers. True, they are called "strikebreakers" and "scabs." These are but ingenuous names, however, names to hide the fact that some men wish to work at the wages being offered and under the conditions that prevail. Usually, they must be the poor, the unemployed, those seeking an opportunity and willing to work. It is against these that the union wrath is directed. The weight of the United States government lies behind this most obvious assault upon the poor.

ITEM:

The poor appear to be the victims quite often of even those government programs not particularly supposed to aid them. The interstate highway program is an example. Has anyone noticed what part of cities these highways go through, if they go through cities? For the most part, they go through those areas where the poorest inhabitants live. There may be financial and logistic reasons for this tendency, but these do not change the fact that it is the poor who have their communities sundered, their houses torn down, their neighborhoods forever destroyed, and their lives disrupted. New housing is difficult to find, apt to be more expensive than the old, and inconvenient to places of employment.

Highways destroy poor peoples housing

ITEM:

One other item will complete the impressions here. It was once claimed that much, if not most, of the direct relief and aid to individuals and families was a temporary expedient, a necessity born of depression, or what not. The numerous other programs were supposed to remove the need for the dole. Farmers were to be made independent; workers were to become self-sustaining; social security was to provide for the aged; and a revived economy would take care of most of those who had once to be directly aided.

Yet it has not worked that way. A book published in 1964 points out that "the scourge of massive unemployment is gone, but the relief problem remains. Programs have expanded and the number in need continues to increase. Since 1953 expenditures for public assistance almost doubled and the number of recipients rose about 40 per cent. Families in trouble have paced that increase. . . ." The author goes on to give a graphic example from his own experience of the extent of the direct relief. "When I was employed as a caseworker in Buffalo's Erie County, the relief budget pushed past the total amount of money needed to educate every child in the city's public schools. It has been ahead ever since."[9]

The thesis of this work is that the War on Poverty is in reality a war on the poor. The main body of what follows will be concerned with the evidence as it bears upon this thesis. The phrase War on Poverty is made into a generic term, then, to refer to programs of government intervention over the years with the avowed intention of aiding the poor. Such programs go back approximately one hundred years in the history of the United States, though the bulk of them have been enacted within the last forty years. But for purposes of setting the stage for the more recent it will be useful to go back to their beginnings and trace them to the present, at least in outline form. This will indicate also that the War on Poverty has been a war on the poor all along.

Government intervention in economic matters did not begin one hundred years ago, of course. All of history is replete with instances of it, and modern history has a much longer background of intervention than a century. But the purposes of intervention have changed over the years; much more than the actual methods, I suspect. And it was about a century ago that government began to intervene for the supposed aid of the poor, though only in a very limited way for a long time. Before that, intervention had usually had other objects in view.

Two related topics will be dealt with first before proceeding

[9] Edgar May, *The Wasted Americans* (New York: New American Library, 1964), pp. 17-18.

to the main business of tracing the story of the government programs and their results. In part, these topics will provide a background to what follows, and, in part, they will answer some questions which otherwise would be left hanging. The questions are these. Why have programs that were supposed to benefit the poor so universally failed of their object? Or, what is it about poverty that makes it so resistant to amelioration by government action? Why have so many believed that government action could improve the situation? And, why have those bent on this course so signally failed to evaluate the evidence and perceive the untoward results? So far as background goes, these two topics will provide us with a brief examination of the nature of poverty and of the intellectual background to the ameliorative programs.

CHAPTER II

The Nature of Poverty

Concisely stated, the reason for the War on Poverty's inevitably becoming a war on the poor is that the government intervention misleads the poor as to what sorts of endeavors are economical. The poor, more than anyone else, imperatively need to act with the greatest economy. They have the fewest resources to invest and need the largest return from them. Government intervention distorts the situation and obscures what action would be most nearly economical. The point may become clearer by an analysis of the nature of poverty, the nature of economy, the nature of war, and the nature of government.

It may be helpful initially to indicate what poverty is not. In the first place, it is not an evil, or, at least, it has not been so considered through the ages. In Christian teaching, wealth and affluence have been described as offering much more dangerous temptations and pitfalls than have poverty. Indeed, those who have devoted themselves to lives of greatest purity have often deliberately taken upon themselves the condition of poverty. Monks and nuns in the Roman Catholic church have usually taken vows of poverty, as well as of chastity and obedience. In more sophisticated circles, the phrase "involuntary poverty" has been concocted to exempt those who deliberately choose poverty from the War on Poverty. It might be appropriate to denominate monks and nuns as "conscientious objectors" to the War. But in the popular political effort no attention is called to the possibility that virtue may attach to the condition.

It may be well to note, too, that men may choose to be poor on other than religious grounds. They may prefer poverty to onerous toil, to moving to a new location, to the discipline involved in saving or in acquiring skills, or for other reasons. If the pretensions of those who declare war on poverty were to be taken seriously, they would have to be understood as meaning that once the victory had been won no one would be permitted to be poor any more.

Second, poverty is not a being. Ontologically, it does not have the same standing as a bear, a dog, a house, a farm, a man, or any other corporeal being. Nor is it of the character of a collection of these, i.e., of a pack of wolves, a city, a tribe, or a country. The point is most important. If poverty were a body, or a collection of bodies, it could be made war upon, though it might not be desirable to do so. The nature of war is such that it must be waged against actual beings. War involves, in case we have forgotten, the employment of armies, navies, artillery, mortars, rifles, bazookas, bombs, and other explosives against an enemy in the field. Since poverty is not a being, it is not at all clear how troops can be arrayed against it, artillery aimed at it, or bombs dropped upon it. It should be obvious that war cannot be made upon something incorporeal.

It may be objected that those who speak of a "war" on poverty are speaking figuratively. They do not mean to conduct an actual war, to use artillery or mortars against it, to send an army into the field to overcome it. Is the War on Poverty, then, only a figure of speech? Have politicians turned poets in our day? The point should not be so readily granted. Even metaphors have a way of containing unsuspected truth when used by those who do not take care in their use of language.

As a matter of fact, governments do use force or the threat of force in their operations. It is the nature of government to use force. Government uses force (or the threat of it) to apprehend law violaters, to punish those found guilty, to collect taxes, to enforce its programs, and to wage war. Any major offensive by government against an enemy could be called war, by extension at least, for any major offensive by government would be a large scale use of force; and that is at least one of the identifying features of war. Nor should it be doubted that a major offensive, and a large scale use of force, has been mounted in the War on Poverty. Taxes are levied, numerous agents of government sent into the field, laws enacted, and force employed. But against whom or what?—that is the question. Force can only be used effectively against bodies of one kind or another. Poverty is not a body; thus, it is possible to know from the outset that whatever the war is being forcibly waged against, it is not poverty.

This becomes even clearer when poverty is defined. One dictionary defines poverty as "the condition of being poor with respect to money, goods, or means of subsistence." It says, further, that poverty "denotes serious lack of the means for proper existence: *living in a state of extreme poverty.*" Poverty, then, is a *state* or *condition*, not, as has been pointed out, a being.

It is analogous to such other states or conditions as hunger, pain, and fever. Each of these may have different sensations associated with it, but they are all alike in nature. Poverty, hunger, pain, and fever are analogous to one another in that they are general conditions. Even more important, they are alike in being signs or signals. Hunger is a sign that the body craves food, pain the sign that something has penetrated, struck, or is attacking the body from without or within, and fever the sign of disease. Poverty is a sign, too, but let that wait for a bit.

It would be foolhardy in the extreme for government to

attempt to abolish hunger, pain, or fever. If hunger were abolished, we would all starve, since we would not receive the signal of our need. If pain were abolished, we would lose a most important source of knowledge about what is going on within or without our bodies. If fever were abolished, many, if not most, would die from diseases because of the lack of a signal, as well as losing whatever benefits there may be in the power of high temperature to heal the body.

There is another vital way in which fever and poverty are alike. Neither of them has a specific cause. In general, fever is caused by an infection. But the infection can be caused by many different species of germs. An attack, even by government, could be launched against the carriers of a particular germ, as, for example, the carrier of typhoid, and a program of innoculation against the disease can be financed by government. But such an attack is not on fever; it is upon *typhoid* fever. In like manner it can be said that poverty has, in general, a single economic cause. But the specific causes are as varied and numerous as there are poor people. Analogy must be carefully used, however; it does not follow that because of these similarities government can be used to attack the specific causes of poverty.

The essential similarities of hunger, pain, fever, and poverty are that they are all *signals*. Hunger, pain, and fever are most important signals for maintaining bodily health; poverty is an equally important signal for economic health or well being. If men get the fruits of their labor, poverty is one of the signs of the lack of productivity. Poverty indicates, in general, the low productivity of an individual or family. More specifically, the condition of poverty is a sign that an individual or family is non-productive, produces very little, produces commodities or provides services for which there is little or no demand, or produces something or offers a service in an area where there is little or no market for it. In general, again, poverty indicates to those in that condition who wish to become more prosperous that they should increase their pro-

poventy is a sign of lack of productivity

ductivity, learn some new skill or offer some new service, change their location, and so on.

Again, poverty is a sign of economic failure, just as prosperity is a sign of economic success. Economics has to do with the most effective means of employing one's resources so as to increase the supply of goods and services at one's command. Political economy deals with the legal conditions within which one may receive the rewards of his labor. If the conditions of political economy prevail, then the extent of one's poverty is the measure of one's failure to employ his resources (such as they may be) sufficiently well to make him prosperous. It should be clear that the mental or physical debility of an individual may be so severe that he either has no resources to employ or that he will be forever (or temporarily) incapable of employing them so as to improve his condition. For such a person to receive the rewards of his labor would mean anything from starvation to varying degrees of poverty. Since even those who are in some way disabled vary as to the degree of their disability, so it follows that the degree of their poverty will vary.

A notion to which some economists subscribe must be discarded. The notion is that if prosperity is general in society this will alleviate poverty, or bring prosperity, for everyone. This is not so, nor can it be so. Poverty is particular and personal, just as prosperity is particular and personal. It is true that general prosperity contributes to the availability of *useful* employment and return from it, but general prosperity, so long as one is dependent upon the rewards of his labor, cannot benefit those who do not labor, nor prevent men from failing because of the misapplication of their resources.

Can poverty be abolished, then? Jesus said not. In a much quoted passage, he said: "For you always have the poor with you. . . ."[1] This statement is not a particular favorite of many contemporary churchmen, and it is not in accord with a prevailing mode of thought. Churchmen of past centuries have

[1] Matthew 26:11.

Poor will
always be around

often been belabored in our time for using this passage as an excuse for opposing social reform. In 1964, the Council of Economic Advisers (to the President) proclaimed that the statement is not true. They said:

> There will always be some Americans who are better off than others. But it need not follow that "the poor are always with us." In the United States today we can see on the horizon a society of abundance, free of much of the misery and degradation that have been the age-old fate of man.[2]

Dean John C. Bennett attempts to dispose of the theological problem in this way: "Jesus' own words: 'for you always have the poor with you' have always been a comfort to those who do not want to change the institutions but these words at the time were no more than a common sense observation about the world as it was."[3] Professor Bennett does not give us the authority for his conclusion that a statement universal in form is really an historical observation. Even if he could, there would be this rejoinder: One may still make the common sense observation in the Year of Our Lord 1968 that the poor we have with us always. That is, so far as my historical information goes, the poor have always been with us. Even in prosperous America, the poor must still be with us, else why the War on Poverty? Nor is there any evidence on record that a change in institutions will succeed in abolishing poverty. There is widespread poverty in those lands that have made the most drastic changes in institutions (e.g., Cuba, the Soviet Union, China, and so on.).

It is possible, of course, to think of the matter in such a way as to convince oneself that poverty could be abolished. Illusions and mirages are so common that we all have heard of or experienced them. For example, it is possible to press one's finger against the eyeball in such a way as to induce an optical illusion. In the same manner, the mind can be made to sus-

---

[2] Robert E. Will and Harold G. Vatter, eds., *Poverty in Affluence* (New York: Harcourt, Brace and World, 1965), p. 11.

[3] *Ibid.*, p. 269.

pend the data which it is considering in such a way that it will
appear possible to eliminate poverty. One may by working
with statistical abstractions calculate how poverty could be
abolished in America. It is possible to take the "national
income" (an abstraction arrived at by adding up the incomes
of Americans), divide it by the total population, and show
that if each of us got an equal share there would no longer be
any poverty in America. Or, the goods and services produced
and provided in a year in America might be divided among
the population in such a way that there would no longer be
poverty.

That those who calculate in this way are working within an
illusion should be clear to everyone, though apparently it is
not. The illusion is that the production of a people is separate
or separable from the conditions which move people to produce. It is only in the imagination that the fruits of production
can be taken from those who produce them and divided
equally among the population and that those who have produced will continue to do so at their present level. To the
extent that such a redistribution reduced the incentives to production—an extent close to one hundred per cent—it would
produce widespread and universal poverty in short order.
While the makers of War on Poverty in America rely upon
the illusion that production can be maintained when the incentives have been removed or reduced, they are not so rash
as to propose an equal distribution of the "national income,"
not all at once, at any rate. Instead, they speak of poverty as a
limited phenomenon—existing in "pockets"—and hold that it
can be eliminated by much less drastic measures. Only *some*
of the wealth of Americans must be redistributed, *some* programs adopted, and poverty will recede before gradual ministrations. The principle is the same, but the consequences are
delayed and made more difficult to detect by the gradualism.

Poverty cannot be eliminated (though, interestingly
enough, prosperity can be). If men receive the fruits of their
labor, poverty is, in general, the failure to produce what is

wanted in sufficient quantity to rise above the level of poverty.

Poverty cannot be eliminated, in the first place, because there are those who are incapacitated by reason of age or infirmity from producing enough to sustain them in affluence. They can be made affluent by government action only by taking from those who produce and giving to those who do not. Such action would result in greatly increasing the incentives for attaining the status of infirmity or incapacity, and reduce in proportion the incentives of being productive. Rather than eliminating poverty, the effect would be the universalizing of it as production declined.

In the second place, poverty cannot be eliminated because much of it is the result of poor management or investment of energy, materials, and capital. In the best of circumstances, some investments turn out to have been unwarranted speculations. Even the wisest of men misjudge the potentialities of the situation on occasion, overestimate the market for a product, enter businesses when demand is declining, carry too large inventories, and so on. At worst, some men's enterprises invariably fail. The poverty which results from malinvestments could only be eliminated by guaranteeing all investments. This would not, however, eliminate poverty, it would only bankrupt the guarantor. It would be an attempt to eliminate the consequences of actions. If this could be done it would only succeed in making it impossible to know what was economic and what was not. There would follow a universal waste of resources which would result in poverty.

In short, the possibility of poverty is an essential condition for economic behavior. Without poverty, one of the crucial signs of what is economic and what is not would be removed. The poor we *will* have with us always; the poor we *must* have with us always.

All of us are under the necessity of acting economically if we wish to improve our material well being. It is especially important for the poor to act economically. Economics has to do with the allocation of the short supply of capital, labor, and materials so as to make the greatest increase of goods and services at our disposal. The wealthy, depending upon the extent of their wealth, can be improvident in disposing of capital, labor, and materials for a considerable period of time. It is not so with the poor. They need to get the most out of the small amount of capital and materials they have when their labor is added to them. They need to effect the greatest increase in production at their disposal. They need to know as quickly as possible the consequences of their endeavors. They cannot afford costly mistakes in investment, and the poor who labor *are* investors. The poor need the widest possible opportunity for their endeavors, to be able to buy as inexpensively as possible and to sell in the market where they can get the highest return. Every economic signal needs to be available to them as clearly and as quickly as possible.

The above are reasons why, at the most obvious level, the War on Poverty is a war on the poor especially. Government intervention in the economy produces distorted signs from the market. Any attempt to eliminate poverty by government action interferes with the signaling devices by which men calculate where to invest their time and money. If government subsidizes this, makes grants for that, offers a bounty for one thing, ameliorates the consequences of effort for another, all sorts of false signs abound to lead the unwary astray. The rich man may hire a clutch of experts to help him wind his way successfully through the maze of government programs. The poor do not have the resources to do this, plus the fact that they are likely to be the most unsophisticated and ignorant portion of the population. They are easily victimized in an increasingly complex situation. It is a common observation that the wealthy quite often benefit from government programs—quite often, indeed, they may be the only apparent beneficiaries. It is equally common for those who interpret such phenomena to rush to the conclusion that the laws were perverted to such an end by "selfish interests" who hired lobbyists or otherwise influenced legislation. This certainly need not have been the case, though it sometimes may be. It must be understood, however, that government intervention, however acutely and humanely conceived, increases the complexity of operating in an economy. It makes the signs more difficult to read, offers much greater opportunity for some men to benefit at the expense of others, and has the most devastating effect on the poor.

The poor are often drawn deeply into the lines of uneconomic activity before they become aware of the mistake, enticed there by supposedly benevolent government programs. They may decide to take up farming because the government is offering free land, not realizing that the additional production will increase the supply of farm produce and reduce the price. With the supplement of government subsidies a farmer may continue to eke out a bare livelihood on his land long after he should have abandoned it for some other endeavor. Eventually, the economics of the situation catches up with each of us, but government intervention can delay the final accounting so long that many of the poor lose all hope of bettering their situation by their own efforts. Governmental programs aimed at eliminating poverty quite often produce the very indigence which they are supposed to remove.

In sum, government cannot make war on poverty. Poverty is incorporeal and inaccessible to the force which government can bring to bear. If poetic language were in order, it would be more nearly correct to say that the government has been making war on economy. This is true enough, so far as it goes, but economy is no more corporeal than is poverty, and no more accessible to government power. Men continue to behave economically, as best they can, even in the face of the government assault. The difference is twofold. In the first place, as has been noted, it becomes much more difficult to discern what is economic. And secondly, government programs quite often make it individually economical to do what is socially harmful. Thus, even the war on economy is subverted by human beings.

In the final analysis, then, the War on Poverty is largely a
war on the poor. Such a war can be conducted. The poor are
bodies; they can be made war upon. Government can tax
them, mislead them, subject them to propaganda, use force
against them and, in fact, conquer them. That this is, in large,
what has been going on in America, it is the burden of this
work to prove and demonstrate.

Before proceeding to a more detailed demonstration of
this, however, there are some matters to get out of the way.
Among these, one that is most germane is the matter of helping the poor. To say that government intervention in the
economy is detrimental to the poor is not the same as saying
that no aid may be given to people in need. If a man is hungry, food may be provided for him. If he is exposed to the
elements because of lack of clothing or shelter, these, too,
may be made available to him. If he is unable to provide for
himself because of mental or physical debility, or both, others
may take care of him.

Roughly speaking, the necessities of life may be provided
for those who are in want of them either privately or by governments. Privately, indigent individuals may be taken care of
by their families, by relatives, by benevolent individuals, or by
charitable organizations. Or, governments may provide relief
from tax monies. As such, neither of these approaches are
designed to *eliminate* poverty. They may be only efforts to
relieve or *ameliorate* the effects of being poor. Such efforts
remain relief measures so long as aid is minimal and those
who receive it are supported at a level of bare subsistence.
When governments provide such relief it may be somewhat of
a drain on taxpayers, but its effect on economy tends to be
slight. If, however, governments should attempt to eliminate
poverty by some kind of relief payment device, the effect
would be quite different. The payments would have to be so
large that the recipient would be moved from poverty to affluence. This would not only place a heavy burden on the productive, but it probably would also drastically reduce those
who are productive, for there would be great incentive to

enjoy affluent leisure. Further discussion of the impact of relief can be reserved for the historical examination. The main point here is that relief payments as such are no part of a War on Poverty to eliminate poverty, nor are they directly a part of what I am calling a war on the poor.

A second point to be made is this: By calling a great variety of programs a war on the poor, it is not my intention to engage in "class struggle" pronouncements. There is no implication here that the wealthy have conspired to make war on the poor. Nor does it follow that the wealthy generally have benefited. Indeed, many programs which were supposed to benefit the poor have been financed by virtually confiscatory taxation on the rich. It is true that those who are better off financially have often taken advantage of the programs, some of whom may be even numbered among the very wealthy. But it will be my contention that conventional class analysis tells us very little, if anything, about what is going on. At any rate, this is not a tract devoted to the machinations of some class.

The other point is of such magnitude that it will constitute the subject matter of the following chapter. Namely, the war on the poor has not been the result simply of malice or ill will towards the poor. On the contrary, there is every reason to believe that many of those who have contributed to developing the outlook and the drawing up of programs have been most sincere in their desire to help the poor. In the nature of things, we do not know with certainty what is in the hearts of men. An appearance of sincerity can be faked; men who are most sincere may appear only "corny" to some interpreters. At any rate, it is my intention to give the benefit of every doubt to those who have fostered programs supposed to aid the poor. The results of programs are the same regardless of the intent of those who have enacted them, and it is the results with which we are properly concerned. Moreover, this writer is as convinced as he can be that a reasonable reading of the evidence indicates that many of those who have fostered the government programs have been sincere.

But to grant sincerity raises more questions than it answers. Why would anyone wage war on the poor if they are sincere? Why would they not evaluate the programs in such a way as to see that they are frequently harming those whom they wish to help? Why would patently harmful programs be continued year after year? Why would the poor not rise up in revolt against programs which are harmful to them? In short, what are all the programs about if they are not beneficial to the poor? These questions might have been deferred for much later discussion, if it were not necessary to place the government intervention in its historical perspective from the beginning.

CHAPTER III

The Hundred Year's War

THE CURRENT WAR ON THE POOR GOES BACK WELL INTO THE last century. Any attempt to date with precision the beginning would be somewhat arbitrary, but 1862 has something to commend it. In that year the Homestead Act was passed by Congress. For the first time, the United States government made free land available to the settlers. In the same year a Bureau of Agriculture was created, a Pacific Railway Act was passed authorizing government support for building a transcontinental railroad, and the Morrill Act was passed providing for the endowing of land grant colleges. In 1861, the Morrill Tariff was passed which made tariffs definitely protective. What these acts had to do with starting a war on the poor requires explanation which will be forthcoming in a later chapter. The point here is that the war on the poor has been going on for quite a while, that it has been, loosely, a Hundred Year's War.

But the "War on Poverty"—the phrase used here to refer to the *claims* by which the government intervention is supported; or the "war on the poor"—by which the *results* of the action are described, has proceeded on more than one level.

At the surface level, it has been carried on by legislative acts, by presidential decrees, and under the auspices of bureaus, boards, commissions, and courts. At a deeper level, there has been a contest of ideas in which the ideas supporting the government intervention have been advanced and have eventually come to dominate. The government action is, in a sense, a reflection of ideological predilections which have become dominant.

It is necessary to explore something of the ideological underpinnings of the War on Poverty to get the background of it, to understand why men have come to believe that economic behavior is not necessary, to grasp why it came to be supposed that government could intervene for the benefit of the poor. We must perceive the vision which has impelled such an extended effort, and comprehend why in the face of so many failures there has been such determined persistence. Back of the vast government effort lies a vision of utopia. Accompanying this vision and intertwined with it is an ideology which can be referred to generically as socialism. It is in terms of this ideology's prescriptions that a war on economy has taken place, having had its direst impact on the poor. It is the ideological coloring of reality which leads to a failure to recognize results and correctly evaluate experience.

At this deeper level, the War on Poverty goes back considerably more than a hundred years. It is as old as the vision of taking action to abolish poverty. Robert Owen, Scottish manufacturer and visionary, declared in 1816: "I know that society may be formed so as to exist without crime, without poverty, with health greatly improved, with little, if any, misery, and with intelligence and happiness increased a hundredfold; and no obstacle whatsoever intervenes at this moment, except ignorance, to prevent such a state of society from becoming universal."[1]

But Owen was hardly the first to envision a society without

[1] Quoted in W. H. G. Armitage, *Heavens Below* (London: Routledge and Kegan Paul, 1961), p. 77.

poverty. This vision is none other than the utopian vision. It goes back at least to the early sixteenth century, to the publication from which utopias get their name, Sir Thomas More's *Utopia*. More claimed that "in Utopia, where every man has a right to everything, they all know that if care is taken to keep the public stores full, no private man can want anything; for among them there is no unequal distribution, so that no man is poor, none in necessity; and though no man has anything, yet they are all rich. . . ."[2] If this pronouncement had any but esoteric significance, it would be more nearly correct to describe the War on Poverty as a 400 year's war. But for more than 300 years, Sir Thomas More's work remained largely an exercise of the imagination, with little or no practical import.

Indeed, there is a great gulf between Robert Owen's utopian vision (stated about 150 years ago) of a world without poverty and President Johnson's War on Poverty. To most of his contemporaries, Owen was an impractical visionary, one to be taken advantage of by cynical joiners of his communities or to be avoided by more upstanding people. President Johnson, on the other hand, would certainly be reckoned to be a "practical" politician. The difference between Owen and Johnson is clearly not in the vision they held forth; it is that in the meanwhile many men have apparently come to accept the possibility of poverty's being abolished. The gulf has been bridged. What was once clearly visionary is now being pursued with all the instruments of power of centralized states, and is even the stock in trade of the most corrupt politicians.

Paradoxical as it may be, most people have not consciously accepted the possibility that utopia can actually be achieved. Nor have they been told in so many words that it can be. What has happened has been much more subtle and complex than that. Over the years, Americans have been gradually acclimated to much of the content of the utopian vision with-

---

[2] Quoted in Joyce O. Hertzler, *The History of Utopian Thought* (New York: Macmillan, 1923), p. 135.

out its being called that. They have been led to believe that by
government action *this* improvement can be made, *that* innovation can be introduced, *this* control will improve things,
that commission will better conditions, and so on. They have
been led to believe by politicians that they can have a Square
Deal, a New Freedom, a New Deal, a Fair Deal, a New
Frontier, a Great Society, and, finally, that government can
end poverty and deprivation. The vision is utopia, but the
words are by now the familiar rhetoric of political candi-
dates.

Again, the abolition of poverty is an old socialist dream,
from Morelly and Saint Simon to Karl Marx, Edward Bernstein, and the Webbs, through Eugene Debs, and Norman
Thomas. Socialists have dreamed of a world without tensions,
of societies without hunger, of life without struggle—a world
of peace and plenty. [Though socialists were originally frequent opponents of governments, they, or their descendants,
in the course of time, came to accept governmental power as
the principal means of attaining their ends.] Twentieth century
socialists have, by and large, accepted the necessity and even
desirability of ever larger measures of government power to
achieve the great society of which they dream. Gradualists—
and that is what most socialists are outside of the Communist
Chinese or Soviet spheres, and some within them—are content
to see the great society achieved bit by bit and piece by piece.

How socialist ideology entered into the stream of American
thought to such an extent that it could be a major determinant
of courses of action is a subject too complex and extended to
be entered into in detail here. Except for one strain of the
development, taken up below, only the outline of the process
can be suggested. In the main, it happened in this way. In the
latter part of the nineteenth century and the early twentieth
various American thinkers came under the sway of one or
another facet of the ideology, often from European sources,
where the ideas had far more currency. They developed
various angles of it and fitted it into the American experience.

Among those who adjusted various socialist ideas to the American scene were Lester Frank Ward, Edward Bellamy, Henry Demarest Lloyd, Walter Rauschenbusch, George Herron, Thorstein Veblen, Herbert Croly, John Dewey, Upton Sinclair, Richard Ely, and so on. The muckrakers presented the picture of America in crisis; the social gospellers brought religion to bear on social reform; novelists, such as Jack London, advanced socialist ideas; progressive educationists turned education to the purpose of remaking society; theorists reconstrued democracy so as to make it into a collectivist dogma. Third parties introduced their notions of social reform in their political platforms. And, then, populists and progressives began to advocate various measures which were taken up by major parties. Presidents, such as Theodore Roosevelt and Woodrow Wilson, began to advocate various reforms which had their underpinnings in socialist ideas, though they were not usually referred to in that manner. Since 1933, more and more reforms which had their inception in ideology have become a part of the American legal spectrum.

One aspect of the development and spread of this ideology is most germane to the subject of the war on the poor, and it needs to be examined in greater detail. That aspect has to do with economic thought. The War on Poverty becomes a war on the poor because it is premised on the belief that economy leads to contradictions, that it is undesirable, and that interventions must take place to obviate its bad consequences. The roots of such beliefs are found in the history of economic thought. Before going into that, it will be helpful to get the nature of economics clearly in mind.

Economics has to do with scarcity. This character of economics is indicated by the conventional uses of words related to it. For example, one dictionary defines "economical" as "avoiding waste or extravagance; thrifty." It "implies prudent planning in the disposition of resources so as to avoid unnecessary waste. . . ." To "economize" is to "use sparingly or frugally." "Economy" refers to "thrifty management; frugality

in the expenditure or consumption of money, materials, etc."
Economics can be defined as the study and exposition of the
most effective means for men to maintain and increase the
supply of goods and services at their disposal. These goods
and services are understood to be scarce; and economics has
to do with the frugal management of time, energy, resources,
and materials so as to bring about the greatest increase in the
supply of goods and services most desired.

There is every reason to believe that man is naturally inclined to be economic. That is, he is naturally inclined to use
as little energy and materials to produce as many goods as he
can. If this were not the case, it is easy to believe he would
long since have perished from the face of the earth. But this
penchant gives rise to a social, or economic, or human, problem rather than resolving all problems. The problem arises
in this way. There are two ways for an individual to augment
the supply of goods and services at his disposal. (1) He can
provide them for himself. (2) He can acquire them from
others. Again, there are two ways for an individual to acquire
them from others. (1) He can acquire them by exchange (in
which we may well include free gifts). Or (2), he can take
them from someone who possesses them.

It is this latter option that raises hob in determining what is
economic as well as accounting for what is socially uneconomic behavior on a large scale, despite the fact that men
incline to behave economically. Strictly speaking, robbery can
be quite *economical* for an *individual*. By stealing, an individual can greatly augment the supply of goods and services
available to him with only a very little expenditure of energy
and materials. A bank robber may, for example, spend half
an hour using a twenty dollar gun and enrich himself, say, to
the extent of $20,000.

Of course, we do not describe such behavior as economy;
we call it thievery. By convention, economics is a social study,
not an anti-social one. It deals with how the actual supply of
goods may be increased, not with how one individual may

increase his supply at the expense of others. The bank robber
increases his potential supply of goods at the expense of those
from whom he has stolen. Moreover, he may actually reduce
the general supply by the threat he poses to trade and the loss
of incentive men have to produce when they are uncertain
that they will be able to keep the rewards of their labor. For
these reasons, theft should not be considered economical. By
economy, then, is meant *social economy*, or measures and
actions which actually increase the supply of goods and services. Forceful transfers of goods and services (theft and
slavery) are uneconomic or diseconomic for reasons given.

With the above definitions in mind, a partial summary of
the history of economic thought relevant to the war on the
poor can be given. A great advance in economic thought took
place in the eighteenth century, coming to a peak with the
publication of Adam Smith's *The Wealth of Nations* in
1776. It was only during and after this that economics became a systematic study and discipline. What Smith codified
in his work were conclusions which a great many people were
reaching at about the same time. What Smith held, succinctly,
was that if men pursued their own interest without the use of
force or violence that the results of their efforts would be
useful to all. If they could not use force or fraud, their efforts
would increase the general store of goods. Much of his writing
was devoted to disproving mercantilism, a theory that held
that one country's wealth was obtained at the expense of another. Thus, according to mercantilist theory, trade might be
likened to economic warfare. On the contrary, Smith held
that trade is by nature peaceful, that the wealth of a people is
not obtained at the expense of other peoples, that when peoples of one country trade with those of another, both benefit.
He could see clearly the advantages of specialization. By this,
each people could produce that item or those items which
they could most efficiently produce, and obtain from others
that which they could most effectively produce. He maintained that when trade is free from arbitrarily imposed ob-

stacles, when each man may buy at the lowest price anywhere in the world and sell to the highest bidder on the world market, when competition is allowed free play, all will benefit.

Adam Smith, along with many of his contemporaries, perceived his principles by looking at the nature of things. There is a natural order in the universe, they held, which springs from human nature and the nature of the universe which, if unhindered, will bring harmony out of the diverse actions of men. There is no need for some earthly power to intervene to produce the good of society, by directing the economy to this end or that. On the contrary, Smith said, "The natural effort of every individual to better his own condition, when suffered to exert itself with freedom and security, is so powerful a principle, that it is alone, and without any assistance, . . . capable of carrying on the society to wealth and prosperity. . . ."[3] In a properly ordered society: "The sovereign is completely discharged from a duty, in the attempting to perform which he must always be exposed to innumerable delusions, and for the proper performance of which no human wisdom or knowledge could ever be sufficient; the duty of superintending the industry of private people, and of directing it towards the employments most suitable to the interest of the society."[4]

One of the calumnies, oft repeated, against Smith is that he was surreptitiously advancing the interest of some special class, perhaps the merchant capitalists. Yet it was the very class character of mercantilism that he brought into the light so that it could be clearly seen. Regarding the benefits of this system of special interests, he said:

> It cannot be very difficult to determine who have been the contrivers of this whole mercantile system; not the consumers, we may believe, whose interest has been entirely neglected; but the producers, whose interest has been so

[3] Adam Smith, *The Wealth of Nations*, II (New Rochelle, N. Y.: Arlington House, Edwin Cannan, ed.), p. 126.
[4] *Ibid.*, p. 290.

carefully attended to; and among this latter class our merchants and manufacturers have been by far the principal
architects. In the mercantile regulations . . . the interest of
our manufacturers has been most peculiarly attended to; and
the interest, not so much of the consumers, as that of some
other sets of producers, has been sacrificed to it.[5]

The thrust of his analysis is to show, however, that both the
consumers and other potential producers are sacrificed to
those who have special privileges from government.

It is appropriate here to observe that the war on the poor is
an exceedingly old one, too. Those who have been in positions to influence government have ever and again used that
power to keep enterprise down, to keep the poor "in their
places," and to consolidate their own position for themselves
and their heirs in perpetuity. Modern (or classical) economics ran counter to this age old tendency. It taught that
special privileges should be removed, that each man should be
permitted to pursue his own interest but be denied the use of
force and fraud in doing so, that each man should have the
fruits of his own labor, that through this system of natural
liberty each might improve his position and contribute to the
well being of society.

The attraction of such a natural system of economy to
man's reason is great, and the arguments for it are perhaps as
conclusive as human reason can make them. The benefits to
individuals and societies of freedom of enterprise can be
demonstrated in the lives of numerous men who have risen
from poverty to affluence, or, at least, material ease, and in
the history of societies which have made some experiment
with it. Almost any man can be led to see that it is desirable
that *other men* get the fruits of their labor, and *only* the fruits
of their labor. No man, presumably, wants force and fraud
used upon himself to take away what is his. Special privileges
for others would hardly be the heart's desire of any man.

Yet each of us has in his bosom a fatal flaw, a flaw which

[5] *Ibid.*, p. 262.

leads to efforts to evade the requirements of economy. It is a truism that you cannot get something for nothing, but this does not keep us from trying to do so. The practice of economy inclines us to its evasion, in one sense, for economy is a first cousin to laziness and sloth. So close is the kinship that some suspect the man who practices economy of really being slothful. There is a major difference, however. Economy involves the least expenditure of effort to get an effective job done. That is legitimate. Sloth is the illegitimate cousin. He sees that he could increase *his* supply of goods and services most effectively by the judicious use of force and fraud. When individuals or groups can use government to employ such methods in their behalf, they are not called force and fraud, of course; they are called tariffs, subsidies, bounties, relief, aid to somebody or other, and so on. It is easy to see how economy becomes its opposite.

Moreover, economy may appear quite attractive when it is abstractly described, but in practice it is always a severe discipline. In trade or exchange, he who would follow the dictates of economy must please the consumer. He must submit himself to the requirements of others, must *serve* others, if he would get what he wants in exchange for what they have. This means that he must be continually changing his product, making expensive improvements, competing with others in the field, and catering to what may appear to him uninformed wishes. It is easy for us to persuade ourselves that we should not have to do this. Each of us, after all, can readily persuade himself that he knows what is best for others. Indeed, few things are clearer to us than that other people's taste is defective. That is particularly true when they do not want what we have to offer, when they will not pay the price for what we would purvey, when they consistently underestimate, as they seem invariably to do, the value of our services. It is small wonder, then, that men are ever and again attracted by attempts to escape from the discipline of economy by the use of force. Government, which usually denies us the direct use of

Force by Gov.

by

force by ourselves in our behalf, always lies near at hand, temptingly offering the use of force without the penalties which are ordinarily attached to it, if we can only bring it into play on our behalf.

But the use of force, even the force of government, is subversive of economy when it interferes with what would otherwise be peaceful production and exchange. It increases the price of goods to consumers, causes funds to be allocated in ways not chosen by people generally, introduces rigidities, closes opportunities, and establishes privileges. So Smith had shown; and there were many of his contemporaries who agreed with him, even some who had said much the same thing before him. The impact of Smith and those of like mind was great upon Western Civilization in the 19th century, nowhere more than in England and the United States. For a while, it almost held in abeyance in some places the penchant of men to use government to their selfish ends. Great improvement was noted in the material well being of people where this occurred.

But however solid the edifice of economy disclosed by Smith and others of like mind, ere long thinkers were beginning to lay it under siege. To this day, any study that can by any stretch of the imagination lay claim to being called economics must trace many of its principles and methods to Smith. But these have been subjected to such twistings, turnings, and distortions that Smith would hardly recognize them as lineal descendants today. There has been more than a hundred year's war on economics, hence, on economy. This is not to say that some have not held fast to economic principles, but that the main trend has been away from them to the justification of the use of force. All these assaults have the common denominator of holding that if men are left free to operate economically great social harm will result.

Contemporary with Smith, there were economic thinkers, operating from a very similar outlook to his, who were making an account of economy which could, in the hands of some, be a justification for government intervention. This economic theory was physiocracy, and those who advanced it were called physiocrats. A Frenchman, Quesnay, was its leading spokesman, but he had many followers among his contemporaries, including a number of Americans. They, too, proceeded by looking at the nature of things and attempting to discover a natural economy. A natural economy, they held, was an agricultural economy. All true increases of wealth were produced by the soil. Manufacturing did not increase the true wealth of a people; it only produced luxuries which would, in the course of time, corrupt a people. Physiocracy was a reaction to and vigorous rebuttal of mercantilism. Physiocrats did not necessarily, or even usually, favor government intervention on behalf of agriculture in the manner that mercantilists wanted government to promote manufacturing. They were usually libertarians, believing that without artificial supports agriculture would naturally prevail. Their theories, did, however, lend themselves to use, by abstraction, to those who would promote agriculture by government activity. There are echoes of physiocracy in the populist movement in America in the late nineteenth century, in the speeches of William Jennings Bryan, in the talk of the farmer as the backbone of America, in the silverite inflationist movement, and in twentieth century interventions to "save" the farmer and "preserve" agriculture.

Smith gave physiocratic agrarian theories short shrift in his account, and so did most others in the mainstream of the development of classical economics. However, troublesome ideas were not long in making their appearance in that stream. Smith's conception of the effects of economy, for any people who had the wit to establish a modicum of liberty within which the natural bent of man to economy could have some sway, was hopeful and optimistic. Economy would conduce to the general prosperity and material well being of a people. Even so, the hopeful discipline of Adam Smith rather quickly became the dismal science of David Ricardo and Thomas Malthus.

They thought they saw a worm in the apple of prosperity-by-economy. Ricardo was the immediate successor to Adam Smith, in the late eighteenth and early nineteenth century. He made great headway in making a systematic exposition of economics. But Ricardo's premises led him to a rather gruesome conclusion. He held that the price of labor must ever and again fall to a level that will maintain workers at a bare subsistence of livelihood. He arrived at this conclusion by a grotesque bit of ideological hocus pocus. According to classical economics, commodities have both a natural price and a market price. The natural price of a commodity is the cost of producing it. The market price is what a commodity will bring in the market under actual conditions of supply and demand. Under conditions of free competition, the market price will tend to approximate the natural price.

Ricardo proceeded to apply this theory to the price of labor. The cost of production applied to labor comes out as the cost of maintaining life. "The natural price of labor is that price which is necessary to enable the laborers, one with another, to subsist and to perpetuate their race, without either increasing or diminution."[6] The market price of labor will fluctuate, he held, due to the operation of supply and demand. When wages rise above their natural level, he thought, population will increase because more life can be maintained. That is, the supply of labor will increase, thus driving the market price of labor down to the natural price, or even below it, for a time. In short, the price of labor will tend toward the subsistence level.

(It would appear that Ricardo had the matter backwards. Though utilitarian economists dispensed with such conceptions as natural price, it would be possible in the light of both experience and marginal theory to maintain that the natural price of labor is not the cost of maintaining it but what labor contributes to the price that a good or service will bring in the market. At any rate, the price which labor can command rises [or falls] with the productivity of workmen.)

    [6] David Ricardo, "Principles of Political Economy," *The Age of Reason*, Louis L. Snyder, ed. (Princeton: D. Van Nostrand, 1955), pp. 153-54.

Malthus carried Ricardo's dismal view a long step further by envisioning spreading famine as population increased. Indeed, he proposed that there were exact laws governing population increase as well as the possibilities of the increase of subsistence.

TO WIT:

> It may safely be pronounced that the population, when unchecked, goes on doubling itself every twenty-five years, or increases in a geometrical ratio. . . .
>
> The means of subsistence, under circumstances the most favorable to human industry, could not possibly be made to increase faster than in an arithmetical ratio.[7]

Ricardo did not believe that anything could be done to correct the situation. The best that could be hoped for would be that enterprise would be free to enable men to produce as much as they could. Malthus held out little hope for intervention, either. The Iron Law of Wages might be expected to keep the bulk of the population in, at best, a state of subsistence. The equally inflexible laws of population increase would contribute to deprivation and suffering.

The flight from economics was soon underway in earnest. The actual course of development in the nineteenth century certainly did not bear out the gloomy predictions of Ricardo and Malthus. Population did increase, but production rose faster. There were a great many more people to be fed, clothed, and housed, but this was done, generally, ever more effectively. This is not to say that there was not malnutrition and deprivation—these there had always been—but that the situation was improving. The gloomy view would not down, however. Utopians began to espouse the view that poverty could be finally banished. Men began the search for the flaw or flaws in the "system," or in economy, which prevented this heady development from taking place. Economy became an enemy to be overcome. Probably, the mainstream of thought for much of the nineteenth century remained libertarian,

[7] *Ibid.*, pp. 150-51.

tending to favor free enterprise and free trade, but there was a
mounting clamor for changing the ·"system," for correcting
the flaws of economy, for reform, even for revolution.

It is not practical here to undertake a history of economic
thought for the last hundred or so years. It is necessary only
to highlight some trends that developed into a war on economy. Karl Marx and Friedrich Engels thrust themselves into
the stream of this development by the middle of the nineteenth century. In *The Communist Manifesto*, they converted
some of the doctrines of classical economics into a call for
revolution. They accepted Ricardo's explanation of how
wages were determined:

> The average price of wage-labour is the minimum wage,
> i.e., that quantum of the means of subsistence which is abso-
> lutely requisite to keep the labourer in bare existence as a
> labourer. What, therefore, the wage-labourer appropriates by
> means of his labour, merely suffices to prolong and repro-
> duce a bare existence.[8]

In consequence, they held, "The modern labourer . . . ,
instead of rising with the progress of industry, sinks deeper and
deeper below the conditions of existence of his own class. He
becomes a pauper, and pauperism develops more rapidly than
population and wealth."[9] This was not a product of the working of economic laws, they declared, but of the control of the
means of production by the bourgeoisie. The bourgeoisie "has
resolved personal worth into exchange value, and in place of
the numberless indefeasible chartered freedoms, has set up that
single, unconscionable freedom—Free Trade. In one word,
for exploitation, veiled by religious and political illusions, it
has substituted naked, shameless, direct, brutal exploitation."[10]

Most of the ideas which have been the stock in trade of

[8] Richard H. Powers, ed., *Readings in European Civilization* (Boston:
Houghton Mifflin, 1961), p. 355.
[9] *Ibid.*, p. 354.
[10] *Ibid.*, p. 350.

reformers and revolutionaries for the last hundred years can be found in Marx and Engels: the labor theory of value, that all true value of products is given to them by "labor"; the exploitation of workers theory, that all profits from capital are gained at the expense of workers; the notion that the rich get richer and the poor poorer; the claim that in a free system business will become ever more highly concentrated in the hands of fewer and fewer people; the ideas of overproduction, underconsumption, warfare to keep bourgeois society prosperous, and so on.*

Very quickly, some writers began to try to fit the American experience into the framework of such ideas. One of the first to make a large impact in America was Henry George. George's work was done independently of Marx, but it was like it in descrying a dismal prospect for the poor and finding the flaw in the "system." In his most famous work, *Progress and Poverty,* published in 1879, George interpreted developments in this way:

> And, unpleasant as it may be to admit it, it is at last becoming evident that the enormous increase in productive power which has marked the present century and is still going on with accelerating ratio, has no tendency to extirpate poverty or to lighten the burdens of those compelled to toil. It simply widens the gulf between Dives and Lazarus, and makes the struggle for existence more intense. The march of invention has clothed mankind with powers of which a century ago the boldest imagination could not have dreamed. But in factories where labor-saving machinery has reached its most wonderful development, little children are at work; wherever the new forces are anything like fully utilized, large classes are maintained by charity or live on the verge of recourse to it; amid the greatest accumulations of wealth, men die of starvation, and puny infants suckle dry breasts; while everywhere the greed of gain, the worship of wealth,

---

* These tenets are ideological, rather than the result of observation of conditions—which were improving, observably, even as Marx and Engels wrote. Some persons easily ignore facts if their theories are at stake.

shows the force of the fear of want. The promised land flies before us like the mirage.[11]

The flaw in the system, according to George, was the unearned increment on land. George was a neo-physiocrat, taking from the physiocrats both the idea of a natural economy and of the central place of land in production. No one has a right to the product of the soil, as such, George claimed. The land was here from time immemorial, and its products belong to all of us. He distinguished, or attempted to distinguish, between the product of work and product of the soil. The latter he called the unearned increment on land. It was the receipt of this unearned increment, by way of private property arrangements, which was supposed to account for the alleged increasing poverty which was supposed to accompany progress.

Henry George's view had only a limited impact in its specifics, but it did lead many of his hundreds of thousands of readers to believe that the situation was bad, and that the system needed correction. Writers were soon forthcoming to provide vivid accounts of all sorts of things that were wrong in America; in their wake came others to prescribe what should be done. The main line of development in America from the latter part of the nineteenth century to the present has been for reformers to proclaim that government should intervene in the economy in some way. Government should, they have said, control big business, regulate rail rates, own public utilities, inflate the currency, appropriate much of the wealth through graduated income and inheritance taxes, grant subsidies to farmers, exempt labor unions from laws, give massive relief to the poor, and, finally, make all out War on Poverty. The numerous interventions from that time to the present have been under the sway of these ideas.

There is no body of thought which demonstrates that it is economical for governments to intervene in the affairs of people. Even the most undisciplined claims of those who have

[11] Henry George, *Progress and Poverty* (New York: Schalkenbach Foundation, 1955), p. 8.

favored intervention have rarely been buttressed with arguments that it would be economic. Instead, the main justifications for intervention have been twofold. One, reformers have claimed that economy unregulated by government produces bad effects, as indicated above. Two, *there is no longer any need for economy.* It is this latter view that justifies calling these ideas a war on economy.

Economy would be in order, demonstrably, if the basic problem was a shortage of goods. There has, however, been a large body of influential thought to the effect that this is not the problem. Interventionist thought has been based, mainly, upon the view that there exists an abundance of goods and services. Even the idea that mankind is confronted with a glut of goods and services is not particularly recent. It goes back at least to *The Communist Manifesto* (1848). In that document, Marx and Engels claimed that in modern crises "there breaks out an epidemic that, in all earlier epochs would have seemed an absurdity—the epidemic of overproduction." . . . Because there is too much civilization, too much means of subsistence, too much industry, too much commerce." But it has had its particularly American articulation. This was provided mainly by that school of "economists" known as institutionalists. Prominent leaders of this school have been Thorstein Veblen, John R. Commons, Stuart Chase, and, lately, John K. Galbraith.

Their basic position is that conditions have changed, that it was once true, indeed, had been true from time immemorial, that societies were confronted with scarcity, but that this condition is no longer the case for some societies, notably the United States. Stuart Chase held that the United States reached a condition of abundance in 1902. "Abundance," he said, "is self-defined, and means an economic condition where an abundance of material goods can be produced for the entire population of a given community."[12] Rexford G. Tugwell, the irrepressible New Dealer, described the change

[12] Quoted in Charles S. Wyand, *The Economics of Consumption* (New York; Macmillan, 1937), p. 54.

to plenty in this way: "Our economic course has carried us from the era of economic *development* to an era which confronts us with the necessity for economic *maintenance*. In this period of maintenance, there is no scarcity of production. There is, in fact, a present capacity for more production than is consumable, at least under a system which shortens purchasing power while it is lengthening capacity to produce."[13]

John K. Galbraith, who plays Stuart Chase to post World War II America, describes the development as historical in the following: "Nearly all people throughout all history have been very poor. The exception, almost insignificant in the whole span of human existence, has been the last few generations in the small corner of the world populated by Europeans. Here, and especially in the United States, there has been great and quite unprecedented affluence."[14] Vance Packard, who is to Galbraith as Galbraith is to Chase and Veblen—that is, derivative—states the development with his usual dramatic flair:

> Man throughout recorded history has struggled—often against appalling odds—to cope with material scarcity. Today, there has been a massive breakthrough. The great challenge in the United States—and soon in Western Europe —is to cope with a threatened overabundance of staples and amenities and frills of life.[15]

The evidence which purports to support these claims of abundance has run the gamut from Veblen's conspicuous consumption of the leisure class to Packard's charges that industrial waste makers prey upon the gullible public with their shoddy merchandise with its built-in planned obsolescence. The terms which have received the widest acceptance for describing abundance are overproduction, unemployment,

[13] Rexford G. Tugwell, *The Battle for Democracy* (New York: Columbia University Press, 1935), p. 7.
[14] John K. Galbraith, *The Affluent Society* (Boston: Houghton Mifflin, 1958), p. 1.
[15] Vance Packard, *The Waste Makers* (New York: David McKay, 1960), p. 7.

ver production

surpluses, unused industrial capacity, and underconsumption.

The following is some of the evidence Stuart Chase submitted in 1931:

> *oil*
>
> American oil wells are capable of producing 5,950,000 barrels a day, against a market demand of 4,000,000 barrels, according to the figures of the Standard Oil Company of New Jersey.[16]
>
> *coal*
>
> The real problem in coal is excess capacity. The mines of the country can produce at least 750,000,000 tons a year, while the market can absorb but 500,000,000 tons.[17]
>
> American shoe factories are equipped to turn out almost 900,000,000 pairs of shoes a year. At present we buy about 300,000,000 pairs—two and one-half pairs per capita. . . . Yet if we doubled shoe consumption—gorging the great American foot, as it were—one third of the present shoe factory equipment would still lie idle.[18]
>
> *farm surplus*
>
> Jumping now across the economic front to agriculture, we find that the basic problem of the American farmer lies in his "surplus." The government at the present writing has bought and holds in storage millions of bushels of wheat in a heroic and possibly calamitous attempt to keep the surplus from crushing wheat farmers altogether.[19]

According to Mr. Chase, there was not only a veritable glut of goods but also a surplus of workers as well:

> What threatens to continue unabated, in good times and bad, is technological unemployment with its three faces—the machine, the merger, the stop watch. In four years oil refineries increased output 84 per cent, and laid off 5 per cent of their men while doing it. . . .
>
> It can mean only one thing. An equivalent tonnage of goods can be produced by a declining number of workers,

[16] Stuart Chase, *The Nemesis of American Business* (New York: Macmillan, 1931), p. 88.
[17] *Ibid.*, p. 89.
[18] *Ibid.*, p. 79.
[19] *Ibid.*, p. 76.

and men must lose their jobs by the thousands—presently by the millions.[20]

Some writers, such as Stuart Chase, quoted above, have written as if there were an absolute surplus of goods. This has not usually been their meaning, however. Instead, they have viewed this "overproduction" as an indication that something was fundamentally wrong. Charles Wyand described the situation in this way:

> More goods are being produced than can be profitably sold. On the other hand, it can be clearly shown that most people are consuming at but a fraction of their potential capacity. . . . As will be shown later, the consumer's buying power cannot absorb all that the nation can produce because (1) incomes are insufficient, (2) too much of the nation's income is saved, and (3) prices are too high.[21]

What lies behind all this talk—whether it be of overproduction, underconsumption, maldistribution, wastefulness, or unemployment—is the view that government must intervene in one way or another to correct the situation. The "system," these men hold, produces these unwanted consequences, and action must be taken to set it straight.

Simon Patten, an early advocate of the notion that a surplus exists, and a teacher of Rexford G. Tugwell, advocated the absorption of the surplus by taxation. He declared that taxation should "be placed not on particular forms of prosperity, but on general prosperity. The State should not try to hunt up the individual who profits by each of the improvements it makes, but should make taxation a reduction of the general surplus of society." His justification of this was that "we can conceive of the State as a factor in production, and hence entitled to a share of the undistributed produce of industry. It has helped to promote general prosperity, and can

[20] *Ibid.*, pp. 15-16. An early nineteenth-century solution to the fear Chase expresses here was supplied by the Luddites, who smashed their machines.
[21] Wyand, *op. cit.*, p. 40.

demand a part of the surplus of society along with landlords, employers, capitalists and laborers."[22]

John R. Commons, an early and late reformer, called in 1893 for a guaranteed right to employment in order to take care of the "surplus" of laborers:

> The right to employment when enforced would have the effect of guaranteeing to every worker, even the lowest, a share of the total income in excess of his minimum subsistence. It would give steady work through the year, which would increase the wages of the lowest labourers by 30% to 50%. And by overcoming the chronic excess of labourers beyond the opportunities for employment, it would raise the marginal utility of the marginal labourers, thus raising the wages of all.[23]

Stuart Chase proclaimed that the situation called for detailed planning:

> In my judgment the only final way out lies through planned production. We have to scrap a large fraction of *laissez-faire*, and deliberately orient productive capacity to consumption goods. . . .[24]

Rexford G. Tugwell said,

> Let me summarize: In this era of our economic existence, I believe it is manifest that a public interest . . . commands the protection, the maintenance, the conservation, of our industrial faculties against the destructive forces of the unrestrained competition . . . For today and for tomorrow our problem is that of our national economic maintenance for the public welfare by governmental intervention. . . .[25]

In sum, the argument is this: Economic action has produced surpluses and maldistribution. This being the case,

---

[22] Simon N. Patten, *Essays in Economic Theory*, Rexford G. Tugwell, ed. (New York: Alfred A. Knopf, 1924), p. 98.

[23] John R. Commons, *The Distribution of Wealth* (New York: Reprints of Economic Classics, 1963), pp. 84-85.

[24] Chase, *op. cit.*, p. 95.

[25] Tugwell, *op. cit.*, p. 9.

government must now intervene. There is hardly an implication that further economic measures are in order. If the problem were one of production, which it would be if there remained fundamental scarcity, it would then be a matter for economics. Where scarcity is the problem, there needs to be frugal management, saving, investment, balanced budgets, calculations as to the best means to use to get the greatest return from materials, and determinations as to how to produce the most goods with the least expenditure of energy. But if the situation were reversed, if abundance has replaced scarcity—as the gentlemen quoted above argue—economic behavior would no longer be in order. It might be helpful to spend more than was taken in, to employ more workers than the task at hand required, to use more materials than would be called for by the undertaking. In short, economy might be placed under assault and rooted out.

While governmental force cannot be used to intervene and produce economic action, it can be used to thwart economy; it cannot be used to get the most effective production, but it can be used to distribute abundance. If there were only the problem of distribution, it would be feasible to argue that governments can intervene to improve the situation. Governments can redistribute; they can take goods from some and give them to others; they can spend, appropriate, set aside lands and resources, confiscate, and even waste rather effectively. These are tasks which governments alone, because of their monopoly of the use of force, would be suited to perform, if anyone had to perform such tasks. No longer are these ideas restricted to the reformers' tracts—they have become operative principles of government.

That the United States government, as well as state and local governments, have taken strenuous measures along these lines against economy for many years should be patent. Governments have adopted crop restrictions, controlled and inhibited industrial production (as, for example, Texas limits oil production), subsidized commodities already in "surplus," engaged in deficit spending to produce prosperity, inflated in order to increase "purchasing power," followed easy money policies to induce spending, promoted higher wages by union exemptions and the minimum wage, established prices, placed graduated income taxes on the productive members of the society and penalized most heavily those most productive.

In short, back of the war on economy lies the claim of abundance. The charge has been that when economy holds sway there will be a glut of goods, which in turn cannot be acquired by those in greatest need because of a maldistribution of purchasing power. Government must intervene, it has been alleged, in order to right the situation. That this intervention is diseconomic is fairly obvious, but the charge is supposed to be nullified because economy is no longer necessary. This war of words on economy underlies the political action which produces a war on the poor. The problem of the poor is economic, as has been stated, but a counterthrust is set up by these programs which tends to negate their effects in behalf of the poor.

The claim that economy is no longer necessary is not correct. It is based upon an illusion, an illusion drawn from an ideology. The illusory character of the notion can be exposed by a brief examination of it. It is an illusion which gains its credibility by ignoring the dimension of time. When that dimension is filled in, the fallacy is obvious.

For the sake of argument, let us suppose that America has abundance in 1968, or, even, to be as generous as possible, that such abundance has been the case since 1902. Surely, however, abundance is not a permanent condition. We all know better, if we would only give it thought. If all production were to cease, the fabled abundance would vanish like a mirage as it is approached. Within a day, there would be great shortages of fresh milk, within a week of fresh vegetables, and within two months even new automobiles could not be had. However well supplied a people may be momentarily, the supply must be continuously replenished or it will melt away.

No amount of redistribution of the supply of milk after a week or so of no production would feed starving babies. We are so accustomed to the daily miracle of continual dependable production that we rarely stop to consider that absolute stoppage would bring universal privation in a brutally brief span of time.

Production and effort must be continued, then, if goods and services are to be available to us. These, by their very nature, require economy. Production requires continuing decisions about what materials to use in what manner by which workers to produce what is most wanted. As soon as this ceases, at any level, the production which will supply our wants also is curtailed. Production can be separated from distribution only by bringing chaos and universalizing deprivation. Communist countries have provided abundant proof in our century of how instant universal poverty can be brought about by attempting to separate distribution from production

Economy, then, is vital for all of us. It is, as I have said, most essential for those who have the least reserves—i. e., the poor. Government can interfere with economy; it can produce distortions; it can send false signals into the economy; it can discourage production; it can, in short, wage a kind of war on economy. It is my contention that this will bear, and has borne, especially hard upon the poor.

Illusion born of ideology begot the notion that economy was not needed and gave rise to the numerous programs of government intervention. The results of these programs are disadvantageous to the poor, as we shall see. Why, then, when they fail, are they not abandoned? Indeed, why in the face of so much evidence of an unfavorable kind is the whole assault on economy not stopped?

The answer, in considerable part, is to be found in the inhibiting effect of a pervasive ideology. Ideology not only begets illusions which serve as the basis for action but also contains built-in illusions which inhibit evaluations and mightily propel believers in the set direction regardless of the catastrophes which result. We should all be familiar with this impact of ideologies from the history of Communism. Modern Communism has usually been introduced with catastrophic violence and has produced failure after failure, while at the same time holding many of the old and gaining new adherents. Every failure can be explained, of course, if it has to be admitted. But the failure is never the failure of Communism. It is a catastrophe incident to the early stages of revolution, or produced by reactionary resistance, or the result of insufficient zeal by bureaucrats, and so on. Never, but never, is the ideology itself to be called into question. To question the ideology and finally to abandon it would be to give up the only justification there could be for the suffering, hardship, and effort devoted to the cause—a thing which men can hardly bring themselves to do.

In a similar fashion, though more subtle, the ideology underlying the interventionist effort in America inhibits evaluation and forestalls abandonment. This ideology is a compound of utopianism and socialism, however much these have been watered down in their advocacy to make them palatable. Those under the sway of the ideology, wittingly or not, hold that all problems can be solved and that poverty and suffering can either be abolished or reduced to insignificant proportions. It is an article of faith with them that government intervention can conduce to these ends. The shortcomings of any program are explained without recourse to an examination of premises. Not enough money was spent, it may be alleged, or the particular program was faultily conceived, or it was sabotaged by boards or commissions whose members were not really committed to it, or unreconstructed elements took advantage of it for their own benefit, and so on.

The bridle for a horse has blinders on it to cut down or limit the peripheral vision of the horse. By cutting down his vision, the driver is better able to steer the horse where he wants him to go, to control the animal for the ends of his master, by making him oblivious of peripheral dangers. Just so does the ideologue wear blinders when he puts on his ideology. He has his eyes focused upon the particular goal—improving the lot of farmers, aiding the handicapped, or what have you—and never surveying the scene as a whole.

The ideological blinders are much more effective in America because the wearer does not even know that he has them on. Socialists don't usually refer to themselves as socialists in America. Ideas drawn from socialism are not usually identified as such. In consequence, those under the sway of ideology do not usually know that they are. They have not even examined the basic ideas by which their vision is limited and do not know that it is limited.

But it is not ideology alone which perpetuates and extends programs which common sense would long since have relegated to the junk heap. Ideology provides the rhetoric which serves as blinders, but the motive power for the effort comes from perverted self-interest. It is not possible to know the inner motives of men directly, but it is possible to discern how they benefit from a particular course of action.

The most obvious beneficiaries of the government programs are the politicians who advance them. They have acquired a vested interest in moving the United States toward socialism. Not only does it provide them with prestige and power, but it helps them get elected to office. Politicians run for office on the basis of benefits, favors, subsidies, exemptions, grants, and so forth which they did or will provide for the electorate. Notice how this impels us toward more and more governmental activity, for the man who would continue to be elected should promise ever greater benefits to his constituency.

At the apex of this structure of power and privilege is an elite of politicians, intellectuals, labor leaders, scientists, military men, and assorted leaders of various privileged minority groups. At the pinnacle is the President and those who enjoy his favor. Here, the benefits are such as would dazzle and tempt a saint. There are the obvious perquisites of

office, of course: the black limousines, the jet planes, the heli-
copters, the Marine band, the medical care at Walter Reed
Hospital, the admiring crowds, and the fawning assistants.
Surely, much of this establishment is maintained on the
grounds of the wonders that government can perform for the
economic well-being of the people.

Those with a vested interest in government behaving in this
fashion may well evaluate programs in a quite different way
from the generality of the citizenry. The farm program, for
example, may not have worked to achieve its stated aims, but
it may have worked to keep politicians from farm states
in office. In the same manner, politicians may reap votes from
benefits passed on to numerous other special interests. In
terms of an accretion of political power, government intervention has worked quite well for those who drive the
blinkered horse.

One other point needs to be disposed of before going to a
more specific account of the war on the poor. Many may find
the logic presented already and the evidence to follow unas-
sailable yet still be troubled by a nagging question. The question might be succinctly phrased in this way: If government
intervention is diseconomic, then how account for the affluence and abundance in the United States? Some of the interventions have been going on for quite a while now, and they
have been extended and increased over the years. Yet there
can be no contesting the fact that America is the most
prosperous land in the world. Moreover, politicians frequently claim credit for the abundance, and that it is a result
of the government programs.

It should be obvious, however, that such abundance as
exists in America could not be the result of these government
programs. Crop restrictions would hardly, of themselves, contribute to the abundance of food; it is their obvious purpose to
reduce the supply. Higher wages do not make the production
of goods and the provision of services easier; instead, they
make them more expensive. Graduated income taxes do not
increase the incentives to production; they reduce them.

Higher prices are not a boon to trade generally; they inhibit it. Redistributionist schemes can serve as a basis for spreading the bounty around, but they neither increase it nor even maintain it. Instead, they are powerful deterrents to production— so powerful that various subsidies to some industries at the expense of others generally result in a net loss in production.

It should be obvious then, that the great productivity in America occurs *despite* the controls, regulations, restrictions, and interventions rather than because of them. Adam Smith knew that a certain degree of political interference could be to some extent overcome. He declared that "the natural effort of every individual to better his own condition" is capable "of surmounting a hundred impertinent obstructions with which the folly of human laws incumbers its operations. . . ." In his day, there were those who claimed that mercantile intervention produced English prosperity. His answer to this was succinct and worth repeating:

> Though the period of the greatest prosperity and improvement of Great Britain, has been posterior to that system of laws which is connected with the bounty, we must not upon that account impute it to those laws. It has been posterior likewise to the national debt. But the national debt has most assuredly not been the cause of it.[26]

On the contrary, he held, it was the relative degree of freedom and security, so far as government was concerned, that made it possible.

Regarding the impact of interference, an American, Henry David Thoreau, made a similar observation to that of Smith. "Trade and Commerce," Thoreau said, "if they were not made of India-rubber, would never manage to bounce over the obstacles which legislators are continually putting in their way. . . ."[27]

[26] Smith, *op. cit.*, II, p. 126.
[27] Henry D. Thoreau, "On the Duty of Civil Disobedience," pub. in *Walden*, Norman H. Pearson, intro. (New York: Rinehart, 1948), p. 202.

So great, then, is the bent of men to economy that they may be expected to overcome many obstacles to it in their efforts. Such prosperity as America enjoys should most surely be attributed to the ingenuity of entrepreneurs, to the determination of men to produce at a profit, to inventions which set at naught for a time some of the governmental handicaps, to the ability to adjust to restrictions and make the most of them. The story of American agriculture and industry in the twentieth century is an amazing chronicle of such adjustments in overcoming obstacles to production.

These adjustments have been made possible by the gradualist character of the intervention. This enables producers to come to some sort of terms with some of the interventions before they have to wrestle with others. They have been facilitated, also, by the greater relative security to property in America than in most other lands. This does not mean either that the potentialities for adjustment are endless, or that prosperity has been generally what it might otherwise have been without the obstacles. After all, the interventions of the 1930's created considerable havoc in America. The pace of intervention has generally been slower since, and adjustments have been accomplished with less obvious harm to economy.

But—and this is the crux of my thesis—all people are not equally well equipped to cope with intervention. A great corporation, such as, for example, General Motors, with its lawyers, economists, and experts of one kind or another, can quite often keep its management informed of changes in the laws, their probable effects on economy, and the best means of survival in the face of them. A great corporation can quite often take advantage of an intervention to better its position vis a vis its competitors, to increase its share of the market, or to turn the application of the law to its advantage. By contrast, the poor are usually sitting ducks to be misled by every false signal sent into the economy, to be misguided by the rhetoric of politicians, to be drawn into uneconomic endeavors to their hurt and to their sorrow. Whatever the state

Big Corp. can take advantage of intervention

of general affluence, they are often led to board a train going away from it.

In sum, then, a hundred years war on economy has been going on. It has been conducted at two levels: the surface level of government programs and the underlying level of ideas. This chapter has been a summary of that war as it has been conducted in the realm of ideas, and tells of how these ideas serve to justify the political effort and forestall evaluations of it. Attention can now be turned to the various battles conducted at the level of political programs.

CHAPTER IV

Farmers at Bay

A generation of "farm policy" adds up to hopeless tinkering, fantastic losses, planned chaos, a lost war against Nature's laws. The battles have been man's laws: the Fordney-McCumber Tariff, the NcNary-Haugen bills, the Farm Marketing Board, the Smoot-Hawley Tariff, the A.A.A., soil conservation, the ever normal granary, the Food-Stamp Plan, 90 per cent of parity, the Brannan Plan, flexible parity, the Soil Bank, overseas surplus disposal. These man-made laws have snares. . . .

The irony is that the farmer to be saved wasn't; since the New Deal, one of every three farmers has quit.[1]

RECENTLY, I TOOK A COUPLE OF DRIVES THROUGH A PART OF the countryside in Alabama in which I had grown up in the 1920's and 1930's. They started out, I suppose, to be what poets would call trips down memory lane, for I expected to capture a pleasant glow of nostalgia, mingled, as it invariably is, with a tinge of sadness of days gone beyond recall. My disappointment and disenchantment was almost total. There was almost nothing to be seen to evoke either pleasant memory or the sadness of a life put behind me.

[1] William H. Peterson, *The Great Farm Problem* (Chicago: Henry Regnery, 1959), pp. 217-18.

The transformation that had occurred within a generation was so complete that I might have been driving through a country never before seen, except for an occasional landmark still standing. In my memory, houses had dotted the landscape surrounded by fields of cotton and corn. Cultivated farm had followed cultivated farm, broken here and there by a scope of woods and occasionally a stretch of wooded or pasture land on countryside that did not lie well for cultivation. In something like a 20 mile drive, I saw one field of cotton. Here and there, a rundown, and usually abandoned, house pokes out of the surrounding woods. Some of the land is now devoted to cattle growing, but mostly it is lying idle or growing trees, or, most likely, doing both. Once thickly inhabited country has an occupied house only here and there, the occupants mostly retired, on relief, or commuting to work in the towns thereabout. Franklin D. Roosevelt's promises to restore the balance between rural and urban dwellers have an empty ring to them which the remembered resonance of his voice can no longer give content.

I grew up amidst the death throes of farming in that country, though knowledge of the impending end was mercifully denied us. We wrestled—in the 1930's—with red depleted soil, with the boll weevil, the grub worms that followed legumes, with drought that dried out the upland crops and then overabundant rains which flooded the bottoms, with weeds, with sun, and against time. Then there were the government programs: the cotton allotments, the soil conservation checks, the crop loans, vague talk of parity and higher prices and soil improvement. The government seemed to be doing everything it could to help farmers. Yet, by and large, the more it "helped" the more desperate became the situation of the farms. The sons were leaving the farms to work at sawmills or in factories, the daughters to clerk in stores or to work in clothing factories that were beginning to make their appearance. Younger farmers began to leave the farms also for work elsewhere. There was nothing dramatic

about the death of agriculture there; it was more like a lingering and wasting sickness from which its victims just faded
away. Any connection between the government programs and
the decline of agriculture was too remote and subtle for anyone to figure out. Communities did not make general analyses
of their plight; individuals, whether they stayed on the farms a
little longer or left early, simply sought to improve their situation as best they could.

Of course, farms have not been abandoned in like degree
all over the United States. There are large areas where the
land is still cultivated, and there are even prosperous farmers.
Still, a great deal of land in America that was once planted to
grow crops, particularly in the East, now lies idle or has been
turned to other use. Economists have a term which they apply
to the above situation. We were, they would say, marginal
farmers who became submarginal. They quite often suggest
that it was inevitable that many should leave the farms, that
technological and nutritional changes dictated the exodus. If
government had not intervened, some say, the exodus from
the farm would have been greatly accelerated and, perhaps,
achieved with less suffering. At any rate, the phenomenon is
apt to be dismissed with a nice, hygienic abstraction—
marginal farmers.

Those who are somewhat aware of the impact of government intervention might not dismiss the situation as casually
as that. They should know that the meaning of "marginal" is
related to economy, and that government intervention is uneconomic. In short, when government intervenes, it is no
longer possible to determine who is marginal and who is not.
To be more precise, government intervention changes the
content of the marginal category. It may make land and labor
uses marginal which were not and would not have become
marginal, or vice versa. Government intervention has been
going on for a long time in the farm situation, and it has long
since come to pervade it. No one knows how many farmers
and of what kind there should be in the abstract. No one

knows how many should live on farms and how many in the cities. That is something which men would decide for themselves, if there were no intervention, and which they might decide in terms of the best information on the subject. My point is that long term intervention has increasingly obscured for us the information which would enable us to know who were marginal farmers in an economic sense, and who were not. It is time now to tell some of the story.

The history of government intervention in agriculture goes back much earlier than the 1860's. Indeed, it goes back to the beginning of the colonies, to the English mercantile system, to the promotion of the growing of staples and commercial farming. But there is an interval, of sorts, between the intervention of the colonial period, spurred by mercantilistic concepts, and the intervention which got under way with new impetus in the latter part of the nineteenth century, spurred by new social doctrines. In the period from the War for Independence to the Civil War, intervention was at a minimum. It picked up considerably in the latter part of the nineteenth century and has, of course, reached unprecedented heights in the last forty years.

Farmers have long been an object of sentiment and special solicitude in America. From the early days of the Republic, the Jeffersonians lavished praise upon them. Men such as Benjamin Franklin, Thomas Jefferson, and Hector St. Crevecoeur created what Professor Richard Hofstadter has called an agrarian myth. He described the myth in this way:

> Like any complex of ideas, the agrarian myth cannot be defined in a phrase, but its component themes form a clear pattern. Its hero was the yeoman farmer, its central conception the notion that he is the ideal man and the ideal citizen. Unstinted praise of the special virtues of the farmer and the special values of rural life was coupled with the assertion that agriculture as a calling uniquely productive and uniquely important, to society, had a special right to the concern and protection of government. The yeoman who

owned a small farm and worked it with the aid of his family, was the incarnation of the simple, honest, independent, healthy, happy human being. Because he lived in close communion with beneficent nature, his life was believed to have a wholesomeness and integrity impossible for the depraved population of the cities.[2]

It was to this belief, and more, that William Jennings Bryan appealed in his famous Cross of Gold speech in 1896:

> You come to us and tell us that the great cities are in favor of the gold standard; we reply that the great cities rest upon our broad and fertile prairies. Burn down your cities and leave our farms, and your cities will spring up again as if by magic; but destroy our farms and the grass will grow in the streets of every city in the country.[3]

Franklin D. Roosevelt relied upon such sentiments for the evocative power of his notion of restoring the balance between rural and urban population.

Fact, sentiment, and sympathy have all been appealed to in the promotion of intervention supposedly on behalf of the farmer. It is true, as it has ever been, that farmers produce most of the basic necessities of life, that without the food and materials that flow in from the farms there could be no cities. The reliance of all of us upon agriculture for sustenance should not be doubted. There are, also, values peculiar to farming: closeness to nature, the honesty of a relation between workman and harvest uncorrupted by human failings, the close relations between parents and children, and so on. Many Americans, if they are no longer farmers, cherish memories of farm life, and, in their reveries, envision a retirement one day to the peacefulness of the farm. There is, too, a sympathy for farmers, for the hard work, for the uncertainty of the harvest, for the long hours and the lonely life.

---

[2] Richard Hofstadter, *The Age of Reform* (New York: Alfred A. Knopf, 1955), p. 24.
[3] Marvin Meyers, *et. al.*, eds., *Sources of the American Republic*, II (Chicago: Scott, Foresman and Co., 1961), p. 95.

The above has to do, of course, with justifications for interventions in agriculture, not with the necessity for them. There
was more involved, too, than sentiment and sympathy, such
as, for example, farm lobby groups, the desire of politicians to
be elected, and a general bent to reform. But the justifications
have usually been couched in terms of sentiment and sympathy.

Even supposing, however, that all of the government action
had been spurred by disinterested good will, that all who had
favored the programs had been animated by the desire to
relieve the hardship of farmers, that farming has a unique
place and importance, the consequences of intervention
would be about the same as if the acts had been done by
selfish monsters. In the final analysis, to farm successfully is to
act economically. Every man who would get his livelihood by
farming must do so by economy. The interventions have been
efforts to remove all or some of the economic considerations.
The consequences of uneconomic actions fall equally upon
the just and the unjust, like the rains.

Economically, the farmer is a businessman or an entrepreneur. He works with three basic ingredients from which his
production comes: land, labor, and capital. He must decide
how much of these to apply and in what ways. That is, he
must decide how much land to cultivate, what crops to plant
where, how much fertilizer to use, what equipment to employ,
and how often and in what ways to cultivate his crops. These
are all economic decisions because everything is scarce. Land,
and particularly arable land, is in short supply; labor is
scarce, and capital resources are limited. They are not all
equally scarce, however; land may be relatively plentiful
while labor and capital are in much shorter supply. The situation will alter from time to time, and, when it does, the farmer
must change with it to remain successful. Indeed, each farmer
is confronted with his own peculiar land, labor, capital "mix"
—as it is called—to be decided. Again, not all farmers are
equally well equipped to make the change. Government inter-

vention can shift the "mix" to the disadvantage of some and to the advantage of others, as we shall see.

Farmers have a particularly complex economic situation. They are particularly vulnerable to the elements. Crops may be ruined by a few minutes of hail. Too much or too little rain may ruin a year's work. How much farmers will produce is uncertain, and what they can sell it for is also difficult to determine in advance, when it is not impossible. Farmers have ever been lookers for signs and portents. In the spring, they look hopefully for signs that the spring rains are coming to an end that they may get the spring plowing and planting done. Then they look for signs of coming gentle showers that will turn seed to plant and keep the young plants green and growing. When harvest time comes, they would stay the clouds with hard looks to permit them to complete their work and gather the crop in good condition.

There are other signs of equal importance to farmers, the economic signs. The most important signs here are called prices. How much land to use is governed to some extent by the price of land. The use of capital is conditioned by the cost of money—interest. Cost of transportation is an important sign of what to grow and whether to move on. The price of commodities is a rough indicator of what to grow and in what amount. Sentimental people may groan if they hear that a farmer in Nebraska must pay 8 per cent interest on money while a Wall Street banker can get money for 5 per cent. It is unfair, they say, for the poor farmer who earns his living by the sweat of his brow to pay so much for money. The sentimentalist thinks he would be helping matters if he could, say, make 5 per cent money available to farmers. Such thinking frequently undergirds the thrust to government intervention.

It is not so easy to help people, a fact which should have long since borne itself home upon the human race. A man who has to pay a higher interest than someone else is being proffered a sign. The bank is saying, in effect, that he is not as good a credit risk as someone else. It may be that the

Interest
rate to whom & what
how much clue to what
kind of credit risk

judgment is personal, that by past performance the man is known to be slow to pay. Or, it may be that the banker judges that the object for which the man wants the money is not one that is most likely to be profitable. At any rate, the man who is expert in investment—the banker—has given his assessment of the possibilities when he announces the conditions of a loan. Low interest, on the other hand, should indicate that a good investment is involved. If, by intervention, the government makes low interest rates available to farmers, it is, in effect, sending out false signals. It proclaims good investments where they do not exist and misleads those who borrow this money.

[handwritten margin note: False Signals by Gov't offering Low interest rate.]

Government intervention, then, short circuits the signaling devices in an economy. It distorts the picture as to what "mix" to use of land, labor, and capital. It promotes uneconomic ventures, prolongs the agony of necessary adjustments, misallocates funds, and misleads men as to the most promising endeavors into which to put their energy. Misleading signs will bear most heavily upon the poor, as has been pointed out, for they are the ones most apt to be misguided by them.

The year 1862 will be taken as the point of departure for the beginning of programs of intervention to be examined. The Homestead Act, passed in that year, makes a good starting point. For the first time in history, the United States government made land generally available virtually free. By the terms of this act, homesteaders could have up to 160 acres from the public domain for the payment of a ten dollar fee. If they lived on the land for five years, they would own the land free and clear. By 1900, somewhere in the vicinity of 80 million acres of land had been homesteaded.

In 1862, the United States government took official notice of agriculture as an interest by establishing a Bureau of Agriculture. The responsibilities of this Bureau, the act pointed out, "shall to be acquire and diffuse among the people of the United States useful information on subjects connected with agriculture in the most general and comprehensive sense of that word, and to procure, propagate, and distribute among the people new and valuable seeds and plants."[4] From these humble beginnings sprang the Department of Agriculture, which was raised to that rank in 1889. Along the same lines, the Morrill Act was passed in 1862, providing land grants to the states from the public domain for the purpose of establishing agricultural colleges.

In the same year, the Pacific Railway Act was passed by Congress. As supplemented by later legislation, it provided for land grants to the railroads building in the west, plus large loans. Four transcontinental lines had made connections to the Pacific by the end of 1883—the Union Pacific, the Santa Fe, the Northern Pacific, and the Southern Pacific. The West had been rather effectively opened to settlement.

There were other interventions and involvements of government with agriculture in the ensuing years which may as well be put on the record at this point. During the Civil War, the Federal government issued $450,000,000 in unsecured United States notes, that came to be known as Greenbacks. This inflationist effort was later supplemented by the Bland-Allison Act of 1878 and the Sherman Silver Purchase Act of 1890. The Homestead Act was supplemented by the Timber Culture Act of 1874 which made 160 acres of additional land available for everyone who kept 40 acres of the land in timber. The timber requirement was shortly reduced to 10 acres. The Desert Land Act of 1877 authorized homesteaders to acquire 640 acres of land for 25 cents an acre if the land was irrigated within 3 years.

On the surface, the above have the appearance of being the acts of a generous and benevolent government. Moreover, they look as if the poor might be the direct beneficiaries of them. Surely, the poor would get land for almost nothing under the Homestead Act. Surely, it would be helpful to the poor to become more productive with the aid of colleges and a Bureau of Agriculture. The railroads opened up a vast new

[4] Peterson, *op. cit.*, p. 58.

domain in which men might find many new opportunities. From the outward appearance of things, a great era of farm prosperity should have been forthcoming.

Yet the record does not show that this was the case. On the contrary, all historians seem to agree that The Great Farm Problem arose in the latter part of the nineteenth century, simultaneously with the supposedly beneficial government programs. Book after book repeats the tale of woe of the farmers. "The country was growing," one writer says, however, "one important group in society was suffering increasingly as the years rolled by—the farmers. . . . Long the backbone of American society, the farmer was rapidly being left behind in the race for wealth and status that dominated the post-Civil War era. The number of farmers and the volume of agricultural production continued to rise, but agriculture's relative place in the national economy was declining steadily."[5] In the same vein, another textbook says: "By 1890 western farmers were becoming desperate. The great industrial development of the period was bringing wealth to the financiers and manufacturers and higher wages to urban workers. Farmers on the other hand had never recovered from the panic of 1873. In fact their situation seemed to be growing worse."[6]

The story that history books tell of the plight of farmers is even more devastating and revealing in detail. The Beards recount the story of the rise of tenancy and farm indebtedness:

> In 1880, the year of the first census of tenancy, twenty-five per cent of all the farms in the United States were tilled by renters; at the opening of the twentieth century the proportion had risen to thirty-five per cent and the curve was clearly upward. . . .
> Even though about two-thirds of the farmers owned the

[5] John A. Garraty, *The American Nation* (New York: Harper and Row, 1966), p. 609.
[6] Ralph V. Harlow and Nelson M. Blake, *The United States from Wilderness to World Power* (New York: Holt, Rinehart and Winston, 1964, 4th ed.), p. 503.

land they tilled at the opening of the twentieth century, a large proportion of these more fortunate individuals labored under heavy debts which imposed servitudes on them no less real, if more euphonious, than the burdens laid upon the cottars and bordars of the middle ages.[7]

The story, as usually told, is one of "overproduction," "surpluses," and declining prices. As one writer says, "All through the period there was a strong tendency for farm production to outrun demand and, consequently, for farm prices to be depressed."[8] In more detail, another writer says: "Between 1860 and 1910 American farm acreage doubled (to 900 million), while corn and cotton production tripled and wheat quadrupled. . . . Overexpansion . . . was not confined to cotton and wheat but appeared in nearly every farm product. The case of the corn-hog cycle was then and has remained since very much the point. . . . At any rate, there were alternate surpluses of corn and hogs with consequent risks to the farmer, and the surpluses and losses became great as corn-hog farming expanded."[9] The general trend of farm prices was downward from the Civil War to the late 1890's. One history book notes the trend in these words: "The prices of staples began to sag in the 'eighties. In the depression years of the 'nineties they hit bottom. Wheat, for instance, brought $1.20 a bushel in 1881, and 50 cents in 1895; cotton, 10½ cents a pound in 1881, and 4½ cents in 1894."[10]

I have quoted at length from history textbooks to show that there is general agreement that the agricultural situation deteriorated and worsened in the latter part of the nineteenth century. It would be possible to show, also, that most historians have been aware of the government efforts that were supposed to benefit farmers. Yet the cause and effect relation-

---

[7] Charles A. Beard and Mary R. Beard, *The Rise of American Civilization*, II (New York: Macmillan, 1933), pp. 275-76.

[8] Robert R. Russel, *A History of the American Economic System* (New York: Appleton-Century-Crofts, 1964), p. 389.

[9] Leland D. Baldwin, *The Stream of American History*, II (New York: American Book Co., 1957), p. 194.

[10] Richard Hofstadter, *et al.*, *The United States: The History of a Republic* (Englewood Cliffs: Prentice-Hall, 1967, 2nd ed.), p. 559.

ship between these two developments is left generally unexplored. History books attribute what happened to such things as an "agricultural revolution," following the Beards in this, to high interest rates, to discriminatory rail rates, to the failure of farmers to organize for reducing production, and so on.

There is, it should be clear, a close relation between government policy and the deteriorating farm situation. It should be obvious that free land contributed to the great increase in production that, in turn, led to lower prices. The cost of land is one of the deterrents to going into farming. Farming can be made to look most attractive if this cost is removed or reduced to a minimum. A prime economic consideration is removed from the initial decision to go into farming. The effect of this was for many to be lured into farming for whom it was not an economic pursuit, or who would make farming uneconomic for those already in it.

Those who suffered most from this would be the poor. In the first place, the production of those who received free or inexpensive land which led to decline in prices made many new marginal farmers. Of the older established farmers in the east, those with the smallest holdings, the poorest soil, and the least effective equipment—in a word, the poor—became the marginal or sub-marginal farmers. Many of those who settled in the west quickly became marginal farmers themselves. One writer indicates their plight: "Because of the steady decline of the price level, farmers in newer settled regions were usually worse off than those in older areas, since they had to borrow money to get started and were therefore burdened with fixed interest charges that became harder to meet with each passing year. In the 1870's farmers in states like Illinois and Iowa suffered most. . . ." In the 1890's, thousands "lost their farms and returned eastward, penniless and dispirited. The population of Nebraska increased by fewer than 4,000 persons in the nineties, less than four-tenths of one per cent!"[11]

[11] Garraty, *op. cit.*, pp. 610-11.

One other point about the government's free homestead policy needs to be made. A vigorous and profitable cattle industry had developed on the Great Plains in the late 1860's and the 1870's. These cattle had been grazed on the open range. The coming of homesteaders disrupted this development, for homesteaders tried to farm their small holdings, threw up fences, and sundered one part of a ranch from another. Many of these farmers did not succeed on their plots of land in arid country, but they did denude the land of its covering and prevent what was probably the most economic use of the land.

Virtually free land probably was less significant in leading farmers down the garden path than another intervention: the subsidizing of the railroads. To encourage the building of the Union Pacific and Central Pacific the Federal government gave each road a 400-foot right of way and free timber and materials from public lands. In addition, for each mile of railway completed the roads got 12,880 acres of land. They were also provided loans ranging from $16,000 to $48,000 a mile. Some other railroads in the west were encouraged in a similar manner. The largest land grant was to the Northern Pacific, which received 42,000,000 acres of land.[12]

The government subsidies for railroad building affected the fate of farmers in several ways. In the first place, the land grants and loans relieved builders of the major initial economic considerations. Railroads were built to carry people and goods. Anyone contemplating building a railroad, if he is to do it with his own money, will be likely to calculate the possibility of profitable returns. This means that the railroad must be able to provide the service at a price that patrons can pay. He would be wise to follow or accompany settlements and enterprises which would potentially make the railroad an economic undertaking, taking care to follow a route with the greatest potential returns. Ordinarily, then, it would be

---

[12] See Gilbert C. Fite and Jim E. Reese, *An Economic History of the United States* (Boston: Houghton Mifflin, 1965, 2nd ed.), pp. 328-30.

plausible to interpret the building of a great railroad through a region as a sign that this was an area with great immediate potentialities.

But the government bounties largely relieved builders of the necessity of these calculations initially. They had maximum incentives for laying as much track as possible over the easiest routes to lay it, and were enabled largely to ignore the future. Moreover, there were possibilities of quick profits from building, profits at the expense of the future stability of the railroad. Credit Mobilier was the famous scandal, involving the Union Pacific, of builders reaping a huge return by milking the railroad of its assets. But even if such shenanigans had not occurred, the railroads would still not have been economically built, most likely, for the incentives ran counter to this.

The railroads had huge acreages of land to dispose of as a result of the land grants. They went to great lengths to lure settlers into the area. One writer says, "Land was offered at prices as low as $2.50 per acre, and sometimes lower, with attractive credit features. . . . Land-seekers' excursion tickets were sold on the understanding that the price paid for the ticket might be counted as a downpayment on any purchase of railroad land." An advertisement addressed to "emigrants" contained these eye-catching promises to settlers: "Farms at $3. per acre," Farms on ten year credit," "Lands not taxable for six years," "Schools and churches," "Best watered and timbered tract of land in northern Kansas," and so on.[13] Settlers were drawn into the west in great numbers.

The necessities of economy can be deferred, but they will sooner or later make themselves felt. As soon as a railroad is in operation, it must begin to take account of costs and profits. Rail rates were considerably higher in the west than in the east. "For example, it cost more to ship a bushel of corn from central Nebraska to Omaha, a distance of some 150 miles, than from Omaha to Chicago, a haul over twice as

[13] John D. Hicks, *The American Nation* (Boston: Houghton Mifflin, 1955, 3rd ed.), p. 212.

long." Moreover, "in 1880 ton-mile railway rates from
Chicago to the Missouri River were only 1.08 cents, compared to 3.15 cents west of the Missouri."[14] A hue and cry
arose that the railroads were gouging the farmers, and pressure mounted for governments (state and national) to regulate rail rates. One thing should be clear, however, that it was
much more expensive for railroads to provide service in the
sparsely settled agricultural west than it was to provide it in
the much more thickly inhabited industrializing east. At any
rate, my point is that railroads had been built without economic justification, that settlers were lured into their regions,
and that economy eventually caught up in rail rates. Undoubtedly, many farmers were caught in a squeeze between
high rail rates, high storages costs, high interest rates, on the
one hand, and declining prices on the other, for the commodities that made their way to the market contributed to the
depressing of prices.

The establishment of land grant colleges and a Bureau of
Agriculture by the Federal Government hardly appear com-
prehensible in the situation. The effect of these, if they had
any effect, would be to increase production. They were to
engage in research projects and to disseminate information to
farmers, and potential farmers, about improved seeds, better
techniques, and higher productivity. It is quite understandable
that individual farmers might wish to increase their productivity, but to make general increases in productivity could
only aggravate the situation. Be that as it may, such programs
by the government are attempts to remove, or reduce, economic considerations from the attaining of information.
Again, the impact would be to contribute to an increase in the
number of farmers as well as the extent of production. Those
farmers who would be least likely either to get or use the new
information, techniques, and materials would be the poorest,
for they are apt to be the least educated, would have the least
capital to spend for new seeds or equipment, and would likely
be the most resistant to adopting new methods. Such farmers

[14] Fite and Reese, *op. cit.*, p. 438.

may become sub-marginal in any case, but the process would be accelerated by government-fed information.

Inflation—an increase of the currency supply—was the main panacea offered by politicians and agitators to suffering farmers. In the latter part of the nineteenth century, the inflationist program was advanced by Greenbackers and Silverites. The results of their efforts were the keeping of Greenbacks in circulation and two silver acts, of limited impact. The argument for inflation in order to aid debtors is most intriguing. Cheaper money should enable debtors to pay off their debts more readily. In general, that probably would be its effect for the moment. Morality aside—and there are rather strong moral objections to be raised to retiring debts with cheaper money than that borrowed—, it must be made clear that there is a false premise in this line of reasoning. This notion of debt reduction by way of inflation is based upon a static concept of an economy, as most panaceas tend to be. If all farmers would *cease* to borrow money, if the currency supply were greatly increased, if the increased money obtained by way of higher prices were applied to debts, most debts could surely be retired. But—and this is a definitive and all-embracing *but*—men do not cease to borrow money when the currency supply is increased. On the contrary, borrowing may be expected to mount for two reasons. First, other things being equal, interest rates will drop,* and loans are more easily acquired. Secondly, prices rise in general, and those who wish to borrow money will need more to make their purchases. Thus, indebtedness could be expected to rise in a period of inflation. The historical record tends to bear this out. For example, farm indebtedness rose greatly between 1910 and 1920, a period of drastic inflation.

Inflation does not tend to decrease indebtedness over a period of time, though it reduces the relative value of a debt once contracted; but it does send misleading signals into the

---

* Temporarily, at least. They rise again when creditors discover that the inflation is eating up the value of the money they have loaned. Then the price of money (interest), like other prices, rises with the inflation.

economy. Easier money may enable a sub-marginal farmer to hold out a little longer as well as draw others into farming. This point, however, requires further examination later on, since it becomes much more relevant when government intervenes more directly to reduce the interest rates.

Governments frequently follow the adage of not letting the right hand know what the left hand is doing. At any rate, there were deep contradictions in the programs of the United States government in the latter part of the nineteenth century. On the one hand, government promoted agricultural production by the homestead laws, by the subsidizing of railroad building, by occasional forays into inflation, and by encouraging research and the dissemination of information. On the other, it made materials and equipment more expensive and reduced the market with the protective tariff. As in so many other things, action taken during the Civil War signaled the onset of full-fledged protective policies. The standard work on the history of the tariff says, "Before the war we had a tariff of duties which, though not arranged completely or consistently on the principles of free trade, was very moderate in comparison with the existing system." This had not been true throughout earlier American history, but the act of 1846 capped a trend in the direction of lower rates. "The act of 1846 had been passed by the Democratic party with the avowed intention of putting into operation, as far as possible, the principles of free trade." This was done even more consistently a few years later. "The act of 1857 took away still more from the restrictive character of our tariff legislation. . . . The maximum protective duty was reduced to twenty-four per cent; many raw materials were admitted free; and the level of duties on the whole line of manufactured articles was brought down to the lowest point which has been reached in this country since 1815."[15]

In 1861 and 1862 the trend was reversed, and tariffs of a

[15] F. W. Taussig, *The Tariff History of the United States*, David M. Chalmers, intro. (New York: Capricorn Books, 1964, 8th rev. ed.), pp. 156-57.

more protective nature were passed. It was, however, the Tariff of 1864 which established the protective trend for so many years thereafter. Taussig says, "The identical duties fixed in 1864 were left in force for a long series of years. When a general revision came to be made, in 1883, they had ceased to be thought of as the results of war legislation. . . . Hence the war tariff, though from time to time patched, amended, revised, not only remained in force in its important provisions for nearly twenty years, but became in time the basis for an even more stringent application of protection."[16]

Since the Tariff Act of 1864 was the standard for the latter part of the nineteenth century, it will be useful to examine it in some little detail. In general, the rates were in the vicinity of 50 per cent though there was considerable variation from commodity to commodity. Of considerable importance, however, was what was covered. A partial list of items covered will reveal the general character of the tariff. Among those named were: tea, sugar, molasses, syrup, snuff, tobacco, bar iron, wire, galvanized iron, tin plates, anvils, chains, trace chains, halter chains, fence chains, hammers and sledges, nuts and washers, axles, bed screws, hinges, nails, spikes, rivets, bolts, horseshoe nails, tacks, brads, pig iron, stoves, pipe, scrap iron, steel wire, skates, cross-cut saws, hand saws, knives, needles, coal, wool, woolens, belts, hats, blankets, dress goods, shirts, oil cloths, cotton and cotton cloth, spool thread, cotton bagging, china, glass, cloves, pepper, salt, gunpowder, and lemons.[17]

Duties, of consequence, were levied on two orders of items: manufactured goods, and materials not produced in quantity in the United States, as, for example, tea. There was a tendency in later decades to drop or lower the rates on materials not grown in the United States. As time wore on, and criticism of the tariff arose, more American agricultural pro-

---

[16] *Ibid.*, pp. 169-70.
[17] *Tariff Acts 1789 to 1909* (Washington: Government Printing Office, 1909), pp. 230-47.

ducts were placed under tariff "protection." However, it should be abundantly clear that major American staples—that is, cotton, corn, and wheat, along with many less durable products such as eggs—could hardly be effectively "protected." The United States was an exporting country of major agricultural staples; therefore, duties on imports would hardly protect farmers who grew them. Taussig's comment on the Tariff of 1890 is to the point: "The duty on wheat went up from twenty to twenty-five cents a bushel, and that on Indian corn from ten to fifteen cents; changes which obviously could be of no consequence whatever."[18] More pointedly, a writer makes this caustic comment on the Tariff Act of 1883: "As far as any significance of these duties on most of these agricultural products, either to the agricultural producer or the consumer, they were at that time of no economic importance whatever. They served only to throw dust in the farmer's eyes, and foster in him a sort of pacific feeling that he was sharing the benefits of the protective system."[19]

In so far as the protective tariff was effective in doing what it purported to do, it had these effects on American farmers. In the first place, it raised the price of goods that the farmer bought. Many items protected were such as farmers are most apt to use, e.g., crosscut saws, trace chains, hammers, nails, galvanized iron, and so on. All mechanical equipment would be affected by tariffs on metals. Clothing would be higher, otherwise there would be little justification for "protecting it." Even farm products which might be effectively raised in price, e.g., sugar and wool, would only "protect" some farmers at the expense of others, and of consumers in general.

Secondly, so far as the tariff did its job, the market for agricultural products abroad would be reduced. America was a major exporter of farm products in the nineteenth century, most famously of cotton, tobacco, wheat, beef, and so on. But

[18] Taussig, *op. cit.*
[19] Clarence A. Wiley, "Economics and Politics of the Agriculture Tariff," *Agriculture and the Tariff*, Julia E. Johnson, comp. (New York: H. W. Wilson, 1927), p. 40.

the extent of the exports was limited by the ability of people elsewhere to pay for them. Foreigners can pay for American goods, in general, only to the extent that they can sell goods of approximately the same amount in the United States. (To a limited extent, of course, trade between nations can be balanced by carrying charges, interest, loans, precious metals, and so forth.) When foreign goods are excluded, that reduces the ability of those who produced them to pay for American goods. In short, exports declined over what they *might have been*, not necessarily over what they were at an early time.

Thirdly, the reduction in the market has the effect of reducing prices. Price is the outcome of supply and demand. When foreign peoples do not buy as many American commodities as they might have, the demand is reduced. If the supply remains the same, or increases in greater proportion than demand, as it did with some agricultural products, prices will fall. American production did, indeed, increase faster than effective markets, domestic and foreign, in the latter part of the nineteenth century. That prices did tumble is a matter of record. (Though, of course, with lower prices the goods were sold, quite often at rates unprofitable to producers.)

Farmers, then, were buffeted by the contrary winds of government intervention. By one policy, they were encouraged to produce as much as possible, to go into farming, to move onto western lands, to settle and bring more land under cultivation. By the tariff policy, what they bought was priced in a protected market while most of what was sold was on the world market. Hence, there was a great expansion of agriculture, followed by declining prices and often accompanied by the heavy indebtedness of farmers.

Eventually, adjustments were made to the situation. From 1898 to 1914 has long been reckoned a kind of Golden Age for American agriculture. According to the later view, this was the period of the ideal ratio between farm prices and prices of manufactured products. No great change in government policy had occurred, but economy had asserted itself over all the obstacles, and adjustments had been made. The words sound innocent enough, but they mask numerous private hardships. The deflation, or depression, of the mid 1890's finally succeeded in driving out many marginal and submarginal farmers. The innocent word, "adjustment," hides the dashed hopes, the years of struggle amidst dreams turned to nightmares, the bankruptcy, the shattered lives of those who had staked all on a homestead in the west, and the shameful returns to the east. "That is war," say the French, as they shrug off misfortune, but few have recognized the subtlety of the war on the poor.

In any case, the Golden Age was brief. It reached its peak, or had its Indian summer, so to speak, during World War I. The coming of the war in Europe brought temporary depression in America, but the trend was shortly reversed, and prices of agricultural products shot upward at an almost unprecedented pace. Cotton had been a little over 12 cents per pound in early 1914; by early 1920 it was bringing 40 cents per pound. Wheat jumped from a little over a dollar per bushel in 1916 to $3.40 in 1917. Corn eventually sold for $2.00 per bushel and hogs for $19.00 per hundredweight. Shortly after the end of the war, the drop came as swiftly as the rise. Wheat brought $2.76 per bushel in 1919, but it dropped to $1.44 in 1920. Cotton dropped from 40 cents per pound to fourteen cents. Nor was this the end. "Prices of manufactured goods also declined but recovered in a year or so. In contrast, prices of farm products remained low for a generation. For the farmer, wartime prosperity was over. . . . In the cold winter of 1921, Dakota and Nebraska farmers burned corn for fuel and bartered meager commodities for clothing."[20]

There is no reason to doubt that there was widespread agricultural depression in ensuing decades. The following is a typical textbook description of the situation. "Beginning in the fall of 1920 agriculture slumped into a severe depression,

[20] Peterson, *op. cit.*, pp. 81-84.

and at no time in the following decade did farmers, especially the producers of staple crops, achieve full recovery. In fact, the position of farmers was poor when compared to other aspects of the economy until agricultural prices were driven upward under the impact of World War II."[21] The major exception to be taken to such statements is that, of course, not all farmers fare alike, and that some prospered while others grew poorer.

Nor is there any good reason to doubt where the source of the new difficulties lay. Government intervention had, this time, produced its distortions and the accompanying difficulties swiftly. As one writer says, "Much of the damage to the farmer can be credited to the direct action of the government."[22] Another says, "The roots of this depression are not hard to find."[23]

During the war, the Federal government used numerous devices, some old, some new, to encourage maximum agricultural production. It was possible now to get a homestead with 320 acres rather than 160, and nearly a quarter of a billion acres of public land was opened for farms and herds. The government financed the war mainly by inflation, vastly increasing the money supply, sending false signals into the economy. The Federal Farm Loan Act provided easy credit for farmers; in consequence, farm indebtedness doubled. Government supported prices of crops most wanted; one billion dollars was appropriated in 1919 to maintain the price of wheat.

The program was at least partially successful in stimulating production. Twenty million added acres of wheat was brought under cultivation and five million acres of rye. Cattle and hog population was increased by 20 per cent. Food exports rose from 7 million tons before the war to 19 million tons in 1919. The total farm debt stood at $4.7 billion in 1914; by 1920 it

[21] Fite and Reese, *op. cit.*, p. 551.
[22] Henry C. Taylor, "Agriculture and the Tariff," in Johnson *op. cit.*, p. 65.
[23] Peterson, *op. cit.*, p. 83.

had risen to $8.5 billion.[24] Farmers had been drawn into great production and were, no doubt, equipping themselves for much more.

But the government gives and the government takes away. In 1920, the inflation was brought to an unceremonious halt, at least for the time being. The price supports were dropped. The foreign market for agricultural products declined precipitately. To further aggravate the situation, a much higher tariff was passed by Congress in 1922, the Fordney McCumber Tariff. The farmers were left holding the bag, or, more precisely, their debts, their lands, their depleted returns. "The gross income of agriculture declined from $17,677,-000,000 to $13,031,000,000 between 1919 and 1925, or 26.6 per cent. The net earnings of farmers declined to a greater extent than the gross income. . . . The expansion of agriculture was brought about during the war by appeals to patriotism and by . . . promises to sustain the price levels. This expansion having taken place, the reduction came slowly and brought with it enormous losses. The farmer's only chance of salvaging anything out of his life-long savings was in hanging on with the hope that there would be a turn for the better."[25]

An adjustment needed to be made to the changed situation. Increased foreign wartime demand with higher prices drew what was otherwise marginal land into cultivation, while easy money induced many to go into debt. With the decline in prices, much land and many farmers became marginal or submarginal. The normal course of events would be for these lands and farmers to drop out of agricultural production. As production fell, prices would either rise or those who remained in production would be efficient enough to stay in farming at the prevailing prices. Such an adjustment was neither pleasant to contemplate nor to carry out. It meant mortgage foreclosures, bankruptcies, changes of residences and employments, and loss of investments. At best, such an

---

[24] See *ibid.*, pp. 82-83; Fite and Reese, *op. cit.*, pp. 519-22.
[25] Taylor, *op. cit.*, pp. 64-65.

adjustment would probably not have occurred quickly. As the writer above points out, many would hold out year after year, hoping against hope that the situation would improve, that prices would rise, and that they could again effectively compete.

The Adjustment has never been made, at least not in the normal way. This is not to say that many adjustments have not been made; they have. Millions have left the farms in America. Millions of acres of land have been taken out of cultivation. But the Herculean effort has been made to prevent normal adjustment, to raise prices, to keep marginal farmers on the farm, to enable the poor to buy farms, and so on. The adjustments have taken place under conditions induced by government to prevent the adjustments. Thus, lands which would be submarginal without interference have been kept in production by interference and lands that would have been profitable to cultivate have been driven out. In short, normal adjustment has not taken place.

In the abstract, a case can be made that the Federal government should have done something to rescue the farmers. After all, the government had done much to produce the mess. It may be pointed out, also, that the programs during World War I were adopted to advance the war effort, to feed allies, and speed the day of victory. In that case, the farmers might be likened to war casualties. To help them might be compared to aid given to war casualties, to pensions provided for the disabled, to hospitals maintained for those wounded, to aid the families of those killed in combat. The analogy is not a perfect one, however, and the differences are worth pointing out for showing how efforts to aid farmers go astray. Payments to the disabled are not likely to encourage many men to actually become disabled. Maintaining hospitals for the wounded will not induce many men to become seriously wounded, though it may encourage malingerers. Certainly, there is little likelihood that many men will get themselves killed in combat in order to provide their survivors with in-

surance. Men are, by nature, disinclined to disablement, dis-
figurement, and violent death. Aid to farmers mobilizes
human inclinations in a different direction. If prices are raised
for what they produce, they will try to produce more. If they
are enabled to pay off their farms with a government grant,
they will be enabled to stay in farming that much longer. In
short, government aid only makes the situation worse. Even
so, there has been a massive effort to "aid" farmers.

Gov makes farming worse

In the abstract, again, a case can be made that farmers
should not have let themselves be drawn into increased wartime production. They should have known that the prices they
received were wartime prices, that the expansion would eventually have to be curtailed, that they were incurring debts at
wartime prices, and that cheap money would give way to
dearer money. In short, an abstract case can be made that
farmers ought to be rigorous economists, deeply learned in
history, and expert psychologists and philosophers. An
equally likely case can be made that politicians ought not to
mislead the electorate, that men should not have wars, or that
they should not take the steps they consider necessary to win
wars. The fact is that most farmers are not expert economists
or historians. They know little more, in this regard, than that
higher prices are a signal that they have a better chance of
profiting with greater production. And, if men ever stopped
acting upon this information, we should all likely starve.

The best case of all can be made for the view that government should not have interfered in the post World War I
situation, that the adjustment that would then have followed
in that time would have been hard, but that there was no help
for it, and that efforts to prevent misery only prolonged and
added to it. Be that as it may, this was not to be. Many
farmers had fallen under the sway of the notion that intervention could relieve the situation. There were vocal farm leaders
of organizations lobbying for aid. Many politicians from farm
states were promising benefits. The reform impetus, even in
the apparently non-reformist 1920's, was gaining headway.

The Federal Reserve Board was already established to interfere with the money supply. Many farmers had come to
believe that the protective tariff offered possibilities for use in
their behalf. (The wartime interventions were there in the
mind as models for peacetime use.)

At any rate, pressure mounted in the 1920's for government to come to the rescue of the farmer. The thrust of
government into the farm arena would not become an all-out
effort until the 1930's, but there is a continuity in the analysis
of the situation and the direction of the effort from the 1920's
down to the present. Thus, it is appropriate at this point to
summarize the interventionist analysis and proposals.

Reduced to basics, the interventionist argument was sim-
plicity itself. It amounted to the proposition that farm prices
were (or are) too low. Or, farmers got too little for what they
sold and paid too much for what they bought. The argument
is most appealing. It accords with each man's (in this case,
each farmer's) *subjective* analysis of the situation. Each of us
"knows"—more correctly, *feels*—that he is underpaid for
what he sells and overcharged for what he buys. There is a
reason, of sorts, for our belief in this proposition, one that
goes beyond our ingrained selfishness. We know what we
have put into the product or service we offer in a way that we
do not know what other men put into theirs. The farmer
knows the struggle he has made to acquire his land, the debt
that looms over him for his equipment, the long hours of work
in season to bring in his crop. He does not know in the same
way the investment, labor, and struggle that others have put
into what they have to offer.

In any case, the proposition that the farmer got, or gets, too
little for his produce was not an economic one. Economically,
price is what a good will bring in the marketplace in competition with other goods. Economically, a given price indicates to the producer the worthwhileness of continuing
to produce and offer for sale a particular good. A great deal
of energy has been devoted to attempts to make objective

computations of the basic needs of people. Having made such calculations, there have been attempts to render them into a money figure and to decide upon the minimum sum a worker must earn or a farmer must get for each article of produce in order to satisfy these needs. If it amounts to more than some are getting, which is the whole point of such calculations, the claim is that they should be paid more. But this runs counter to every other man's economy. It bids him to pay more than the market price, and, perhaps, to take less than the market price for what he has to offer. The argument has a purely theoretical appeal; in the marketplace men operate upon the economic principle of buying as cheaply as possible and selling as dearly as they can. Only force can induce men to behave otherwise, which is why such schemes rely on government; but force will not make such action economic.

Nonetheless, there have been a host of programs advanced to raise the price of farm produce. These have usually rested upon rationales as to what caused the low prices. Most commonly, it has been held that farmers have overexpanded and overproduced. The solution to this, everyone may agree, would be to curtail production. However, interventionists do not reason, at this point, that inefficient producers should get out of production. If this were the point, no intervention would be called for. Instead, they envision the desirability of curtailing production without reducing the number of farmers. But they doubt that this could be accomplished by voluntary agreements. Farmers are individualists, they say, and will not voluntarily co-operate to reduce production. Instead, a farmer who believes that production is going to be reduced will increase his production in the anticipation of a higher price. Therefore, government must intervene to reduce production.

Most of the arguments for government intervention were based on the supposedly inferior position of agriculture *vis a vis* industry. In contrast to the manufacturer, it has usually been held, farmers cannot determine before-hand how much of a commodity they will produce. Even if they could come to agreement upon acreage to be planted, this would still not have a determinable effect upon how much they would produce. There are the vagaries of weather which will affect the amount. In consequence, they may produce bumper crops, resulting in lower prices. Moreover, farmers frequently sell at that time when the price is lowest for the year, in the period immediately following the harvest when others are also selling. These considerations have led to a number of proposals. One is to make loans available to farmers to enable them to withhold their crops from the market for a period of time. Another related one is to make storage facilities available at little or no cost. Another is the ever-normal-granary idea, to have part of bumper crops stored for lean years. Many reformers have favored co-operatives among farmers to accomplish these things, co-operatives promoted by government with various inducements and special privileges.

One of the claims, hoary with age, has been that the middleman—the processor, the distributor, the owner of the storage elevator, the wholesaler, the retailer—gets the profit. According to this view, the farmers get a low price, the consumer pays a high price, and the middlemen get the difference, an exorbitant profit. Strangely, those who offer this argument do not accompany it with the proposal that some considerable number of people ought to quit farming to become middlemen. If there are such profits to be had, one might suppose that a great many more people could prosper offering these services. But theirs is an argument, of course, which appeals to ingrained prejudices, not to reason, and that makes it more effective as a persuader, not less. Even so, some efforts have been made to cut out the middleman, such as co-operatives for distribution of commodities and sale of goods that farmers buy.

Interventionists have offered many allegations to justify government involvement, but the above are sufficient to show their character. It will be more informative to see how they went about trying to raise prices, curtail production, equalize the position of farmers and manufacturers, and rescue the farmers.

In the 1920's, government intervened in the situation in three ways that were supposed to aid the farmer. In the first place, tariff rates for farm products were raised. There is no evidence, except for a few products and select situations, that this raised the price of farm products. On the other hand, as has already been noted, prices were probably hurt by the reduction in demand resulting from the exclusion or diminution of imports. Second, the government attempted to encourage the activities of farm co-operatives. In 1922, the Capper-Volstead Act was passed, exempting co-operatives from prosecution under the antitrust laws. In 1923, the Agricultural Credits Act was passed. "This measure established twelve Intermediate Credit Banks, financed by the Treasury and operated in conjunction with the Federal Land Banks, to make loans to organize groups of farmers for periods running from six months to three years. In addition, the Act authorized the creation of National Credit Corporations, or private agricultural banks, to serve the special needs of livestock producers."[26] The main purpose of these acts was to enable co-operatives to make loans to farmers on their harvested crops so that they could withhold them from the market in order to raise prices. Again, these appear to have had little effect on farm prices, possibly because of the very limited operations of co-operatives.

The third way was to raise prices by inflation. By 1922, the government had resumed inflationary policies, policies which were to continue with some interruptions through 1928. One economist calculates that the total money supply increased from 45.3 billion dollars on June 30, 1921 to 73 billion dollars on December 31, 1928.[27] While the exact figures would

[26] Arthur S. Link, *American Epoch* (New York: Alfred A. Knopf, 1955), p. 265.

[27] Murray N. Rothbard, *America's Great Depression* (Princeton: D. Van Nostrand, 1963), p. 88.

be a matter of dispute, owing to differences of opinion as to
the kinds of reserves which constitute a part of the money
supply, there should be little doubt that an inflation of these
proportions did occur. This inflation was supposed to benefit
farmers especially. Most directly, in the latter part of 1921 the
Federal Reserve announced that it would extend credits for
harvesting and agricultural marketing. Indirectly, another
"motive for inflation" was "a desire to help foreign governments and American exporters (particularly farmers). The
process worked as follows: inflation and cheap credit in the
United States stimulated the floating foreign loans in the
U. S. . . . Artificial stimulation of foreign lending in the U. S.
also helped increase or sustain foreign demand for American
farm exports."[28] In short, "To supply foreign countries with the
dollars needed to purchase American exports, the United
States government decided, *not* sensibly to lower tariffs, but instead to promote cheap money at home. . . ."[29] Indeed, as we
have seen, the government raised the tariff at about the same
time it began attempting to stimulate exports by inflation.

Government can, under certain conditions, increase the
effective money supply. It *cannot*, however, determine how
and for what the money will be spent. An increase of the
money supply will no doubt result in rises in prices somewhere, but it will not necessarily result in the rise of prices
sought. There was a great deal of lending by Americans to
Europeans in the 1920's. This did enable American exports
to be much higher than they otherwise could have been,
because of the protective tariff. Quite probably, too, farm
prices were higher than they otherwise would have been; so,
however, were other prices. The inflation may have enabled
some farmers to hang on in the 1920's; if so, the evil day was
only being deferred. In any case, the dramatic impact of the
inflation was not on prices to farmers. The prices of farm
lands did not recover their highs of 1919-1920, after the

[28] *Ibid.*, p. 127.
[29] *Ibid.*, p. 128.

drastic decline of 1920-21. The plight of farmers was reflected by that of the banks to whom they were indebted. As Frederick Lewis Allen says, "Thousands of country banks . . . ultimately went to the wall. In one of the great agricultural states, the average earnings of *all* the national and state banks during the years 1924-29, a time of great prosperity for the country at large, were less than 1½ per cent; and in seven states of the country between 40 and 50 per cent of the banks which had been in business prior to 1920 had failed before 1929."[30]

Such temporary benefits of the inflation as there may have been to farmers, then, were highly limited. The impact elsewhere was much more readily discernible. One writer sums up his answer to the question of benefits in this way:

> Who benefited, and who was injured, by the policy of protection *cum* inflation as against the rational alternative of free trade and hard money? Certainly, the bulk of the American population was injured, both as consumers of imports and as victims of inflation and poor foreign credit and later depression. Benefited were the industries protected by the tariff, the export industries uneconomically subsidized by foreign loans, and the investment bankers who floated the foreign bonds at handsome commissions.[31]

Much of the new money went into real estate and building, particularly in the middle of the decade. Speculation in real estate reached its peak in Miami around 1925. Allen says, "There was nothing languorous about the atmosphere of tropical Miami during that memorable summer and autumn of 1925. The whole city had become one frenzied real-estate exchange. There were said to be 2,000 real-estate offices and 25,000 agents marketing house-lots or acreage."[32] With a little less fervor many other cities were being expanded by the building of suburbs, and resorts were developed in many

[30] Frederick L. Allen, *Only Yesterday*, (New York: Bantam Books, 1959), p. 201.
[31] Rothbard, *op. cit.*, p. 128.
[32] Allen, *op. cit.*, p. 192.

areas. Toward the end of the decade, however, one object began to absorb more and more of the inflation: the stock market. The market soared from 1927 through the summer of 1929. Some indication of the increase can be gathered from the following increases in the price of individual common stocks from March 3, 1928 to September 3, 1929. (The prices are adjusted to take care of such things as stock splits.) American Can rose from 77 to a fraction over 181, American Telegraph from 179½ to a fraction over 335, General Electric from over 128 to over 396, Montgomery Ward from over 132 to 466½, and so on.

False economy

Much of the stock market investment was spurred by credit, most directly by buying on margin. In 1929, the Federal Reserve began to try to clamp down. For one thing, they tried to prevent monies acquired by way of the Federal Reserve from entering the speculative stream. On February 2, the Board made this pronouncement: "The Federal Reserve Act does not, in the opinion of the Federal Reserve Board, contemplate the use of the resources of the Federal Reserve Banks for the creation or extension of speculative credit. A member bank is not within its reasonable claims for rediscount facilities at its Federal Reserve Bank when it borrows either for the purpose of making speculative loans or for the purpose of maintaining speculative loans."[33] Its subsequent instructions to member banks did make call money more difficult to acquire. Moreover, there was no significant increase in the money supply for the first half of 1929. The Federal Reserve had from 1928 raised the rediscount rate several times until the New York Bank's rate finally reached 6 per cent. The Federal Reserve's policies did not bear immediate fruit in the first half of 1929; money continued to be available for the market from banks and corporations for a good part of the year. Moreover, the Federal Reserve did not follow a consistent deflationary policy; it backed and filled, raising rediscount rates and lowering the interest on accept-

[33] *Ibid.*, p. 217.

ances. Banks, in general, followed similar inconclusive policies; they tightened margin requirements and placed lower valuations on stocks as securities, meanwhile, interest rates on call money and stock exchange time loans actually declined from August to early October of 1929.[34] No one wanted responsibility for the stock market crash when it came. Yet come it did, as come it must, once the inflation ended. Once more, the government had given and the government had taken away.

Deflation came, in full measure and inexorably, after October of 1929. Men were thrusting for liquidity, for solid value, to meet their obligations and debts. Numerous banks failed, and with them vanished into thin air that part of the money supply that had been carried on their books as deposits. Mortgages that had been renewed year after year could no longer be renewed, for those banks trying to hold out had to translate their accounts receivable into liquid funds. Foreclosure was the route open to them to attempt to accomplish this end. Prices fell, drastically and disastrously, to enable sellers to dispose of goods for the declining money supply.

For many farmers, the day of accounting was at hand, in 1930, in 1931, in 1932, and for that matter, in the years to follow. The inflationary binge of World War I had drawn farmers into heavy indebtedness; the reinflation of the 1920's had enabled them to hang on. With the deflation came the rising demand that the debts be paid, came drastically reduced income to meet fixed obligations, came the apparent necessity for the least efficient to leave farming.

The Hoover Administration, with the aid of Congress, attempted to prevent the effects of the deflation from taking place. The Federal Reserve attempted to reinflate by lowering the rediscount rate, but this time banks and individuals did not behave as they were supposed to. Easier access to money only made it possible for some to establish a more nearly

[34] See Benjamin M. Anderson, *Economics and the Public Welfare* (New York: D. Van Nostrand, 1949), pp. 207-10.

liquid position. There was an attempt to prevent the effects of
deflation by one of the major devices that had set the stage for
the whole course of events, by raising the tariff once again.
The Smoot-Hawley Tariff Act was passed in 1930, raising
rates generally, with particular attention to those that were
supposed to protect prices of farm products. The government
made large loans to farm co-operatives to allow them to hold
on to farm products, keeping them off the market in the hope
of raising prices. But the actions of the Hoover Administration were not analogous to the Dutch boy standing with his
finger in a hole in the dike; they were more like someone
trying to turn back the winds of a hurricane with a fan. Nor
can the ravages of a flood be prevented by building dams in
the path of the onrushing waters. The water will be held only
for a brief time before it goes around, over, or crushes the
dam, to rush forward once more with even more damaging
force. So it was with the Hoover measures to maintain prices
in the face of deflation. Prices moved downward inexorably
toward the level of the reduced money supply, just as flood
water rushes to the lower level, delayed only temporarily by
attempts to prop them up, leaving the tariff, the Federal
Reserve, and the co-operatives like washed out dams to testify
to the futility of the effort.

That the measures of the government failed is a matter of
record. That the plight of many farmers was worse than ever
in the early 1930's is also rather clear. Of their fate, one
historian says: "Already in desperate economic straits by
1929, American farmers lost more in cash income and general economic standing during the depression years than any
other important group. Between 1929 and 1932 gross farm
income shrank from $11,941,000,000 to $5,331,000,-
000."[35] His assessments of the impact of two of the efforts
that were supposed to help farmers are worth quoting. "As
early as 1931 the members of the Federal Farm Board recognized their inability to cope with the situation; by the summer

[35] Link, *op. cit.*, p. 360.

of 1932 the Board had lost some $354,000,000 in market operations and admitted its helplessness. . . ." And, "Hoover's program of tariff relief for agriculture was an even greater fiasco than his illfated effort at stabilization."[36] Another historian, more given to hyperbole, gives this description of the situation in early 1933.

> . . . No group in the population, except perhaps the Negro workers, was more badly hit by depression. The realized net income of farm operators in 1932 was less than one-third what it had been in 1929—a dizzying collapse in three years. Farm prices had fallen more than 50 per cent; and the parity ratio of prices received by farmers to the prices they paid— had plummeted from 89 in 1929 down to 55 in 1932 (in terms of 1910-14 as 100). The seething violence in the farm belt over the winter—the grim mobs gathered to stop foreclosures, the pickets along the highways to prevent produce from being moved to town—made it clear that patience was running out.[37]

One might suppose, then, that farmers had had a surfeit of government interference, that having been buffeted back and forth for seventy odd years by the ill winds of various government interventions they might have finally been moved to violence, if necessary, to end it. Of course, this was not the interpretation put upon the events. The interventionist movement which had been gaining headway for many years found perhaps its greatest opportunity in the travail of farmers, and others. According to what is now the standard history textbook interpretation, the Hoover programs had failed because they were not more widespread, varied, and vigorously pursued. (The tariff should be excepted from these strictures, for reformers were not favorably inclined to it.) What was needed, men who became increasingly influential from 1933 on were saying, was much more thorough government inter-

[36] *Ibid.*, p. 367.
[37] Arthur M. Schlesinger, Jr., *The Coming of the New Deal* (Boston: Houghton Mifflin, 1959), p. 27.

vention. Thus began what has become a perennial chorus since: If the medicine fails, the solution is to increase the dosage. One is reminded of the practice of physicians at one time of bleeding patients. It was not uncommon for a patient, who survived a bleeding but did not get well, to be bled again, and again. Some hardy souls finally got well, in spite of the efforts of the physician. Of course, many did not. Some farmers have survived the ministrations—progressive "bleedings"—of government over the last 35 years, but alas, as we shall see, many have not.

In 1933, the New Deal came, and with it a melange of all the old and some new panaceas, nostrums, solutions, and notions which were supposed to save the farmer and restore agriculture to its former role in American life. There was the Agricultural Adjustment Administration, first and second, with its crop restrictions, subsidies, and soil conservation payments. There was the Commodity Credit Corporation with its efforts at manipulating the market and cartelizing American agriculture. There was land reclamation, people resettlement, rural electrification, co-operative organizations, and irrigation projects. There was the Farm Security Administration to make loans, long and short term, to enable farmers to stay in operation and, perchance, to buy a farm. A whole assortment of words entered the language, or were made more familiar: Acreage allotments, parity, diversified farming, and ever-normal-granary. These ideas were propagated, programs administered, and practices fostered by a host of people: county agents, assistant county agents, local committees, extension service people, and assorted part- and full-time government employees. Over the years, some programs have been abandoned, others modified, new ones added, but in substance the effort begun in the early days of the New Deal is still with us. It has had a rather thorough trial, as experiments go.

[The farm programs have failed to accomplish their purposes, on this everyone may surely agree] Indeed, they have been going on for so long and have gone so far astray from their original purposes that it is necessary here to call to mind what some of those purposes were. So completely have some apparently forgotten that there are now suggestions that the government adopt programs to achieve the opposite effect of what it started out to do. At least one writer says, "Movement of people out of agriculture and farm consolidation has been advocated as a means of maintaining farm family incomes. . . . Some people suggest that public programs should be undertaken to speed up these trends [the trends of migration from the farm]."[38] The writer does not say how "some people" propose to speed migration from the farm, but there would be a wonderful illogical consistency (or logical inconsistency) if they would undertake to adopt measures to drive prices down! [The original purpose of the farm programs was quite the opposite of inducing migration from the farms. On the contrary, they were aimed at "saving" the farmer, maintaining the farm population as it stood, and even getting more people to live on farms. There was a kind of back-to-the-farm notion behind some of the programs. Roosevelt said, as quoted in the first chapter, that he wanted to restore the balance between urban and rural population, restore it by increasing the farm population. One historian notes this romantic penchant in Roosevelt in these observations: "Franklin responded with much greater warmth to chimerical plans to remove slum dwellers to the countryside than he did to schemes for urban renewal. The President, Tugwell has written, 'always did, and always would, think people better off in the country and would regard the cities as rather hopeless. . . .' "[39] Among the more bizarre efforts to achieve the removal of people from the city to the countryside was the ill-fated Subsistence Homestead Division authorized under the National Industrial Recovery Act. Somewhere in the vicinity of a hundred rural

[38] Walter W. Wilcox, "The Farm Policy Dilemma," *American Economic History*, Stanley Coben and Forest G. Hill, eds. (New York: J. B. Lippincott), 1966.

[39] William E. Leuchtenburg, *Franklin D. Roosevelt and the New Deal* (New York: Harper and Row, 1963), p. 136.

communities were built to lure city dwellers. Some did go to live in such places, but as "soon as the pall of the early depression years lifted, people hurried to get back into the 'real' world of the bustling city streets."[40]

Roosevelt not only wanted to stop the clock, so to speak, but also wished to turn it back to an early time. He wanted to make farming an economically rewarding occupation for an increasing number of people, ideally for an increasing proportion of the population. The main line of the effort was more subtle, of course, than homesteading city dwellers, but the purpose was roughly the same. The central informing idea of most of the farm programs was to equalize farm income and opportunity with that of industry. This was the parity idea. The parity idea had been advanced in the twenties and even resulted in the passage of a bill—the McNary-Haugen Bill—by Congress, but President Coolidge vetoed it. Action to implement the parity idea was quickly taken during the early days of the New Deal. The basic notion is that farmers should get a price for their commodities that would enable them to buy industrial products at a kind of set ratio. To calculate what this ratio should be, 1910-1914 was taken as a base or ideal period. The aim was to raise prices for agricultural commodities to the point where a given amount of them would buy the same given industrial product that it had in the earlier period. If, for example, 500 bushels of wheat would buy a farm tractor in the period 1910-1914, the aim was to raise the price of wheat to the level that 500 bushels of wheat would still buy a farm tractor. Of course, parity was not calculated for each individual manufactured product, but for some kind of average of industrial prices. When this ratio prevailed, it was assumed that farming would be profitable, that the balance between rural and urban dwellers would be restored, that agriculture and manufacturing would be on equal footing, and that struggling farmers would be rescued. There were, of course, to be many other supplementary programs that were supposed to help balance the scales.

[40] *Ibid.*, p. 137.

'As I have said, the programs failed, all down the line without a single notable exception. They did not "balance" the rural and urban population. As previously noted in the first chapter, about 25 per cent of the population of the United States lived on farms in 1933. This had fallen to 23 per cent by 1940, to 15 per cent by 1950, and to 8 per cent by 1961. The decrease was both proportional and absolute. The farm population had been about 32 million in 1933 but less than 15 million in 1961. The number of farms, of all classifications, declined from 6,800,000 in 1935 to 6,100,000 in 1940 to 5,400,000 in 1950 to 3,253,000 in 1960.[41]

Nor has the small farmer been rescued, or helped, overall. On the contrary, the larger farms have enjoyed such prosperity as has resulted and poor farmers have left the farms in droves. Regarding the impact of government subsidies in more recent years, one book says: "It has been estimated that the lowest 56 percent of the farmers received only 7 per cent of the subsidies. Most of the aid has gone to the larger commercial farmers, particularly those who produced basic commodities like wheat, corn and cotton. In 1960, 296 cotton growers received more than $30 million in government price supports. The largest amount received by a single producer was $1,236,048, which went to a Mississippi cotton company owned by an English firm."[42]

Nor have vast government programs succeeded in equalizing farm with non-farm income even on that category of farms classified as highly productive. This was the situation several years ago as summarized by one writer:

> Farm operator families on the 2,213,000 commercial (high production) farms received an average income of $5,415 in 1956 while all nonfarm families, including those living on skid row and public relief programs received an average income of $6,900. The realized returns to all farm labor and management was only 69 cents an hour in 1957

[41] See Duscha, op. cit., p. 67; Peterson, op. cit., p. 151; Fite and Reese, op. cit., p. 664.
[42] Fite and Reese, op. cit., p. 665.

while workers in manufacturing industries received $2.07 an hour.[43]

The programs have not even managed to deal with the vaunted "problem of overproduction," despite the millions who have left farming for other pursuits. On the contrary, since the New Deal programs got underway, we have been confronted with true surpluses for the first time. (No surpluses of any consequence ever existed prior to the adoption of direct price supports. What writers mean when they refer to earlier overproduction and surpluses is that many farmers were producing more of some commodities than some of them could afford to at the price they could get. This does not mean that there was a surplus, only that prices fell to enable farmers to dispose of their produce). The following is a summary of the surpluses in storage during a recent period:

> So, as of December 31, 1962, the Government was storing surplus commodities valued at more than $8 billion. . . .
> The biggest items were more than $2.5 billion worth of wheat, $1.8 billion worth of corn, nearly $800 million in grain sorghums, and cotton valued at over $1.5 billion.[44]

The programs did not simply fail to achieve their objects; they did fail, but that is only part of the story. In many instances, they produced the opposite of what was desired. That is, they actually contributed to making farming unprofitable for many, to the migration from the farm, to the marginality of many farms, and to the abject poverty in which many farmers found themselves. The very people whom the programs were supposed to benefit were quite often the ones most directly harmed by them. More than one investigator has noted this strange phenomenon in passing. One writer says, "The AAA brought benefits to almost all commercial farmers. But in limiting acreage and providing the strongest possible incentive for more efficient land use, and thus for better

[43] Wilcox, *op. cit.*, p. 513.
[44] Duscha, *op. cit.*, p. 231.

technology, it forced sharecroppers off the land and worsened the plight of farm laborers."[45] Another says that "New Deal policies made matters worse. The AAA's reduction of cotton acreage drove the tenant and the cropper from the land. . . ."[46]

Closer analysis will show not only why the programs failed but why they had the opposite results, why they were, particularly, a part of the war on the poor. The programs were uneconomic; they were attempts to avoid economic consequences. Operating in an evasion and ignorance of economics, they were fundamentally contradictory. The effort was, at its center, a contradiction. On the one hand, the interventionists from the New Deal down to the present have wished to enable farmers to stay on the farm, that is, to keep as many farmers as there were, or even augment their numbers. On the other, they have sought to reduce production. The same number of farmers, then, were to have higher income from reduced production. This was supposed to be achieved by raising the prices of farm products.

To make the rise in prices possible, the government from 1933 onward has engaged in generally inflationary policies, that is, increasing the money supply. As we have already seen, an increase in the money supply does not necessarily raise those prices one wishes to see raised, or does not raise them in greater proportion than others. Increasing the money supply can only make the money available for the increase. There was an attempt to funnel the money toward farmers by subsidies and various price support activities. In so far as this made growing of the subsidized crops profitable, it led to concerted efforts to produce more and more of them. This, combined with the fact that subsidized commodities were priced above the world market, led to surpluses.

The other device was crop restrictions and acreage allotments. It was these that bore heavily upon the poor. To see

[45] Paul K. Conkin, *The New Deal* (New York: Thomas Y. Crowell, 1967), p. 42.
[46] Leuchtenburg, *op. cit.*, p. 137.

how this occurred, let us take an imaginary cotton farmer and examine the effects of allotment restrictions on him. Suppose that he had forty acres of arable land under cultivation. Just prior to the imposing of limitations he might have planted twenty-five of the acres into cotton. He might have made one-half bale to the acre, a reasonable expectation, or twelve and one-half bales which he could sell, let us say, for ten cents per pound. This would give him a gross return from cotton of $625, not sumptuous surely, but families often survived on much less. His allotment, under the government program, would probably have been something like ten acres for cotton. If his yield per acre remained proportionately the same, he would produce five bales of cotton. In the early years, even with supports, cotton brought no more than, say, twelve cents per pound. At this rate, his gross return from cotton for the year would be reduced to $300.

The obvious solution to this problem would be for the farmer to increase his production of cotton. He could do this in three ways: (1) more intensive cultivation, (2) get more land, or (3) use better seed, more fertilizer, and so forth. The government program made more intensive cultivation most difficult, for it based the allotment on a percentage of the total acreage cultivated. This meant that as much land as possible had to be planted to other things, and these cultivated, in order to maintain the cotton allotment at a given level. In short, for cotton farming to be profitable the government program shifted the land-labor-capital "mix" away from land and labor toward capital. More precisely, it made larger farms necessary for profitable cotton production, put a premium on the use of mechanical equipment to tend larger acreages of land, and encouraged the use of expensive fertilizers and seed. Capital was needed for the land, equipment, and fertilizer. That in which terms men are poor—money—became much more essential in making a living at farming.

The crop allotment system worked a particularly heavy hardship on tenant farmers. Not only were they under pressure from their own circumstance to tend as much land as intensively as possible, but also from the landlords. A landlord wanted to have as much land tended as possible not only in order to make ends meet but also to keep his allotments intact. The burden increased for farmers as they grew older, their children left them, and they were not able to work as effectively themselves as when they had been younger. Landlords had to let them go, and they wandered downward in the scale to farms with poorer and poorer soil. If they lived long enough, it hardly mattered whether they farmed or not; they could no longer produce enough to be significant to themselves or anyone else.

Having shifted the "mix" toward capital, the government made attempts to help those whom it had placed under almost intolerable pressures. The main effort, initially, was along the lines of soil building, land reclamation, and resettlement. Payments were made to farmers for planting legumes, for terracing, and for other land restoration practices. Government supported informational services were expanded, new seeds developed, chemicals used in new ways to increase farm production. In 1935, a Resettlement Administration was set up under Rexford G. Tugwell. "Tugwell's chief assignment was not communitarianism but resettlement; he sought to move impoverished farmers from submarginal land and give them a fresh start on good soil with adequate equipment and expert guidance. The RA, which planned to move 500,000 families, actually resettled 4,441."[47]

Another activity by the government was reclamation of land, most notably by irrigation. This had been going on since the early twentieth century, but it, too, gained in vigor from the New Deal down to the present. The Federal Government had made 3,173,570 acres of irrigable land available in 1926, 3,698,417 by 1936, 5,150,813 by 1946, and so on.[48]

The government began in 1937 a direct effort to narrow

[47] *Ibid.*, p. 140.
[48] Peterson, *op. cit.*, p. 159.

the capital gap for poor farmers. This aid was provided under the Bankhead-Jones Farm Tenancy Act and carried out by the Farm Security Administration. The FSA "extended re-habilitation loans to farmers, granted low-interest, long-term loans to enable selected tenants to buy family-size farms, and aided migrants. . . ." To explain its ultimate failure to achieve great results, one historian says: "The FSA's opponents kept its appropriations so low that it was never able to accomplish anything on a massive scale."[49]

The first thing to observe about all this is that in order to undo some of the damage it had wrought the government was drawn into an effort to prevent the results of its own programs from taking place. It had set out to reduce production. In 1933, crops had even been plowed up and animals slaught-ered to reduce the supply. Then, the government turned to trying to help farmers make their reduced acreage *more* pro-ductive. To the extent that it succeeded in this, it failed in its effort to reduce production. To the extent that government loans kept submarginal farmers in production, to that same extent it either contributed to surpluses in storage or to mak-ing other farmers marginal, or both. Over the years, the government deepened the contradiction with its soil bank pro-grams to take land out of cultivation and at the same time bringing new lands under cultivation with land reclamation projects. It has subsidized farmers, as veterans after World War II, again making it more difficult for numerous other farmers to stay on the profitable side of marginality.

Government programs made many farms and farmers sub-marginal, then induced them to stay on the farms with hand-outs, contributing to the marginality of yet others and pro-longing the agony of those who would eventually leave. They accelerated the adoption of machinery, but with crop allot-ments made it impractical for people on small farms to buy it. (After all, diversified farming requires much more equipment than does one crop farming, besides which there may be no

[49] Leuchtenburg, *op. cit.*, p. 141.

good market for the other crops grown in an area). At least, and at last, some of the migrants had sanitary facilities in the camps along the way on their lonely journeys away from their dreams!

Statistics are abstractions which tell in dramatic and not fully human terms what happened to millions of human beings. They do not tell of the struggle, of the hope each year that the situation will improve, of the worsening condition, of the final sense of failure and futility and migration. From a field investigation in Alabama in 1936 James Agee, writing with vivid imagination which distorted conventional reality, tried to capture the individuality of existence of three tenant farmers and the commonality of their fate. While he gives no indication that he understands how government programs have aggravated the lot of these people, he does note at one point "that this particular subject of tenantry is becoming more and more stylish as a focus of 'reform,' and in view of the people who will suffer and be betrayed at the hands of such 'reformers,' there could never be enough to pry their eyes open even a little wider."[50]

However, he chronicles the declining fortunes of the three families, without comment, in the following words:

> The best Woods has ever cleared was $1300 during a war year. During the teens and twenties he fairly often cleared as much as $300; he fairly often cleared $50 and less; two or three times he ended the year in debt. During the depression years he has more often cleared $50 and less. . . .
>
> The best Gudger has ever cleared is $125. That was in the plow-under year. He felt exceedingly hopeful and bought a mule; but when his landlord warned him of how he was coming out the next year, he sold it. Most years he has not made more than $25 to $30; and about one year in three he has ended in debt. Year before last he wound up $80 in debt; last year, $12. . . .
>
> Years ago the Ricketts were, relatively speaking, almost

[50] James Agee, *Let Us Now Praise Famous Men* (Boston: Houghton Mifflin, 1960), p. 208.

prosperous. Besides their cotton farming they had ten cows and sold the milk, and they lived near a good stream and had all the fish they wanted. [Their condition worsened, for reasons private as well as public, and] for ten consecutive years now, though they have lived on so little rations money, and have turned nearly all their cottonseed money toward their debts, they have not cleared or had any hope of clearing a cent at the end of the year.[51]

Eventually, men must begin to turn elsewhere from such futile employment. Two of these men began cautiously edging toward the change in 1936. As Agee describes it:

Gudger and Ricketts, during this year, were exceedingly lucky. After they, and Woods, had been turned away from government work, they found work in a sawmill. They were given work on condition that they stay with it until the mill was moved, and subject strictly to their landlord's permission. . . . Their landlords quite grudgingly gave their permission on condition that they pay for whatever help was needed in their absence during the picking season. Gudger hired a hand, at eight dollars a month and board. Ricketts did not need to: his family is large enough. They got a dollar and a quarter a day five days a week and seventy-five cents on Saturday, seven dollars a week, ten hours' work a day. Woods did not even try for this work; he was too old and too sick.[52]

What later became of the Gudgers, Ricketts, and Woods is not a part of the record. But of many others we know, in general. They migrated. In the 1930's they left the farms in great numbers, to go to California, to Chicago, to Detroit, and to cities and towns closer by. The most famous migration was that of the "Okies" and "Arkies" to California in the 1930's. As one history tells it: "By the end of the decade, a million migrants, penniless nomads in endless caravans of overburdened jalopies, bursting with half-clad tow-headed children, had overrun small towns in Oregon and Washington

[51] *Ibid.*, pp. 118-19.
[52] *Ibid.*, pp. 120-21.

and pressed into the valleys of California."[53] More, "In the winter of 1939, although the great peregrination had passed its peak, one still saw families huddled over fires along western highways."[54]

Over the decades to the present, the migration from the farms has not ended; it has become a steady stream, unnoticed generally, for it has been going on for so long. In 1967, *Saturday Evening Post* had a feature story on the black migration from Mississippi as it is now taking place. It is the story of the last look of a family at familiar sights, of the quiet vigil at the train station for the train that will take the family north, of the sadness of leaving a life they had known, of the apprehension, and, for some of the children, anticipation, of entering upon the unknown. But there is little hope for them where they have lived. Machinery is doing much of the work they once performed, and this is being accelerated even more now by a minimum wage for farm workers. The family upon which the article concentrated was that of a Walter Austin. There is a poignancy to his description of his reluctance to leave the farm which may give at least a hint of what millions have felt:

> "I don't want to leave Mississippi," Austin said. "I never been out of Mississippi except one time in my whole life, and that was only one week. Tell you the truth, up to the sixteenth day of March, 19 and 57, I never been out of Holmes County. I never been in no kind of trouble, never paid a fine, never been to court. . . .
>
> "I likes to farm. I loves it. I can raise my chickens, raise my hog, I have my garden with peas and beans and potatoes and squash and cucumbers and onions and greens. You can't do that in town. You can't raise a hog in town. I'm just a home child. I just don't want to leave home unless I have to. I'll be frank with you. I like the country."[55]

[53] Leuchtenburg, *op. cit.*, pp. 138-39.
[54] *Ibid.*, p. 141.
[55] Ben H. Bagdikian, "The Black Immigrants," *The Saturday Evening Post* (July 15, 1967), p. 27.

Farming is a hard enough life in any case. For most, it has been a struggle from time immemorial to wrest from the soil enough to make do, not to speak of prospering. Changes would have taken place to some degree and in certain ways in America had government not intervened. But that intervention has now taken a frightful toll: it has accelerated the pace of change; it has made productive farmers marginal or submarginal; it has made it increasingly difficult for anyone to make a go of it at farming (and there is no reason, except for government interference, that farming should not be as profitable an undertaking as any other productive pursuit); it has driven men who loved the farm into crowded city dwellings; it has denied American produce to the world at market prices and denied the world market to American farmers; and it has produced and prolonged a farm problem which might never have been and would certainly have been healed by necessary adjustments over the years. Government programs have contributed to the enrichment of the wealthy and the impoverishment of the poor.

As I rode through the countryside of Alabama, I could not say with certainty of any one place, "there but for the efforts of government would be a house with people surrounded by cultivated lands." No one may know now which land is potentially productive and which submarginal. Yet there are many who have known farming as a rewarding way of life. There is already talk of impending famine in much of the world. According to all accounts, there is hunger and need in many parts of the world. There may yet come a day when the war on the poor will end, when the controls and restrictions will be stopped, when tariffs and quotas will be removed, and lands will be restored to the most meaningful purpose of providing materials for feeding and clothing people. A countryside now abandoned may be at least partially peopled with farmers once again.

CHAPTER V

Wage Workers Under Attack

I N THE EARLY 1950's, THE INTERNATIONAL BROTHERHOOD OF
Electrical Workers' Local 35 was hailed before the Connecticut Civil Rights Commission to answer charges that it discriminated against Negro workers. The Union denied the
charge in one of the most revealing statements ever made by
such an organization. As one writer summarizes the position
of the Union, "Local 35 argued that it had not violated the
law because it discriminated against all races!"[1] The union
attempted to defend itself against a particular charge of discrimination by proclaiming that by its nature it discriminated
against workers of all races. The Commission did not entertain the generic allegation; it brushed it aside. More's the pity,
for had it delved into this claim, it might have discovered
something relevant to the civil rights of all men, not just the
Negroes.

Unions do not simply *discriminate* against workers of all
races, however; when the occasion arises, they actually subject them to harassment and violence and, if they meet re-

[1] Ray Marshall, *The Negro Worker* (New York: Random House, 1967),
p. 75.

sistance, engage them in combat. The following examples are taken from published accounts of such actions. They bring home the fact that unions are organized against other workers and visit both physical and mental suffering upon them when challenged. The first example takes off from an incident in 1962:

> It was just past midnight when the two big tractor-trailers, loaded with cheese and butter, pulled out of a terminal in Birmingham, Alabama, to start on the 10 hour, 365 mile run to New Orleans. At 2:45 they were barreling along Alabama Highway 5 when a cream-colored car passed them, raced on to a junction, turned and sped back. From the car a shotgun was fired point-blank at the cab of the lead truck, critically wounding driver Charles Warren, 31.
>
> It was the latest in a series of bloody episodes that have marked a 12 week strike by the International Brotherhood of Teamsters against Alabama's Bowman Transportation Company, a medium sized trucking concern. Turning down the union's demands on wages and working conditions, the firm hired non-Teamster drivers. Since then, Bowman trucks have been shot at more than 70 times in Alabama, Georgia, Tennessee, North and South Carolina. Four drivers besides Warren have been wounded. More than 20 trucks have been fired at while laboring up a steep grade on U. S. Highway 278 near Piedmont, Alabama; it has come to be known as bullet hill.
>
> Eight striking Bowman teamsters have been arrested, since November. Sam Webb, President of Northern Alabama's local 612 was indicted for assault with intent to kill in the Warren Shooting.[2]

This was by no means the whole story of violence connected with the Bowman Strike, of course. Trucks sometimes carried an extra man as an armed rider, workers were intimidated by Teamsters, and there were attempts to stop shipments from going out. The point, however, is that the harassment and violence was aimed at workers primarily.

[2] "Bloody Strike," *Time* (February 2, 1962).

The following tells an even more pointed story:

> A coal strike marked by gunfire and blasts of dynamite is turning the mountains of Kentucky into something of a battlefield.
>
> The United Mine Workers Union is striking in an effort to get owners of truck mines and coal tipples in 8 counties of Eastern Kentucky to sign union contracts. One county in Northeastern Tennessee is also involved.
>
> Violence has plagued the strike from the start. Two men—a non-union mine owner and a non-union truck driver—have been shot to death. Other men, union and non-union, have been beaten or wounded. . . .
>
> The owners of the truck mines say that if they signed the union contract they would be put out of business. They maintain that profits are so scant that they can't pay the union wage of $24-25 a day and the royalties of 40 cents a ton for the union's welfare fund. Non-striking miners talk the same way. They say that a union victory would put them out of work.[3]

Another publication, reporting on the same strike, says that the miners "earn less than they would make under UMW terms, but they make a bare living they wouldn't be earning otherwise. As a result, they are on the side of the operators, armed and ready and willing to shoot for their right to work for non-union pay."[4] This was in 1959.

Professor Sylvester Petro has written at length about a more famous strike, the Kohler Strike. He describes the onset of this strike in Wisconsin in these words:

> Kohler Village was not quiet on April 5, 1954. Marching in solid ranks before the main entrance to the plant early that morning were some two thousand persons. They were there to prevent anyone from going to work, and they succeeded. As one eye witness put it, "employees attempting to enter the plant were slugged, kneed in the groin, kicked, pushed, and threatened," almost always by the group of mili-

[3] U. S. News and World Report (May 25, 1959).
[4] "Violence Lingers," Business Week (April 25, 1959).

tants who had come from out of town to "help." For fifty-four days, despite restraining orders, agreements by union officials to obey these orders, and efforts of the Kohler management and nonstriking employees, the plant was shut. . . . It was many more months before persons might go to their jobs in peace without fear of reprisals to themselves, their homes, and their families.[5]

All this, and much else, to keep those who wished to work at the wages being offered from getting to work.

The Kingsport Strike, as chronicled by the same author, has been going on since the early 1960's. The strike has been marked by the same sort of violence that anyone who has read of or knows much about such occurrences will have learned to expect: massed pickets at the gates at the outset, name calling, rock throwing, single workers beset by groups of strikers, paint thrown on automobiles, "delegations" of strikers descending upon the home of workers, automobile and home windows broken, and so on. But it may be brought closer to home by recounting some of the trials of a single worker. The Kingsport Strike is a strike against the Kingsport Press. The Press decided to continue to operate despite the strike, with such old and new employees as it could get. The following is the story of one of them as told by Petro:

> In the middle of March, 1963, Joe got talking to Ralph McCoy, a Press executive, at a funeral, and asked him if it was true that the Press was telling the strikers that it was going to start hiring replacements. Ralph McCoy said it was true, and Joe said: "If those people don't want to work at the Press, I do; and I'm willing to cross the picket line." McCoy said that Joe's application would be given serious consideration. It was. Joe said proudly that he was either the first or the second man to be hired during the strike.
>
> Crossing the picket line was wild, Joe said: "Pu-lenty of name-calling. You name it, they called it." There was never a dull moment in his job, for he was a truckdriver and had to

[5] Sylvester Petro, The Kohler Strike (Chicago: Henry Regnery, 1961), pp. 4-5.

cross and re-cross picket lines many times each day. In the early days it was hard because the Press was short of truck-drivers, and Joe had to do by himself—largely after sleepless nights—the work normally done by three or even four truck-drivers. "I had 'em throw eggs, rocks, and everything imaginable at me. They used to gang up, before the injunction, three or four hundred of 'em out thar'—throwing eggs, rocks, what have you. First time, comin' by the warehouse, I had my window down and they threw an egg that splattered all over me. After that I kept the window up, though I didn't like to because if one of those rocks had hit it, the glass would have cut my haid off."

Joe is big and tough. His hands look as if they could tear a man apart. They kept clenching as he recounted his experiences when walking or driving through the picket lines. "They are still saying rotten, filthy things to me at one picket post, which I can't avoid—men and women, too—filthy things about my wife. It makes my blood jump but I know that if I give in there'll be real trouble. If it wasn't for hurting the Press and myself, I'd jump out and let them have it, but that's probably what they want. So I just take it. I've taken two years of it, and I can take two more. In the less than two years I've been here I've made nearly $13,000, while they've been pickcting, and I'm providing for my boy and my wife."

The strikers have provided Joe with some occasion for relief, however. Maybe without it, he would have exploded by now. The relief may be measured in terms of what he has left of three boxes of shotgun shells which he bought shortly after going to work at the Press. There were 25 shells in each box, he said, and there are only six left. "So," he said, "I must have shot 69 or 70 times the first three months of the strike."

"Many a night," Joe said, "I sat up with the bottom window of the storm door up and my shotgun in my lap. One pesty fellow would pull his car up, aiming the headlights right at the house. One night he yelled out: 'Why don't you shoot, Joe?' I said, 'One more time, Ernie, and I'll blow those headlights out.' He never came back."

But others did, night after night, shooting up the front of his house. Joe reported it to the police. They always came quickly, when he called, but they said they couldn't keep a man stationed constantly at his house; for the same kind of thing was going on all over town. Joe said he intended to defend himself, his family, and his house; he was going to load his rifle and "get" the vandals. The police officer said he had every right to defend himself. "But he told me," Joe said, "that I shouldn't use a rifle because the bullets might richochet and hurt innocent people. He said I should use a shot-gun and punkin' balls." (They are extra large pellets.)

After a while, Joe took to stationing himself across the road from his house, on the tin roof of a welding shop. That gave him a better line of fire. A car would show up in the small hours of the morning about every other day, stop in front of Joe's house and fire at it. Joe would return the fire from the welding shop. "There was very few times I would miss," he said. But the cars kept coming back. After a while, Joe took turns standing watch on the welding shop roof with another striker replacement. Staying up all night, every night, was getting to be too much for him and working long hours every day. The assaults came to a climax, and to an end, one morning toward the end of June, 1963. "My friend, Eugene Pyle, and I were standing watch together that night. A black four-door Corvair with four men in it drove slowly up to the front of my house, stopped, and someone shot a big ballbearing through the glass on my storm door. Pyle and I stood up on the top of the shop. He fired twice, I fired three times. We blew the glass out of the left side and the rear of the Corvair. They took off as fast as they could, and there was only one head showing. We jumped down, ran across the street over the broken glass, got in my car, and drove all over looking for that car, but never did we see a black Corvair.

"I was up all night that night, like I had been for most of three months. It was a lousy, lousy way to live. I was a mess, our life was a mess. But I had to stick it out."[6]

[6] Sylvester Petro, *The Kingsport Strike* (New Rochelle, N.Y.: Arlington House, 1967), pp. 154-57.

Such violent episodes have not been frequent and wide-spread throughout the United States since World War II. As a matter of fact, most strikes are not accompanied by violence today. *Only* when there is an attempt to operate struck plants does such violence occur. The management of most companies that are unionized in many parts of the United States do not even seriously consider operating when a strike is called. They comply; they do not throw open their doors to those willing to work.

The limited number of such instances, however, does not take away one whit from their importance when they occur. The above stories are as germane as they would be if each strike were accompanied by such happenings, for they contain the potential course of every strike differing in that most struck companies do not try to operate. The violence that does occur is the veiled, or open, threat behind every negotiation between union and management. The centrality of the threat of coercion is a point to be taken up later.

The stories are recounted at this point because they dramatize the point of whom strikes are basically against, and through that provide an inkling of the antipathy for and conflict of unions with workers. They show that the bulk of violence falls upon workers. According to union lore, a strike is against the employer. So it is, *in part;* there is an attempt to close down his business, to induce him to meet union terms, to make him suffer the inconvenience or even hardship of having his business remain idle if he does not comply with their demands. If a strike goes on long enough and is conducted in certain ways, the employer may actually be driven out of business. On occasion, the owner may be subjected to abuse and even violence. This is, however, exceptional and rare. By convention, and even by mutual agreement, management may usually go and come at will into and out of the struck plant, usually without being harassed. Even when a struck plant is being operated, management is not usually harassed. The ire of strikers is focused upon the workers brought into

the plant; harassment and violence is usually aimed at and
visited upon them. This is not accidental; it is essential. To see
why this is so and to explore its extended ramifications it will
now be useful to examine the nature of the union effort.

The fundamental attempt of the unions is to take the determination of wages out of the market. They strive to have
wages decided by agreement between management and
unions, under the threat of retaliatory measures by the union
if a satisfactory agreement is not reached and, so far as possible, without reference to the market. Thus, their approach is
uneconomic, and it is this that leads, in the final analysis, to
the attack upon other workers. Economically, wages are set
by supply and demand, just as other prices are in a competitive situation. The competition is between or among
workers for a particular job, not between workers on the one
hand and management on the other. This accounts for the use
of violence against would-be workers to exclude them from a
struck plant. The union is attempting to reduce the supply of
available workers to an employer and thereby to increase the
wages they can get. This takes the whole procedure out of the
economic realm. The use of violence makes it into warfare;
whereas, competition is peaceful.

Unionists do not describe their undertaking in this way.
Indeed, those workers who would replace their members are
not called workers. They are referred to as "strike-breakers,"
"scabs," and "rats," among other unsavory titles. The conflict
is classified as if it were solely a contest between workers and
employers. Modern unionist rhetoric is derived from and informed by the class struggle idea. The classes, in the classic
Marxist (or socialist) formulation, are capital and labor. In
America, the terminology has been softened somewhat by re-
ferring to the alleged protagonists as management and labor.
In any case, the justifications offered for organized labor
unions and their tactics are derived from the notion that these
two are in conflict, and, by derivation, engaged in a class
struggle.

[Unionists picture management and labor as representing two different and conflicting interests. On the one hand, management wants to get laborers as inexpensively as possible. (Expense includes not only wages and hours of work but what are referred to as working conditions, which would include all the appurtenances and conveniences provided for workers at the place of employment.) On the other hand, laborers want as high wages as possible, as short hours of work, and as commodius working conditions. So far as it goes, this is an accurate enough statement of the desires of prospective employers and employees.]

The justification of unionism hinges upon the validity of this next proposition, however. The claim is usually stated in some such fashion as this: Since the growth of large factories and the development of giant corporations, individual workers must organize into unions in order to bargain as equals with employers. There is an implied major premise in this formulation, that wages are arrived at by bargaining between employers and employees. This is only the case superficially, when it occurs at all. True, when men are free there is an agreement as to wages to which both parties have consented. It sometimes happens that negotiations precede this agreement—usually this would occur only when highly trained personnel were involved—, but they are not nearly so common as the premise implies. There is, in most localities at a given time, a going wage. It is this wage that an employee expects and an employer will ordinarily offer. It is the wage that an employer has to offer in order to induce the number and quality of workers that he wants to come into his employ. The wage is what it is because of the competition among employers for workers and the competition among workers for jobs. The size of the factories and the largeness of corporations are irrelevant to the determination of wages, so long as there are competing factories and corporations. The picture of an automobile worker standing hat in hand negotiating his wages with, say, a Ford, is as spurious as it is unlikely.

Neither a Ford nor a worker can set wages at will. If what the worker asks is to any significant degree above the going wage for the job under consideration, the employer simply will not hire him at that rate. If the wage offered by the prospective employer to the worker is significantly below the going wage, the worker will not take it; he will go elsewhere. Working conditions may be considered the same as wages in this regard; they are one of the means an employer uses to induce men to work for him.

This does not in the least mean that union activity is economically irrelevant. From one angle, unionists appear to have tacitly accepted the economic truth that wages are determined by supply and demand. What they attempt to do, at the crucial moment, is to reduce the supply of workers available to a given employer in order to induce him to pay higher wages and provide better conditions. They try to do this in a strike by driving other workers away. In essence, unions try to improve the lot of their members by excluding other workers from job opportunities. Everyone could see the impact of this if all activities were unionized. In that case, they could reduce the supply of workers only by keeping some portion of the population perpetually unemployed. Since all employments are not yet unionized, nor presently likely to be, the impact of the union is more subtle and varied.

Before examining further the consequences of unions, it will be useful to examine the role of government in their development. The growth of unions in membership and power has been contingent upon special government favors. Historically, great growth of membership has occurred when government has thrown its weight behind the unions in various ways. Three major growth periods in the twentieth century have been: just before and during World War I and its immediate aftermath, the late 1930's, and World War II. Between 1915-1920 union membership increased from 2,582,600 to 5,047,-800. From 1935 through 1940 it increased from 3,659,300 to 8,100,900. From 1941 through 1945 membership increased from 8,614,000 to 12,724,700. There has been continued increase since World War II, but not nearly so dramatic.[7] What one book says about the growth during World War I can be said in equal measure for the later periods:

> If we examine the figures of growth from 1917 to 1919, we shall find that the war policy of the government was by far the greatest factor, for it was the government that opened the doors to unionism in industries heretofore closed—not that unionism *forced* the doors open by its own strength. The government, by virtue of its war time power and prestige, gave the unions the all-important right to organize against a temporarily confounded and half-rebellious employing group. . . .[8]

Government has promoted union membership growth in four ways: (1) by empowering them to use coercion, (2) by special exemptions or immunities, (3) by special assistance, and (4) by way of inflation.

There are those who maintain, or attempt to maintain, that unions could survive and prosper without the special privileges. Professor Sylvester Petro is the leading advocate of this position. He holds that without the use of coercion or special immunities unions could provide many useful services for their members. He says;

> There are a number of other ways [he had listed several already] in which unions can serve both their members and society as a whole. They could provide employees with a great many useful services. They could be of great help to their members in planning savings and investment programs. If they were run well, they could be trusted with pension and welfare plans. They can and do run training and retraining schools for workers who are anxious to improve their pro-

[7] Irving Bernstein, "The Growth of American Unions," *Readings in United States Economic and Business History*, Ross M. Robertson and James L. Pate, eds. (Boston: Houghton Mifflin, 1966), pp. 362-63.

[8] Philip Ross, *The Government as a Source of Union Power* (Providence: Brown University Press, 1965), p. 18.

ductivity. They could serve as a clearing-house as regards employment opportunities. . . .[9]

Whether or not such viable unions are possible or likely is a moot question.

Unions, as they exist in America, are not essentially of the character Professor Petro would have them be. (If they were, their story would probably form no part of an account of the war on the poor.) They rest upon the potentiality and practice of using coercion. As Petro himself says:

> Coercive conduct has been characteristic of trade unions in this country throughout the history at all levels of union action. At the first level, the organizing level, unions have often depended more upon picketing, secondary boycotts, sit-down strikes, compulsory-unionism contracts, and other kinds of physical and economic coercion than they have upon peaceful persuasion and other civilized methods of inducing employees to join.[10]

They have also relied upon special privileges from government. Union leaders and advocates have worked for years to get these special privileges. They have proclaimed over and over that they could not survive without them. In any case, the nature of the union has been shaped by the use of coercion and the existence of immunities.

Unions employ threats of and actual coercion to attain their ends. They can only do this because governments permit them to. Both the coercion and the permission of government are necessary to their task as they perform it. In the first place, the threat or use of coercion would appear to be necessary to reduce the supply of workers available to an employer. In the second place, it is not clear why an employer would sign an agreement with a union as they are constituted. This latter point needs some background explanation to see its full import.

[9] Sylvester Petro, *The Labor Policy of the Free Society* (New York: Ronald Press, 1957), p. 108.
[10] *Ibid.*, pp. 109-10.

Union members are *not* exempted from the application of the laws of the land in the use of coercion. They are, in some states at least, immune from the operation of trespass laws to some extent. Otherwise, they are no more exempt from the laws dealing with slander, defamation of character, intimidation, assault and battery than is anyone else. True, policemen and other law enforcement officials frequently look the other way when union members employ such tactics. And, diligent enforcement of the laws should sharply reduce the amount of coercive tactics. Members are not exempt from responsibility at law for their acts, but the union is. Not only have unions been immune from prosecution for the coercion but they are enabled by the law to derive advantage from it.

The crux of the matter is this: the courts will enforce a contract between a union and a company, though that contract was only agreed to after the threat and use of coercion by union members. Yet it is a venerable principle of Anglo-American law that a lawful contract must be willingly consented to by all parties to it. If any party to the contract has used force or coercion, the contract is null and void; the courts will not enforce it and may offer relief to injured parties. It is this validation by the courts and enforcement of these contracts that constitutes a central privilege which labor unions enjoy.

Not only can it be almostly endlessly shown that force and the threat of force have been employed by unions to obtain contracts but it should be clear that they could not otherwise be obtained. That companies would willingly recognize unions and enter into agreements with them is at odds both with common sense and the nature of man. This would mean that management willingly consented to having their employees organized to take action against them, to having unions take credit for pay raises and improved working conditions, to limitations upon the use of the work force, to costly procedures, and, quite often, to having their workers alienated from them. What is the *quid pro quo* for such concessions? What does the company get from the agreement that it could not have more readily without it? It agrees to pay such and such wages and to maintain certain conditions of employment. In return, it does _not_ get an agreement from unions to provide it with workers nor does a single member of a union agree to work for one more day for an employer. In return, the union only agrees, however it may be worded, to refrain from using its tactics against the company for a period of time. The contract is not only flawed by being based upon coercion but also by the lack of any recognizable _consideration_ tendered by the union, another requirement of a binding contract. The history of the development of unions substantiates the unwillingness of employers to recognize unions. Most of them have resisted the recognition of unions as long as they could, and stay in operation.

The point has been somewhat elaborated in order to show that for unions to deal with employers as they do they must have exemptions, immunities, and special privileges at law, that their behavior is contingent upon special consideration from government, that government finally bears the onus for whatever ill effects derive from this behavior. There are other ways that government aids and abets unions. One of these is in the matter of monopoly. In order to reduce the supply of labor to an employer a union must, in effect, have a monopoly—that is, be the exclusive seller in that particular market—of labor. It is to gain or maintain this monopoly that unions operate to frighten away or drive out other workers. There are those who would maintain that there is no significant question of monopoly so long as a union is restricted in its operations to a single company within an industry.[11] Be that as it may, unions are organized for whole industries and for particular crafts and skills. These are monopolistic, and it is through these monopolies that unions attempt to attain their goals. There are antitrust laws which were designed

[11] See, for example, Patrick M. Boarman, _Union Monopolies and Antitrust Restraints_ (Washington: Labor Policy Association), Chapter I.

initially to punish such activities. But, again, labor unions have been exempted from their provisions. Government has extended special privileges to unions in the matter of monopoly.

Another way in which government is necessary to labor union organization is through the increase of the money supply—inflation. The major effort, though not the exclusive one, of unions is to obtain higher wages for their members. To keep its following, the union finds it expedient to demand and to get higher wages, i.e., more money, in each successive contract. As an economist has described the dynamics of unionism: ["Laborers who went on year after year receiving the same wages, however good, would soon be aware that they were getting them without any intervention on the union's part] Either they would cease paying dues and the system would disintegrate, or they would elect a new set of officers who would get on the job."[12] Union officers will also wish to increase union membership, or at the least, maintain it at its current level, for the salaries of officers come out of the dues paid by members and the effectiveness of the union is tied to its financial resources.

These two goals—perennial money wage increases and stable or increasing union membership—are incompatible in the short run and impossible in the long run, except under one condition, a regular and continuing expansion of the money supply. All other devices can be seen to be strictly limited in their application, and self-defeating when employed over an extended period of time. For example, it is often alleged that wages can be increased by increasing labor's proportion of the take of the gross income of a company. If, for example, labor gets 65 per cent of the gross income (or accounts for 65 per cent of the gross "costs" of production), money wages could be increased by increasing labor's percentage. But this could not

[12] Edward H. Chmberlin, "Labor Union Power and the Public Interest," *The Public Stake in Union Power*, Philip D. Bradley, ed. (Charlottesville: University of Virginia Press, 1959), p. 14.

continue year after year indefinitely, for there is only 100 per cent, and eventually labor would have it all. Long before that occurred, however, the company would have been driven out of business, and union membership reduced by the number disemployed. For an industry as a whole, the process would be less dramatic. The price of the product or service would be increased to cover the higher wage costs (or investment would go elsewhere), or machines would replace workers. In any case, the number of workers would decline. Another device that it is alleged could result in money wage increases would be increased productivity. But overall increases in productivity will not result in money wage increases, in the absence of an increase in the money supply; the result, given competition, will be a reduction in prices. Lower prices would increase the *real wages* of workmen, but unions could hardly claim credit for the increase, since money wages would remain the same, or might even decline. Again, only a regular and continuing increase of the money supply can provide for both perennial money wage increases and stable or increasing union membership. With what consequences to union members and others we will examine later. One other exception should be noted. Even a perpetual expansion of the money supply will not guarantee this result in a particular industry. The relative demand for a good or service may diminish over a period of time, and price increases will only worsen conditions in that particular industry and reduce employment.

In sum, unions depend on inflation for their growth, and, within narrow limits, even their survival. In the United States, government now controls the money supply. Once again, then, unions are dependent upon government succor. The historical record bears out this analysis. The periods of dramatic union growth—World War I, the 1930's, World War II and after—have been periods of inflation. The only extended period of continued large scale union membership in our history has been one of a continued and long-term increase of the

Union cause inflation through higher demand of wage or production costs money supply, namely, from the 1930's to the present. Statistics, both of union membership and money supply, indicate that this is the case. To clinch the connection, union membership usually drastically declines in a deflation (or depression). One history book notes this phenomenon time after time. Regarding labor organizations in the early 19th century in the two industries—printing and shoemaking—where there was considerable unionization, it says: "Even in these two industries the mortality rate was high and most if not all of the surviving unions were wiped out in the Panic of 1819."[13] There was notable increase of unions in the early 1830's, but this was short lived. "Although the labor societies were apparently successful in a number of strikes, any real gain in wages was wiped out by the Panic of 1837. This severe depression . . . resulted in the dissolution of virtually all of the unions."[14] Again in the 1850's, "The major depression of 1857 brought this period in the labor movement to a close, and once again many of the unions failed to survive the depression."[15] The 1870's is generally described as a period of depression. These historians describe the positions of major unions this way: "Labor unions as a whole suffered during this decade, and even the better-organized trade unions lost membership. For example, the Coopers' Union had 7,000 members in 1872, but only 1,500 six years later."[16] For the 1890's, "The American Federation of Labor grew slowly until 1898. Internal divisions, loss of strikes in the early 1890's, and the long depression following 1893 all contributed to the organization's slow development."[17] In the twentieth century, there was a slight decline in union membership from 1908 to 1909, following the panic of 1907. There was a large drop-off from 1920 through 1924 during the post World War I recession. Union membership fell off

[13] Fite and Reese, *op. cit.*, p. 227.
[14] *Ibid.*, pp. 228-29.
[15] *Ibid.*, p. 230.
[16] *Ibid.*, p. 398.
[17] *Ibid.*, p. 403.

sharply from 1929 through 1933.[18] Detailed analysis will show that the declines in union membership accompany and follow a decrease of the money supply.

Probably, the initial drop in membership with deflation is not due to disillusionment with the union. What happens is that with the reduction of the money supply employers can no longer afford to employ as many men at the established wage. Men who lose their jobs will simply cease to be union members after a time. Over any long period of stable or decreasing money supply, however, a union will generally be unable to raise money wages, may even have to accept a reduction in wages. In consequence, the union will lose its attractiveness.

It does not follow, however, that inflation, *per se*, will result in an increase in union membership. For example, the inflation of the middle and latter 1920's was accompanied by a continuing minor decline in union ranks. A decrease in money supply is sufficient explanation for a union's loss of members, but an increase in money supply is only one of several conditions for growth. Another of these, of course, is the degree of union militancy. And, as has been pointed out, special privileges from government were necessary to continued or spectacular growth.

The special privileges by which unions have been empowered by national legislation are a result, mainly, of the following enactments: the Clayton Antitrust Act, the Norris-LaGuardia Anti-Injunction Act, the National Industrial Recovery Act, and the National Labor Relations Act. Union powers have been only slightly circumscribed by the Taft-Hartley Act and Landrum-Griffin Act of more recent times. By the former acts, government either exempted unions from the application of certain laws or threw its weight behind unionization. Section 6 of the Clayton Antitrust Act (1914) exempted labor unions from the antitrust laws. It said, in part:

[18] Bernstein, *op. cit.*, pp. 362-63.

That the labor of a human being is not a commodity or article of commerce. Nothing contained in the anti-trust laws shall be construed to forbid the existence and operation of labor . . . organizations . . . ; nor shall such organizations, or the members thereof, be held or construed to be illegal combinations or conspiracies in restraint of trade, under the anti-trust laws.

Section 20 of the same Act limited injunctions against labor unions:

That no restraining order or injunction shall be granted by any court of the United States, or a judge or the judges thereof, in any case between an employer and employees . . . involving or growing out of, a dispute concerning terms or conditions of employment, unless necessary to prevent irreparable injury to property. . . .[19]

The Norris-LaGuardia Anti-injunction Act (1932) is very complicated, but it was a major effort to reduce and severely circumscribe the authority of Federal courts. What it did is perhaps most clearly revealed in Section 6 and parts of Section 7. Section 6 provides that neither unions nor their officers are to be held responsible for acts done by individual members of the union unless it can be shown that they participated in or authorized the acts. Section 7 provides the conditions under which injunctions may be issued. In order for an injunction to be given, the court must find that "unlawful acts have been threatened and will be committed unless restrained," though how a court may know that an act will be committed is somewhat difficult to imagine. Moreover, the court must find

(b) That substantial and irreparable injury to complainant's property will follow;

(c) That as to each item of relief granted greater injury will be inflicted upon complainant by the denial of relief than will be inflicted upon defendants by the granting of relief;

[19] Henry S. Commager, ed., *Documents of American History*, II (New York: Appleton-Century-Crofts, 1962), 100-01.

(d) That complainant has no adequate remedy at law; and

(e) That the public officers charged with the duty to protect complainant's property are unable or unwilling to furnish adequate protection. . . .[20]

By the time a court had established the existence or potentialities of all these conditions beyond reasonable doubt, the need for an injunction would long since have passed, no doubt.

We can safely pass over the labor provisions of the National Industrial Recovery Act since they were superseded by the National Labor Relations Act of 1935. This was the crowning piece of legislation for empowering unions. In the first place, it authorized a National Labor Relations Board with sweeping investigatory powers and broad quasi-judicial powers over companies in labor disputes. The act compels companies to bargain with the majority union, and defines a variety of unfair practices which, if a company commits one of them, can lead to all sorts of penalties for the company. One historian describes the impact of the National Labor Relations Act in these words:

> A barrage of National Labor Relations Board rulings and Supreme Court decisions from 1935 to 1947 steadily encroached on the rights of employers. They almost, but not quite, lost the right to hire and fire without the union's consent. They had to recognize the majority union and bargain only with it, but the minority union could strike if it chose. If they committed one "unfair" act in an attempt to operate a struck plant, they had to take back all strikers with back pay. . . .[21]

In short, the Federal government gave maximum encouragement to unionization.

The major impact of unions is to *create unemployment*. Economists often sum up the whole of the impact by saying

[20] *Ibid.*, p. 236.
[21] Baldwin, *op. cit.*, pp. 604-05.

that unions cause a misallocation of resources, which is the case, but the task here is to spell out the various misallocations. In so far as unions succeed in their efforts, and quite often when they do not, they succeed in producing unemployment. This is true because of their premises and their activities in accord with them. Unions attempt to take the determination of wages and working conditions out of the market. They hold, implicitly or explicitly, that there is a surplus of workers, and that this would drive the wage downward below the living level if all laborers compete for jobs. They would increase wages, and so forth, by denying employers access to the whole supply of workers. To state it bluntly, they would raise the wages of those employed by reducing the number of people employed. They do not say this, but they act upon it.

Unions do *not* make any significant amount of unemployment by driving would-be workers away from plants. It is more indirect than that. Ordinarily, a union, when it is not on strike, would allow the employer to hire as many workers as he would at the union wage. But the union wage, if it is what the union claims, is above the market level. The effect of this upon wage workers is similar to that of government programs on farmers. It makes many workers marginal, or submarginal workers, who would not otherwise have been. This means that the employer will either lay off workers or will not hire those whom he otherwise could have. It means that the employer seeks more than he otherwise would for means to reduce his number of workers in order to keep prices competitive. The union wage accelerates the introduction of technology and the replacement of workers with it. The most dramatic examples of this effect have been in coal mining and the railroads. It is commonly said that John L. Lewis acquiesced in the displacement of workers by machines in order to get the high wages for those who remained in the mines.

Many economists would no doubt boggle at the implications of some of the statements in the above paragraph. For one thing, it raises the specter of technological unemployment which classical, libertarian, and conservative economists have labored so hard to down. They claim that the introduction of new technology increases the possibilities of employment rather than diminishes them. It enables a given worker to produce much more, thus adding to the value of the workman and increasing a given worker's employability. They can cite as incontrovertible proof that technology does not reduce overall employment the fact that there are more people employed in America today than ever before, despite mechanization and automation.

I take it that, as such, the introduction of technology neither increases nor diminishes the potentialities of employment. The potentialities of employment are 100 per cent of the population at all times, and always have been. Practically speaking, anyone who can produce a good or provide a service is employable. The only thing that could prevent him from being employed, if he wished and needed to be, would be government prohibition and rigidities of wages and requirements as to working conditions. The number of potential jobs is as limitless as are the wants of men and the possibility of laboring to satisfy them—that is to say, infinite. The use of new technological means does not, then, increase the potentialities of employment; *it increases the possibility of highly remunerative employment*. It increases the possibility of a workman's getting paid $2.00 an hour, say, rather than $1.50 an hour. Or, to be more exact, it increases the amount of goods and services available to all of us.

In a free labor market—i.e., one where the price of labor is flexible—the introduction of machinery will neither increase nor diminish the number of people employable. It will, however, tend to increase the real wages of everyone, not only those who use the machines. It will do so by reducing the price of goods, for the decision to use machinery rather than more workers will be based largely on reducing the overall cost of production. Reduced costs, in a competitive situation (either actual or potential), may be expected to result in lower prices. It may happen that the lower prices will so enhance the demand for the particular product that more workers will be employed, and that in order to attract them money wages will be raised. For any particular industry, this depends upon the elasticity of demand for a product. In a controlled market— one in which wages are decided to some extent by something other than the market—the introduction of technology does not have all these pleasant effects. The decision to use machinery rather than men is not made in order to reduce overall costs but to reduce labor costs, in order to remain competitive. The gain that would be made by changing to machinery has already or is about to be pre-empted by wages. There may be no reduction in the price of the product even after the purchase of new equipment; indeed, prices may still rise for goods because the savings from equipment do not equal the higher costs of labor. If unions attempt to save jobs by "featherbedding," the costs will be hiked further. Any determination of unions to get the profits from any gains in productivity will make it that much harder to get the money to pay for the equipment, and, as investment dries up, more and more jobs are lost. In short, labor union-induced use of machinery tends to reverse the normal results of the use of technology; rather than maintaining full employment and increasing the value of the money which one may have, it tends to raise prices and reduce employment.

Labor unions, then, are able to raise wages above the market by producing unemployment. One economist notes that "when a union pushes the wage beyond the competitive level, it is not the union which suffers the resulting unemployment nor the members who remain employed at the increased wages. The true sufferers are the workers who are disemployed as a result of the 'false' wage and the workers who will not be hired because the expansion which would normally have taken place at a lower level of wages (and prices) does not take place."[22]

[22] Boarman, *op. cit.*, pp. 162-63.

Perhaps the best period for an historical case study examination of the effect of unions on employment was 1935-1939. The National Labor Relations Act (usually referred to as the Wagner Act) was passed in 1935. There was somewhat of an increase in union membership in 1936, but the percentage change of union membership from the preceding year was an increase of only 10.1. In 1937, however, the greatest jump in membership for a single year in the twentieth century occurred; it was a whopping percentage increase of 53.9 over the preceding year.[23] The main thrust for this increase came from the Congress of Industrial Organizations under the leadership of John L. Lewis with the organization of much of the steel, automobile, and textile industries. As one writer describes this surge: "At the end of two years of activity, in December, 1937, the C.I.O. boasted a membership of 3,700,-000—composed of 600,000 miners, 400,000 automobile workers, 375,000 steelworkers, 250,000 ladies' garment workers, 175,000 clothing workers, 100,000 agricultural and packing-house workers, 80,000 rubber workers. The day of labor giants had dawned."[24] There followed a drastic increase in unemployment. According to one compilation unemployment in 1937 stood at about 7½ millions. In 1938, it rose to 11 million, and in 1939 was still lingering around 9½ million.[25]

A stock market crash of considerable dimensions occurred beginning in the middle of 1937. One economic historian explains these events in this way. There had been an increase of aggregate labor income at the expense of profit income. This had resulted primarily from the great amount of unionization which increased wages of manufacturing laborers rapidly. "A main factor," he says, "on the industrial side in bringing the revival of 1935-1937 to a close was this startling increase in wages . . . , due . . . to a tremendous burst of activity by trade unions under the Wagner Act—a rise in wages unmatched by

[23] Bernstein, *op. cit.*, p. 363.
[24] Joseph G. Rayback, A *History of American Labor* (New York; Macmillan, 1959), p. 355.
[25] Fite and Reese, *op. cit.*, p. 599.

a corresponding rise in the productivity of labor."[26] In consequence, prospects for businessmen declined, investment slacked off, and an increasing number of workers were unemployed.

In this one instance, there is a fairly clear-cut connection between union activity and unemployment. Statistics bear out the results that could be predicted by the use of economic theory. But one swallow does not make a summer. Not every round of wage increases obtained by unions results in dramatic increases of unemployment. The task of the economic historian would be immensely simplified (and some number of them might be disemployed) if economic truths could be so readily ratified with empirical evidence. Let us return shortly to the question of proof of disemployment as a result of union activity.

It is in order, first, to complete the explanation of the business decline and rise of unemployment in 1938. Unions were by no means the only contributing factor in unemployment. As has been indicated in the previous chapter, government programs were driving farmers off the farms and, hence, into the industrial labor market. Moreover, there is something to the conventional explanation of the crash of 1937 as being a result of fiscal activity. One historian gives a convenient summary of this explanation: "In June, 1937, Roosevelt . . . slashed spending sharply. He cut WPA rolls drastically and turned off WPA pump-priming. At the very same time, Washington collected two billions in new social security taxes. The government had not only stopped priming the pump but was even 'taking some water out of the spout.' "[27] Benjamin Anderson has challenged this explanation,[28] but it is plausible to conclude that when the higher wages were required, combined with a slacking off of inflation, that the two things in conjunction accelerated unemployment.

[26]Anderson, *op. cit.*, pp. 444-46.
[27] Leuchtenburg, *op. cit.*, p. 244.
[28] See Anderson *op. cit.*, pp. 439-44.

Government further aggravated the situation in 1938 by the passage of the Fair Labor Standards Act. This established a minimum wage and maximum hours, resulting in higher wages than many workers had been getting in some industries covered. The effect of a minimum wage is the same in kind as a union wage. So far as it works to raise wages above the market level it will result in unemployment. All those workers, or would-be workers, who cannot produce enough to warrant their employment at this wage, cannot be profitably employed. The least skilled, the least productive, the poorest, are once again the victims of government action. The effect of establishing minimum wages in 1938, other things being equal, would have been to add to the rolls of the unemployed.

Government has labored mightily for a good many years now to undo the damage it has done by the empowerment of labor unions and the establishment of minimum wage, maximum hours, and other working conditions—or, failing in its corrective efforts, to hide the results. A good angle from which to tell this story is from that of hiding the results. (Whether this hiding of results is deliberate or not need not concern us, for the effects are the same whether done from innocence or intent to deceive.) The main way in which the results are hidden is by the use of statistics. It should be clear that the statistics on unemployment and employment issued by government agencies are *political* statistics. They are used by politicians in power to claim great victories for their programs and by those out of power to point up the failures of those in power (quite often simultaneously, though by different speakers or writers). Much more seriously they do not tell what they are alleged to tell. They neither accurately record the number of people employed nor the number unemployed. A little examination of some figures should make this clear. Suppose at a given moment, within the last year or so, the population of the United States was announced as being 200,000,000. (These will not be exact figures, but they will surely be near enough that there is no particular reason for concern.) The Bureau of Labor Statistics might announce simultaneously that the number of employed in the country, was, say, 70,000,000, give or take a million or so. The number of unemployed, it might announce, stands at approximately 4,000,000. These figures are close enough to actual ones announced to demonstrate my point without distorting the actual use of statistics that is made.

There is something obviously wrong with these figures. As anyone can see, they do not balance. If the population of the United States is 200,000,000, if the number employed is 70,000,000, then the number unemployed is 120,000,000!, not, as announced, 4,000,000. But, as the bureaucrat who compiled these statistics might object, the figure of 70,000,000 does not purport to include all those employed, only those *gainfully* employed. Very well, but the books still do not balance: there are 70,000,000 gainfully employed and 4,000,000 unemployed. There are still 126,000,000 people in statistical limbo. Let us come to the rescue of the statistician by concocting a third category, say, that of the *ungainfully* employed. Never mind that housewives may be insulted by being told that they are ungainfully employed or that the category is somewhat imprecise as regards infants and the aged infirm. It might fairly describe those in school and college, in the armed forces (or would it?), retired, perennially on relief, and so on. As a matter of fact, it would be a safe bet that some of those listed as unemployed are in reality ungainfully employed: say they are fishing, or some such thing. There is every reason to suppose, even, that some of those listed as unemployed are unemployed gainfully. For example, they might be drawing unemployment checks and selling tickets in the numbers racket.

If it were possible to calculate the number of unemployed in the United States at a given time, the figure would be attained by subtracting the number of employed from the *potential labor supply*. The potential labor supply can be defined as consisting of all those who are capable of rendering a service. It would not, then, include the whole population. Obviously, at any given time the potential labor supply would not include infants and very small children, the bedridden sick, and the incapacitated insane. To turn it around, the category of potential employables would include school children, college students, housewives, elderly retired, and so on. A calculation of such a potential labor supply could be made that would probably be as nearly accurate as figures that are commonly bandied about today, though I have not made such a calculation, nor has anyone else to my knowledge. As a very rough guess, I suppose that if unemployment were reckoned from such a computation it would amount to somewhere between 80 and 90 million people today! If we had such figures, we would have a much more accurate picture of the unemployment induced by labor unions and government intervention.

Many people jump to conclusions, so it should be made clear that this writer does *not*, emphatically does not, if you please, equate the potential labor supply with the number who *should* or *ought* to be productively or gainfully employed. He does not profess to know how many ought to be so employed (since *ought* is a moral imperative, not a quantifiable category), nor does anyone else on this earth. The number of people who ought to be employed is not, never has been, or ever will be a datum of experience. Yet it is precisely such data that the Bureau of Labor Statistics purports to be releasing from time to time. There is an implication that those whom it announces as unemployed ought to be employed. Congress passed an Employment Act of 1946 pledging itself to follow policies leading to full employment. Moralists have for years waxed poetically sorrowful over the number of unemployed, without any clear notion of how many there are or why they are unemployed.

My point is this: the United States government (and many state governments) established conditions under which a large portion of the population could not be gainfully employed. It fostered labor union organizations, established minimum wages and maximum hours, defined minimal working conditions which had to prevail, aided and abetted in the driving of those who would work from the gates of factories and from farms. Then it labored mightily to reduce the labor supply (called labor *force* in sociological parlance) to fit the procrustean bed of its requirements.

Governments have worked for years to reduce the actual labor supply, spurred by labor unions and assorted reformers, though many of the most effective measures to do this have been passed in the last thirty years or so. One of the earliest efforts to keep laborers off the market that bore fruit was immigration restriction. The attempt to exclude Chinese from the United States was embodied in law in the Chinese Exclusion Act of 1882, a measure that is frequently credited to the efforts of the Knights of Labor. In the latter part of the nineteenth century, states began generally to pass compulsory attendance laws for school children, a movement which had reached fruition generally by the early twentieth century. The thrust to immigration restriction reached its peak in the 1920's with the passage and implementation of the National Origins Act. By the early twentieth century, states were passing legislation restricting the hours of work for women and laws prohibiting child labor, sometimes to have them disallowed by the Supreme Court. Employer liability laws made it exigent for employers to select their workers much more carefully, even though they carried insurance to cover themselves. I am not concerned here with what may have been the motivation behind the passage of such legislation, only with the fact that the impact was to reduce the actual labor supply. In the 1930's the Federal government got into the reduction of the labor supply much more vigorously. The Social Security Act, passed in 1935, was a three-pronged attack. In the first place, it levied a tax on employers and employees for the purpose of providing a pension at retirement for industrial workers. This enabled many workers to leave the labor market at age 65, or employers to rid themselves of them with a clear conscience. To attempt to sway retired workers not to re-enter the market, the Social Security regulations over the years have limited the amount a workman can earn while receiving Social Security payments. (Incidentally, this limitation could hardly be aimed at anything else than reducing the labor supply.) Also, the Social Security Act contained provisions and requirements for unemployment compensation, to compensate those who are disemployed under the system for a period of time. It contained, in addition, provisions for Federal supplements to states for what are euphemistically referred to by recipients as old age pensions for the aged poor, thus enabling even those who had set aside little or nothing for retirement to stay off the labor market.

Even these Herculean measures did not succeed in cutting the labor supply to the diminishing procrustean bed of available jobs in the 1930's. Government entered the gap much more directly to provide jobs, or money for those unable to find jobs. The most famous of these stopgap measures was the WPA or Works Progress Administration. As noted before, WPA rolls had been reduced in 1937, but with the swelling unemployment following union wage raises the program was expanded once more. "In November, 1938 . . . , WPA employment reached an all-time high when 3,238,000 workers were engaged on government projects. There were still over one million people on WPA in 1941, and the program was not discontinued until early in 1943. . . ."[29] The Civilian Conservation Corps in the 1930's took up some of the slack in the labor market and induced some men to withdraw from the labor supply for a period of time. Large building programs for government structures were undertaken in the 1930's and since. More recently, the interstate highway program has diverted a part of the labor supply. Defense spending is sometimes dispensed in those areas where it will be supposed to

[29] Fite and Reese, *op. cit.*, p. 601.

help the situation. So thoroughly has the effect of a controlled labor market impressed itself on Americans, that many believe that without the programs there would be widespread unemployment. So there would, so long as the determination of wages was kept off the market.

The Fair Labor Standards Act of 1938 not only provided for minimum wages and maximum hours—which would have the effect of increasing unemployment—, but also prohibited the employment of children under a certain age, which would have the effect of reducing the available labor supply.

Over the years, the Federal government has inaugurated a variety of programs to enable students to stay in school longer. In 1935, the National Youth Administration was set up to dispense funds for the part time employment of young people in school and college. Between 1936 and 1940 something in the vicinity of $325 million was spent on this undertaking.[30] Since World War II, there have been a variety of programs which were to have the effect of keeping people at schooling and out of the labor supply. The most famous and extensive of these efforts has been the G.I. Bill of Rights, which not only paid for tuition and books for veterans to attend college (or high school) but also paid farmers to farm and fostered on-the-job training. More recently, the government has gone into the scholarship program to enable some young people to stay in school and off the labor market. Presently, the biggest inducement for boys to attend college may well be the exemption from the draft. It is not that all the young men are wanted in the Armed Forces, but they are not wanted as a part of the labor supply either.

Even this great multitude and variety of programs would not have, and has not, sufficiently reduced the labor supply to permit those laborers on the market to be paid above market wages without causing considerable unemployment. The government's major device over the years to facilitate the perpetual rounds of money wage increases has been the increase

[30] *Ibid.*, p. 602.

of the money supply. It is, of course, possible to increase money wages if the money supply is increased, in something of the same ratio. It may not even create unemployment. In theory, the increase in the money supply might exactly balance the rise in minimum wage and union wage so that there would be no noticeable effect on employment. In which case, it should be obvious that union leaders and government officials would be engaging in a grotesque deception. They say that they are providing great benefits to workers when in fact prices would rise to compensate for the wage increase, and the worker would be no better off than formerly. For good or ill, it is not that simple. In practice, it is not possible to calculate precisely how much of an increase in the money supply would be needed to balance wage increases (for one obvious reason, all wages are not increased proportionately), though it is perversely intriguing to imagine someone engaging in such diabolical computations. Government must attend to other pressures in regard to money supply than its effect on wages. Moreover, there are, of course, some devastating side effects of inflation on others than workers.

As I have said, unions, as constituted, must have continual rounds of inflation to survive. It is equally true that if government's raising of the minimum wage is not to lead to much greater unemployment than it does it must be accompanied or followed by an increase in the money supply. That this continual round of money wage increases followed by a round of inflation is a vicious treadmill from which nearly everyone loses should be obvious. It is as if one should deliberately take poison and then follow it with the antidote, not once, but time after time. It is by no means clear that even those workers who get the money wage increases benefit from this practice. It is more than probable that the raising of the minimum wage by government follows rather than precedes the inflation. Thus, the minimum wage only serves to compensate, more or less, for a situation the government has already created. If the inflation continues, as it has almost uninterruptedly for the last thirty years, those workers at minimum wages will shortly be getting less rather than more than they formerly were. Union contracts that run for two or three years tie workers more or less to the monetary situation that existed when the contract was drawn. Even when there are cost-of-living clauses or annual increments provided, the rise in money wages tends to follow the rise of prices rather than precede them. There is an element of Russian roulette in giving hostage to inflation with long run contracts. Those whose incomes do not fluctuate with the monetary policies of the government are, of course, likely to suffer the greatest from the inflation—such as retired persons on fixed pensions.

The economic mode for the improvement of the well being of workers, as well as people in general, is the reverse of money supply increases and politically contrived wage increases. It is by way of increased productivity which, if the money supply remains relatively stable, will result in lower prices. In these circumstances, prices of goods and services tend to fall much more readily than wages. Indeed, money wages may remain the same, or actually increase, while prices fall. This was generally the case in the latter part of the nineteenth century when unions were hardly a factor and there was no government minimum wage. One economic historian says that the "index of money hourly wages for men in all industries practically doubled between 1860 and 1890. . . . Since the index of commodity prices fell rapidly [that is, commodity prices fell, *not* the index] after 1865, the purchasing power of wages, 'real wages,' often attained a spectacular improvement."[31]

Unions, then, quite often benefit only those who draw salaries as union officials. In so far as they enable some workers to draw higher "real wages" than they otherwise would, they do so at the expense of excluded workers and, eventually, of the very industry from which they receive the

[31] Edward C. Kirkland, *Industry Comes of Age* (New York: Holt, Rinehart and Winston, 1961), p. 402.

income; for the higher wages are reflected in higher prices which tend to price the product or service out of the market. There are many other unfavorable results of unionization for workers (and others) which can only be touched upon here. Work stoppages by strikes reduce production and result in less income for workers. Union dues are a tax, in effect, on the income of workers, and tend to reduce their income to that extent. Individual workers are kept, in effect, from improving themselves and their wages by the union's insistence upon equality of pay for a particular job and resistance to greater production by individual workers. Union seniority rules reduce the mobility of workers, reduce competition for jobs, and tend to fix the worker in his particular factory. Wages not based on productivity tend to price American goods out of the world market. Unions quite often act to attempt to prevent the equalization of industrialization over the country by opposing the initial move of companies to other parts of the country and then rushing to organize workers in the new plants and raising their wages to the national average. By so doing, they would deny the manufacturer the temporary gain he would make by moving. Slowdowns and stalling by union members deny what is not produced to the country. Unions encourage suspicion of management and inhibit the co-operation between managers and workers which could be mutually beneficial.

But let me return finally to unemployment, which is the most direct and devastating result of union activity and government proscriptions and restrictions upon workers. The devastating effects reach out to touch those whom a benevolent society would wish to help. Almost everyone must have heard, at one time or another, the poignant appeals to employ the handicapped. This appeal is perennially made on television, radio, in newspapers, and by posters. Few stop to ask why it is that the handicapped need such special attention. If there is work that they can do or services which they can perform, we might suppose that this would be well known to employers. Such reckoning ignores, however, the obstacles we have thrown in the way of their employment. Quite often, the handicapped are unable to produce enough to warrant paying them the union wage or minimum wage. They are especially liable to have accidents and thus will drive up insurance rates, which employers take to meet the government requirements of liability for workmen. Their susceptibility to illness may make them a drain on unemployment compensation and company health insurance programs. In short, the scales have been rigged against the handicapped. They become, quite often, the object of charitable appeals when they might be self-sustaining and self sufficient without the arbitrary obstacles.

By the same token, many sections of cities are today made well nigh uninhabitable for civilized people by the presence of the idle. Young ruffians, teen-agers with nothing to do, and lounging gangs make the streets unsafe and life for those who live in their midst dangerous and unpleasant. The reason for this phenomenon is not far to seek. The young are supported in their idleness by government doles. The dull are kept in school far beyond the point of usefulness (turning schools in some districts into a nightmare experience for teachers and less violently inclined students) by compulsory attendance laws, and induced to stay there by massive attempts to prevent drop-outs. When they are old enough to be allowed to work, quite often they cannot find employment. The inexperienced and the unskilled are not sufficiently productive, at least over a considerable period of time, to warrant paying them the minimum wage or union wage. Many employers now find it more profitable to pay the penalty of overtime wages to skilled and dependable employees than to take on new ones who will have to be trained, be paid minimum wages during the period of relative unproductiveness, and, above all, for whom they will have to make additional social security payments and keep additional records to satisfy government. Overtime is now a way of life for many workers in factories, as extra jobs are to craftsmen. The 8-hour day has hardly turned out to be the ideal of workers, though who could resist the original lure of more pay for less work? At any rate, government programs contribute mightily to the unemployment of the unskilled and the young.

How government restrictions even keep young people who are in school from summer employment is illustrated by this letter to the *Wall Street Journal:*

> I am a life insurance salesman, licensed in North Carolina. Of course, my secretaries receive far above any minimum wage. However, in previous summers I had used high school sophomores in the office for routine duties and to give them a chance to get acquainted with business. Because some birthday cards were mailed out of the state, there was a suit which involved two or three years of my time and money and ended with the decision that these girls were under Federal wage control. Consequently, I owed them back salaries because they had mailed some post cards.
>
> Now I wouldn't think of letting a student come in to work. Of course, this means disillusionment and unemployment for students.[32]

In 1967, following a raise and an extension of the coverage of Social Security, many firms reported releasing some of their employees, and a portion of those who did so attributed their action directly to the Social Security change. Letters received by an organization making a survey reveal how some small businessmen have adjusted to the government prescriptions and regulations. The owner of a large food store in Michigan wrote:

> For 38 years I have been in the retail grocery business. I have trained hundreds of young fellows 16 to 20 years old as stock boys, retail clerks, produce managers, meat managers, assistant managers, and finally managers. It was a real pleasure to work with these kids. About three years ago Congress passed a bill making it impossible to hire more than 10 per cent of your total payroll-in-hours at a figure of 80 per

[32] *Wall Street Journal* (June 8, 1966).

cent of the minimum wage. Some of these 16-year-old boys
in our state area are just not worth wages of $1.40 per hour.
We . . . eliminated the part-time students. . . .

A laundry in Utah reported this sobering action:

We have some choice and loyal employees but we have
some who are not able to produce to the necessary capacity,
so we are forced to replace them. This is a most difficult
thing to do to an old employee, but the dollars just won't
reach.

An automotive electrical shop in Nebraska wrote:

I have helped four men through the ranks giving them
education needed for a better job. Under the minimum wage
I cannot afford to hire anyone to train because I cannot
absorb the cost or charge to the customer.

A plant in Wisconsin described the problem this way:

The minimum wage and hour law keeps me from employing high school and college students. Many students seek
work in this area but have no experience. An employer like
myself cannot train the students and pay $1.40 per hour. We
could use them for clean-up personnel and they would be
happy to work for less but it puts our cost too great.[33]

Older workers—those 50 or above—quite often find it
difficult to find new jobs, according to common report.
Campaigns have even been launched to promote the hiring of
older workers. If this is a problem, as alleged, it can be ac-
counted for mainly in the same way as the others, that is, by
obstacles erected in the way of employing new workers: the
minimum wage, the Social Security payments, employer liability for accidents, the extra bookkeeping involved, and so
on. To the extent that these have promoted the use of technology they have made more formidable the employment of
the older people also.

[33] News release of National Federation of Independent Business (August
14, 1967), pp. 1-5.

The assault upon wage workers does not appear to have borne what might have been expected to be its most obvious fruits: namely, declining production, increasing and widespread deprivation, falling standards of living, and, perhaps, widespread hunger and even starvation. On the contrary, it is generally held, and I think this is correct, that the standard of living is higher today in America than ever before (though one must grant that we live in smaller rooms of smaller houses than formerly). Yet there was a time in America, say, 1800, when the proportion of the employed to the total population was vastly greater than today. It is not improbable that in 1800 somewhere between 80 and 90 per cent of the population was gainfully or productively employed for some portion of the year. On the farm, everyone worked all or most of the day except very small children and the bedridden. Children and the aged were employed in factories and in mines. At the present, a liberal interpretation of government statistics would indicate that, perhaps, 40 per cent of the population are gainfully employed. In short, 40 per cent of the population support the rest. This, on the face of it, would not conduce to a higher standard of living. On the contrary, other things being equal, we should be much poorer generally today than in 1800. It is obvious, too, that such prosperity as we enjoy today is not the result of the smaller proportion of workers.

It must follow, then, and it should be as obvious but is not, that our wealth today is not a product of union activity or government intervention in the labor market. The material wealth of a people is surely measured in the goods and services which they can command. Unions do not contribute to productivity by excluding workers from the market, by strikes, by work stoppages, by slowdowns, by resisting the introduction of machinery, by featherbedding, or by reducing the hours of labor. Government restrictions do not increase productivity by pricing workers out of the market, by prohibiting others from entering it, and by supporting still others in idleness. Above all, government does not increase productivity by inflation. If government could enrich us by increasing the money supply it should do so forthwith, and it should cease its penny ante tactics. It should give each of us, say, an annual income of $100,000 by the expedient of printing the money. But if we could each have $100,000 for not working we would not all be rich. We would all be incomparably poor, for our money would be worthless. No legerdemain of monetary manipulation can enrich all Americans one whit. In short, we have neither been enriched nor kept from universal poverty by union or government efforts that have been supposed to benefit workers.

Our prosperity, such as it is, can be attributed to two things. In the first place, all of it can be attributed to those who work with their hands and their minds to provide and increase the goods and services which all of us enjoy. Actually, the Bureau of Labor Statistics does not give an accurate figure for the employment of Americans. There are a great many more employed, at least part time, than the figures tell. The self employed are not included in them. Newspaper boys are not included, most babysitters, many cleaning women, many of the aged who do various and sundry things to increase their income. The moonlighting that goes on increases goods and services available to us greatly over what the situation would be without it. One of the most dramatic adjustments that has been made to artificially high wages and limitations on hours of work is do-it-yourselfing. Sears Roebuck and Montgomery Ward catalogs, as well as building supply establishments, offer a great variety of materials that can be installed by the individual with only a modicum of skill and ingenuity. Even the materials for a house can be purchased pre-cut and ready to be assembled by the do-it-yourselfer. Many men, no doubt, get a sense of achievement and fulfillment by this activity, but, as much as anything else, it marks a movement away from specialization in consequence of the inordinate overpricing of such skills as plumbing, tile setting, carpentry, painting, and locksmithery. Everyman becomes a handyman when he has time on his hands and the inexpensive handyman is kept off the market. Many of those employed by government calculations should be counted as much as 1½ workers in terms of the government's 8-hour day.

But of equal importance is technology. Even if there were twice as many employed today as the Bureau of Labor Statistics claims, the proportion of workers to total population would probably not be as great as it was in 1800, and we would still be poorer than they were if we were dependent upon their technology. The use of technology has enabled one man to produce as much as several used to and, in some instances, as much as many men could. This makes our abundance possible despite reductions of the proportion of workers, deliberate efforts to keep workers off the market, shorter hours, and even coffee breaks.

The greatest irony of all is that the very technology which has largely saved us thus far from the consequences of suicidal government policies has been made the scapegoat for those policies. Unemployment is frequently blamed on technology. Unions have often resisted technological innovations, meanwhile rushing to claim all the fruits of any that is used. Capital which buys and maintains the technology has not only been blamed for the ills of our age (rather, the capitalists have), but those who gather the capital, that is, save, invest, and so forth, have alike had all manner of obstacles thrown in the way of their endeavors. Technology has even sometimes been blamed for the lack of personal services in a society in which machines perform so many of the functions once performed by people, a reaction as eminently sensible as kicking an automobile when it will not run. In point of fact, the blame for much of the lack of personal service is, once again, that government policy which has resulted in the pricing of so many services out of the market.

Thus far, then, we in America have generally been spared

some of the most horrendous consequences which would have befallen a people in any other age following such policies. This does not mean that we have avoided the consequences; we have only diverted and rechanneled them. The consequences are with us in juvenile delinquency, in the boredom of enforced idleness, in the loss of the elegance of personal craftsmanship, in the futility of the unskilled in their quest for meaningful work, in the loss of the contacts of personal service, in the overemployment of some and underemployment of others, in the stunted lives of the old put out to pasture and of the young who have been sated with fruitless efforts to provide them recreation when they have not yet experienced creation. This and much else is all about us in consequence of the assault upon the wage worker.

CHAPTER VI

Roadblocks to Enterprise

RECENTLY, THE "JITNEYS" BECAME AN ISSUE FOR A TIME IN Pittsburgh. A "jitney," in the local vernacular, is a vehicle which serves as a taxi for at least a part of the time but is neither authorized nor licensed to do so. It seems that the drivers of these vehicles were given to driving up to bus stops, picking up one or more passengers, and driving them home, particularly after work in the afternoons. The issue arose after the Port Authority, a sort of government corporation, had acquired a monopoly of street car and bus transportation in Pittsburgh. The "jitneys" were poaching on its domain as well as that of authorized taxis, though the latter does not appear to have been at the heart of the issue. Some "jitney" drivers were apprehended, and there was considerable talk of prosecuting them—of driving them out of business. The matter was handled somewhat gingerly, however, because the "jitney" drivers were mainly, if not exclusively, Negroes, and there was considerable sympathy for them at the moment.

The war on the poor, it turns out, has been conducted on many fronts. The poor left the farms in droves in the wake of government intervention. They have been driven out of the labor market by wages and hours legislation. The enterprising poor have frequently found their path blocked in yet another direction. One of the options open to them would be to go into business for themselves. The case of the "jitneys" illustrates one of the difficulties thrown in the way of those who would like to go into business. As we shall see, the government hurdles which the small businessman must overcome to succeed are numerous, subtle, and varied.

This is the more surprising because for many years reformers and interventionists have weeped and wailed and gnashed their teeth, so to speak, over the plight of the small businessman. They have often pledged all sorts of help to him, and many government programs have been put into operation that were supposed to rescue him. In 1953, the Federal government inaugurated the Small Business Administration with the ostensible purpose of helping small businessmen. Yet many of the hurdles that a prospective businessman must leap in order to make good have been placed there by government.

Let it be clear from the beginning of this discussion, however, that not all the obstacles to enterprise are government made. In the nature of things, going into business on one's own is a difficult undertaking, and would be hard enough if government confined itself largely to the protection of life, liberty, and property. To go into business, it is usually necessary to accumulate capital reserves. This means denying immediate satisfactions for future gains; it may mean that one's family is denied for a time many comforts and luxuries. Any enterprise is risky; all may be lost if the investment is not successful. There is usually competition to be met, and even if there is little at the outset, one's own success is but a sign to others to go into the business. Successful business endeavor requires rigorous self-discipline; being on one's own does not mean that one may do as he pleases—not, at least, if one wishes to succeed—, but rather that he must learn to boss himself rather severely. His store or shop, or whatever, must be open or available during stated hours. He must often be there before it opens and sometimes long hours after it closes. No clock frees the owner from his responsibilities as it does the wage worker. The natural obstacles are great enough; when they are supplemented by arbitrary government intervention, they often become formidable.

One other thing should be said in preface to what follows. It is not practical to discuss the many ramifications of government programs alluded to, nor to make thorough evaluations of them. It would be jumping to conclusions in some instances to conclude that because a government regulation or restriction imposes an obstacle to enterprise that it should be abolished. I must restrict myself largely to showing that a particular program does block enterprise, leaving out of consideration the many controversies that could be called up as to the desirability or undesirability of the program. For example, health and sanitation regulations may indeed be useful and even vital, a case which may not in the least alter the fact that some of them deter enterprise. My thought on the matter is this: that there is usually more than one way to skin a cat, that the customer may be his own best protection in most instances, and that before a program is undertaken it should be examined from as many angles as possible.

The first thing to be done in going into business on one's own is the accumulation of the minimum necessary capital. Almost all undertakings require capital of greater or lesser amounts. To accomplish this, most men must set aside some portion of their earnings as savings. The most discouraging government intervention for savers is our old acquaintance, not to say friend, inflation. Inflation reduces the value of money saved because as the money supply is increased prices rise. This means that the saver could have bought more with the money at the time that he first received it than he could at a later date, if the inflation continues over a period of time. The propensity to save is discouraged by inflation, and the propensity to spend is encouraged. The inflationary policies of the government over the last 50 years have discouraged saving, though, of course, they have not stopped it.

The progressive income tax is another deterrent to capital accumulation. This tax is often talked about as if it were devised to take from the "haves." It should be understood, however, as taking from those who are "getting," or trying to accumulate. A graduated income tax does not, *per se*, tax wealth that has been accumulated in earlier times; rather, it taxes current income. There has been a trend, in recent years, for workers to prefer fringe benefits instead of, or in addition to, wage increases, because direct increases of incomes put men in higher tax categories. Progressive taxation constitutes a war on the poor mainly in two ways. In the first place, it makes it more difficult for them to leave the ranks of the poor by accumulating wealth. More important, perhaps, since progressive taxation does not bear heavily on the very poor, it works against the accumulation which would lead to new investment, new jobs, and more competition among firms for workers. It is such competition that leads to increases in real wages to workers. At any rate, progressive taxation limits and obstructs enterprise by making it difficult to accumulate investment capital.

Another way in which taxation inhibits enterprise is through the subsidies to businesses and farms. There are, today, a great array of government subsidies: to farmers, to airlines, to railroads, to shipping, for house building, to commuters, to entertainment, and so on. More subtly, government subsidizes business by stockpiling of materials and by carrying commercial mail below costs. The point is that these subsidies come from taxes on the general public, that the man trying to accumulate wealth to go into business is charged for keeping others in business, that what he pays in this way comes out of what he might have been able to save.

Social Security payments are an inhibiting tax on potential enterprisers. There are many roads to such security as man can attain in this veil of tears, one of which is to own one's own business. It will not do to argue that a business does not provide absolute security, which is true enough, but then neither does government. The history of mankind is, in large, the story of the rise and fall of governments, of forfeited obligations, of arbitrary confiscations by governments, and so on. Our own century has been replete with governments overturned by war and revolutionaries, of debts and obligations wiped out thereby, of unstable and insecure governments. The young who are burdened with taxation to provide for their retirement have just so much less savings which might serve for investment. The Social Security system is particularly pernicious in this regard, for all that is paid into it is forfeited by the individual; he cannot draw it out for investment; he cannot use it to take advantage of greater opportunities as they come along. In short, he cannot follow his own road to independence and security so readily because he is taxed to provide for his old age at a time in life when he might well be advancing his more immediate well being. Social Security payments fall particularly heavily on the poor, for the tax is regressive in that it only applies to incomes up to a certain point.

Government interferes with the acquisition of capital in yet another way. States usually have maximum interest rates, above which the interest is called usury. The history of laws against "usury" is very long, and they are usually defended as protections of the poor and needy. Their practical effect, however, is to "protect" the poor and needy from getting a loan, or, at least, a legal loan. New enterprisers and new enterprises are not, quite often, the best credit risks, but if there were no ceiling on interest those who are very convinced of their possibilities could usually get money at some price. Maximum interest rates are yet another hurdle in the way of going into business. The Federal government has made some effort to counteract the damage that other governments have done in this respect. The Small Business Administration was founded to make loans to small enterprisers, and it was mainly taking over a function in 1953 that the Reconstruction Finance Corporation had been supposed to perform. It makes money available to some enterprisers at low rates and on favorable terms. It is as economically unwise, however, for government to encourage enterprise by such interventions as it is for it to discourage it by others. A low interest rate should tell a borrower that the lender reckons his undertaking to be a prudent one. On the contrary, government loans can only tell the borrower that he belongs in a political category which entitles him to the loan. He may enter business to compete with other small businessmen, some of whom may be driven out of business by his competition. His loan will be a burden on savers because it will have been subsidized by inflation or taxes, or both. The cure for the effects of a ceiling on interest rates on enterprise is not government-fostered low interest rates but the removal of the maximum interest restriction.

The man who has overcome all these arbitrary obstacles—inflation, progressive income tax, Social Security payments, taxes to subsidize other businesses, and maximum interest rates—to accumulation and actually has his nest egg with which to go into business must next decide upon what to undertake. If he were to make a thorough survey of opportunities, he would find that the field has been considerably narrowed by government monopolies—Federal, state and local made difficult to enter by franchise and special re-quirements, already virtually pre-empted, in some instances, by government competition.

The most general monopoly of the Federal government is that of carrying the mails by the United States Post Office. Of itself, this may not appear to be much of an obstacle to any enterprise that those with few resources might enter. Certainly, no small enterpriser might expect to undertake to deliver the mail throughout the country. It is, however, more in the manner of the present operation of the Post Office than in its overall task that small enterprisers have been shut out. Much of the work of the Post Office could be contracted out to local bidders. It was once common for local enterprisers to deliver mail from post office to post office, and it is still done in some instances. But the government now has its own fleet of trucks to perform this function mainly. It is conceivable that delivery to households could even be made under the direction of private contractors. Of course, the government could divest itself of the whole operation. Be that as it may, here is a vast operation over which the government maintains a monopoly, and little to no opportunity exists presently for small entrepreneurs to enter the field.

Other Federal monopolies are generally limited to areas or in time, as in the case of war time undertakings. The most famous of the monopolies over an area is that held by the Tennessee Valley Authority. In this area, a Federal government corporation acquired, in one way or another, a monopoly of the generation and sale of electricity. It undersold competitors and acquired their transmission facilities. It apparently started out as a competitor of private power companies but became rather quickly a monopoly dispenser of electricity.

Less well known but much more complete as a monopoly has been the sway of the Federal government in the Panama Canal Zone. Not only did the Federal government construct the canal but the railroad as well. According to one writer, "Private parties are not allowed to own any land in the Zone and private businesses do not operate there. Therefore, the many other businesses in the Zone other than the Panama Canal are maintained and operated by the Panama Canal Company. These businesses include a steamship line between New York and the Isthmus of Panama; a railroad across the Isthmus; the cargo docks and piers and harbor terminal facilities on the Isthmus; a coaling plant for ships; an oil-handling plant; commissary stores . . . ; a printing plant; restaurants, theaters, bowling alleys," and so forth.[1]

There are, or have been, other monopolies, of sorts, maintained by the Federal government, but most of those mo-

---

[1] Harold Koontz and Richard W. Gable, *Public Control of Economic Enterprise* (New York: McGraw-Hill, 1956), pp. 684-85.

nopolies that are best known are maintained by state and local governments. The most dramatic of state maintained monopolies occurs in those states that operate liquor stores. Something on the order of one-third of the states have a monopoly of the sale of some of the alcoholic beverages. Usually this does not include beer, but often includes wines. In these states all private enterprisers are rigorously precluded from competition by the police force, and numerous small and large businesses that might otherwise thrive do not exist. Where there are state liquor stores, those who are considering going into business on their own legally must put this avenue of operation out of mind.

In connection with the liquor business, there is in effect another exclusion of the small entrepreneur, or so it would seem, though I am not certain where in this thesis it should be discussed. Small operators appear to be effectively excluded from the manufacture—distilling—of liquor. There was a time in American history when many farmers were also distillers and when the sale of alcoholic beverages was undertaken by many entrepreneurs. This does not occur legally any more to my knowledge, though there are still such operations carried on illegally. The problem in explaining this is that the manufacture of alcoholic beverages is still done by private concerns. But they are mostly large industries, and none of them, to my knowledge, would be described as small and local in character. The reason for this must be the great maze of restrictions and regulations which one must go through before being allowed legally to distill alcoholic beverages, plus the scale on which one must operate before being successful. In states where there is a liquor store monopoly, the difficulties of getting a brand on the shelves must be great. For it to be offered on the level of a whole state, the manufacturer must be big business already. The situation is probably not much better in states where there are private stores, for franchises and licenses are usually difficult to obtain and those in the business are carefully regulated. The basic taxes on liquor are so high that it is difficult to compete effectively in price with established brands, since the portion of the total price that goes to the producer is frequently less than that going to taxes. In any case, it is not practical for a distiller to start small, to sell to local patrons, to build a reputation for his product, and to expand gradually. After all, those who have gone into distilling have usually found themselves beset by the police and lucky if they have been able to escape prison. Small wonder that they might not know that it is somehow legal for some people to make liquor for sale in some places.

To return to state and local monopolies, states sometimes have other monopolies than that of the sale of liquor. The following are examples:

> The state of New York has long maintained a system of barge canals 525 miles in length, which it operates at public expense, charging no tolls. The Commonwealth of Massachusetts, since 1918, has operated the transit system of Boston and neighboring cities and towns. Harbor facilities at ocean ports—wharves, docks, warehouses and the like—are usually owned by state governments. At New Orleans a State Board of Port Commissioners, formed in 1896, operates grain elevators, coffee terminals, banana conveyors, cranes, derricks, a belt-line railway, a canal, and a free trade zone. . . .[2]

Moreover, "Multipurpose projects including the generation and sale of hydroelectric power have been constructed by state governments in Nebraska, Oklahoma, Texas, and South Carolina. The people of Nebraska are served exclusively by publicly-owned electrical utilities."[3] All such monopolies, of course, make it difficult, if it is not prohibited, for private enterprisers to enter the field.

Local monopolies, however, are apt to be the ones that could be challenged by small enterprisers, sometimes with

---

[2] Clair Wilcox, *Public Policies Toward Business* (Homewood, Ill.: Richard D. Irwin, 1960), pp. 805-06.
[3] *Ibid*, p. 807.

little capital, if it were not prohibited. Municipalities frequently have a monopoly of trash collection, water distribution, sale of electricity, distribution of gas, and sometimes of the running of busses, trolleys and streetcars.[4] In recent years, an increasing number of cities have taken over the operation of street railways and busses. In the first place, they tended to drive the firms into near or actual bankruptcy with rate regulation and service requirements. Then, a government corporation of some sort would usually take over the systems, operating transportation facilities. Sometimes, this involved taking over "feeder" lines operated by a number of small bus companies. Not only were companies driven out of existence and their assets taken from them for a governmentally determined price, but also this aspect of transportation was closed to enterprisers. So it has been, depending upon local action, with trash collection, water distribution, electricity distribution, and so on. Only rarely will a government provide a service even in competition with private enterprises.

The field of enterprises open to beginners is further narrowed by government granted monopolies to private companies and by limited entry to fields by franchises and special restrictions. The most common instances of government granted monopolies to single companies are telephone, street railway and bus, radio and television stations (when there is only one in a vicinity), electric companies, trash collection, and so forth. The usual argument for this sort of thing, at least at its inception, was that a natural monopoly was involved, that it would be impractical to have competing telephone companies, street railways, and so on. In practice, governments now frequently go beyond the natural monopoly argument to the question of how many companies can be afforded or may operate with economic success in a particular area. Let us not concern ourselves with the validity of the arguments but merely note that such franchises do limit enterprises which an individual may enter.

[4] See Koontz and Gable, *op. cit.*, pp. 702-03.

Of much more general importance, however, are industries in which there is and can be competition but to which access is limited by franchises, charters, or special permits. These include such diverse activities as banking, radio and television, bars and saloons, trucking and moving, liquor stores, airlines, and so on. The restrictions upon hauling goods in interstate commerce may be taken as illustrative of the difficulties of going into such businesses. Anyone who carries goods over state lines for someone else has come into the vicinity of being a common carrier. Not only is he subject to buying special licenses but also to special taxes of one sort or another. Congress passed the Motor Carriers Act of 1935 providing for the certifying and control of common carriers in interstate commerce, placing them under the control of the Interstate Commerce Commission. The Act contained a kind of "grandfather" clause providing that those who were common carriers at the time should be issued certificates if they applied for them within a specified time. After that, common carriers have had to meet the following general requirements: "(1) 'the applicant is fit, willing, and able properly to perform the service proposed and to conform to the provisions of the law and rules of the Commision; (2) the Commission finds the 'proposed service . . . is or will be required by future convenience and necessity.' "[5] Contract carriers would also have to have permits, and those were to be issued upon somewhat similar grounds.

It should be clear that such regulations constitute considerable obstacles to beginners. It does not require much capital to buy a truck; one may even be rented. But to go into the hauling business is something else again. Those who are already established have been given a vested interest by government. The man who has bought or rented a single truck would have great difficulty showing that he was "fit and able" to conduct the business. As to the future necessities of his service, even Solomon in all his wisdom would have

[5] *Ibid.*, p. 128.

trouble answering such a conundrum. In short, for a man to go into the business he needs to demonstrate that he does not need it, in the first place, and that someone should have been performing his service all along, in the second place.

A great variety of restrictions limit entry into the field of owning and operating a taxicab. This, too, is an undertaking which might be begun with very limited resources. But there are quite often formidable obstacles erected by state and municipal governments. At the least, there is likely to be an expensive license to acquire. At the most, entry may be so restricted that there is no immediate opening in the field. New York City is a notorious example of the difficulties of becoming a taxicab owner. Permits may be sold by those who acquire them in that city. A single permit has been sold for upwards of thirty thousand dollars, many times the price of an automobile!

But the field of enterprise is not only narrowed by government monopolies, by private monopolies granted by governments, by charters, franchises, and licenses but also entry into many kinds of business is made exceedingly difficult by government competition. When governments enter a field to sell a good or purvey a service they do more than add to the number of competitors. They have resources and use methods which make it exceedingly difficult for private persons to enter the field or to successfully compete with them. This is more than ironic, for the Federal government has for many years adopted measures to enforce what it is wont to call fair competition. The Federal Trade Commission Act, passed in 1914, declared "That unfair methods of competition, in commerce are hereby declared unlawful." The Robinson-Patman Act of 1936 "prohibits sales at unreasonably low prices for the purpose of destroying competition or eliminating a competitor."[6] Moreover, fair trade laws enacted by states have quite often been aimed at price cutting and under-

[6] Dudley F. Pegrum, *Public Regulation of Business* (Homewood, Ill.: Richard D. Irwin, 1959), p. 272.

selling. Yet governments regularly enter fields to provide services without direct cost to the user or at greatly reduced prices. It would not be hard to define government in business as unfair competition. But then, one supposes, governments are above the law.

At any rate, any prospective enterpriser will find his way made much harder by government competition in a host of lines of business or endeavor. Some of this competition is so common or so long established that hardly anyone thinks of it as competition. The most general and pervasive case is government maintenance of schools. Formal schooling is not generally thought of as an area where private enterprisers might enter; education is not generally sold as if it were an economic good. It is generally priced much below its cost. This has almost always been the case throughout American history, for it has generally been subsidized either by governments or private charity or, as is frequently the case today, by both. Private colleges are having an increasingly difficult task today in competing with *government supported* institutions, and, indeed, many of them are taking government loans and various subsidies. In any case, any private enterpriser who thought of entering the field with his own school would be in for rough competition. This is increasingly true even in the area of trade schools, which were not so long ago mainly private undertakings, and quite often probably profit makers —e.g., barber schools, radio schools, and so on.

The building of hospitals is another area where government is making it difficult for competitors. The Federal government has been maintaining hospitals for veterans for many years. It got into the subsidizing of local hospitals on a large scale with the Hill-Burton Act. Local communities have been building and maintaining hospitals for a good many years. Private hospitals are still fairly numerous, but their days are probably numbered.

Governments at all levels are vigorous competitors in providing recreation facilities. This is particulalry true in the maintenance of parks, zoos, golf courses, swimming pools, lakes, and waterways. Many buildings in which recreation activities take place—e.g., auditoriums, ball parks, civic centers—are now being built with tax funds. Not only does the prospective enterpriser find his potential savings taken away in taxes to support such undertakings but also his entry into such enterprises made difficult by competition.

The Federal government is in the research and information business in a big way. The Government Printing office is enormous, and keeps busy printing numerous pamphlets, making available research reports, publishing agricultural treatises, and providing information for businessmen. A United States Senator points out that the Commerce Department gathers around 100,000 research and development reports each year, and that the government spends approximately $10 billion each year on research. He explains how it can be put to use:

> . . . Suppose you are like Charlie McQueen, who operates a small canning factory in Wisconsin. Charlie was having trouble with his beets: the flavor wasn't just right and people were complaining of a certain sour quality. When Charlie simply couldn't pin down the reason for this, he wrote me about it. My office got in touch with Commerce, and we sent a sample of Charlie's beets to the Technical Services Department.
>
> For a small fee, technicians turned up 300 articles on beet processing—from all over the free world. Then Charlie's beets were sent to the Department of Agriculture for analysis. This provides a fine example of how the various agencies can work together.[7]

We are not told whether Charlie McQueen's cannery survived or not, but we are pleased to learn that government agencies co-operate. It may be, as the Senator alleges, that government agencies can sometimes provide aid to small businesses seek-

---

[7] William Proxmire, *Can Small Business Survive?* (Chicago: Henry Regnery, 1964), pp. 100-01.

ing information, but my point is that if this information is of value, private researchers could be in businesses to provide such aid. Indeed, there are many men who make their living in private consulting firms, but the field has heavy competition from government in some areas. There are many private publishers, too, who find themselves competing with the government's give-away or below-cost booklets.

The government has been in the housing business in competition with private builders, landlords, and real estate agencies for many years. As one book points out: "In addition to assistance to private builders of houses and other buildings, the federal government has gone into the business of constructing and operating housing projects. In order to stimulate low-cost housing developments, it supplemented its favorable loan policy by actual construction of many housing projects."[8]

A man going into business frequently needs land on which to situate. He finds himself in competition—though it hardly seems to be the right word—with Federal, state, and local governments for the dwindling supply of lands. Governments were once the great sellers of land in America but they have now reversed the field and become major buyers: for military installations, for parks and forests, for housing projects, for lakes and dams, and for an increasing variety of undertakings. As one writer puts it, the Federal government "is the biggest landlord on earth, aside from the communist countries."[9] This does not, of course, include the lands owned by lesser governmental divisions. Governments, as I have implied, do not compete for land in the usual way. They exercise the power of eminent domain to acquire whatever lands are wanted. But they do make land more expensive for the private buyer by reducing the supply of land.

The Federal government is in numerous other activities. It is no doubt the leading banker in the country. "In 1955 the

[8] Koontz and Gable, op. cit., p. 695.
[9] Wilcox, op. cit., p. 796.

Hoover Commission found 104 agencies with 40,000 employees and $17 billion in federal funds engaged in the business of making loans or providing insurance against various types of risk."[10] The Federal government is deeply immersed in the trading business. As one writer says:

> The government's principal trading agencies are the Department of Agriculture and the Defense Materials Service in the General Services Administration. Agricultural commodities acquired by the Commodity Credit Corporation are sold at home for interior uses or abroad in return for dollars, for foreign currencies, or for strategic materials. The Defense Materials Service contracts for expanded production of metals and minerals in the United States, for the development of new metallurgical processes, and for the maintenance of manufacturing facilities.[11]

As the same writer says, "The government is also involved in manufacturing activities. The Navy builds ships and produces paint, rope, ship's stores, and the like. The Army and Navy manufacture weapons, ammunition, uniforms, and other military goods. The Post Office makes its own mail bags."[12] In addition to these activities, the Federal government competes with private companies by providing certain kinds of insurance (as do some states), by hauling freight known as Parcel Post, by providing electricity, and so on. A man trying to go into business may even find himself competing with a cooperative which enjoys special exemptions and privileges from government. Many, if not all, of these activities could be done by private entrepreneurs, and the fact that they are not forecloses many opportunities of the prospective enterpriser.

A man who has surveyed the opportunities for going into business on his own, who has noted the government monopolies, franchised activities, and government competition, may decide that he could improve his chances of success by chang-

---

[10] *Ibid.*, p. 797.
[11] *Ibid.*, p. 800.
[12] *Ibid.*, p. 803.

ing localities. Local and state interference with business do vary from place to place. Then, too, the grass is always greener on the other side. Anyone thinking in this way should make a pilgrimage to his prospective new locale and look into the situation before making his move, however. This would be particularly true if his projected move took him across state lines. There is not only the difficulty of establishing a business among strangers but there is also the rather unpleasant fact that states have erected various barriers to discourage newcomers. Some of these have the suspicious look of being deliberate obstacles erected by legislators to protect the local citizenry from competition. But whatever their intent, they can be quite troublesome to newcomers. There may be a large sign on the highway entrances to the city bearing the legend that "Middletown," or whatever the name of the town may be, welcomes industry, but even the goodhearted people who erected the sign may be largely unconscious of the obstacles their lawmakers have thrown in the way of such industry. These range from regulations and requirements that are a nuisance to those that are very nearly prohibitive.

One of the first obstacles that a newcomer to a state encounters is that state's rules, regulations, and restrictions upon owning and operating an automobile or other motor vehicle. These vary greatly from state to state and range from consuming some time and going to a little expense to involving a maze of requirements with which one must comply and to being quite expensive. Pennsylvania's motor vehicle regulations, while not typical, are an horrendous example of the latter possibility. In the first place, the newcomer must establish ownership of any vehicle which he claims as his. If the vehicle is old, this means tracing backward to the bill of sale. If it has been recently acquired, it may be necessary to pay the Pennsylvania 6% sales tax, though the vehicle was bought in another state. (An interesting variation of this occurred in Texas in times past, and may still be in effect; newcomers had to pay an import tax on vehicles). When ownership is established, the owner then has the privilege of buying a license plate. Before the vehicle can be operated on the highways and byways of Pennsylvania under the cover of that license, however, it must be inspected. There is a fee for the inspection, and if the car doesn't pass, there may be costly repairs to make. If, for example, there is a crack in the windshield, however obscure, the whole windshield must be replaced, at considerable expense. At this point, one is ready to go through the maze of requirements to become licensed as an operator. It is necessary, first, to purchase a "learner's license," no matter how long or in how many states one has operated a vehicle. Then there are formal applications to be made, duly notarized, a physical examination to be taken and, finally, if all goes well, at least an oral examination to be passed on the Pennsylvania regulations, with particular attention to any peculiarities or eccentricities of them. Those who have persevered beyond this point may find themselves sud denly and inexplicably, as it were, authorized to own and operate a vehicle on the highways of Pennsylvania. As often happens in the cases of those who have been submitted to an ordeal, they get a wry and sadistic pleasure ever after in seeing to it that everyone else in their former condition has to endure a like degree of hazing. This obstacle course may be quite amusing to old residents of the state, but it should be emphasized that it can be quite burdensome to poor newcomers who have come in as wage earners or to those starting into business who need all their savings for their new undertaking and their time for learning the intricacies of a business.

Many states and localities have a great variety of restrictions and regulations for engaging in particular pursuits. It will be sufficient here to indicate the general character of some of them. Barbers may have had to be trained for a particular period of time, nurses to have undergone a particular regimen, teachers to have taken certain education courses, real estate salesmen to have served an apprenticeship, beauticians to have taken a particular course, saloonkeepers to have conformed to certain moral standards, and so on. A particular locale may have zoning laws which prohibit the use of residences for the conduct of business. Some states and localities have health laws which restrict the moving of foods or the buying and use of second hand dining equipment, and such like. Anyone who wishes to buy and sell old mattresses may have a shock in store for him when he studies the health regulations surrounding such commerce. Lawyers usually find themselves at a considerable disadvantage if they have not studied in the law schools of the state in which they wish to practice. Those in the medical profession must often submit themselves to the approval of their peers in a new locale. Each undertaking has its own set of difficulties. However desirable any or all of these restrictions may be, one thing they all have in common: they are roadblocks to enterprise.

Let us suppose, now, that our prospective enterpriser has somehow managed to set himself up in business. However improbable it may seem, however much of at least a minor miracle it surely is, some men are actually able to begin new enterprises. Indeed, a considerable number manage to do so each year. They manage somehow to accumulate the savings necessary despite the inflationary thrust, the progressive income taxes, the burden of Social Security and other taxes. They manage somehow to settle upon an undertaking that is not monopolized by government or that government competition has not made it completely impossible to enter. They get franchised, certified, licensed, authorized, permitted, qualified or whatever, and actually find some land upon which to locate. By hook or crook, they succeed in satisfying the local authorities that they are citizens worthy to reside in the locality and carry on some worthwhile pursuit.

Such an enterpriser is by no means out of the woods because he has managed to open his doors for business. It would be more correct to say that his troubles have just begun. The man who enters business discovers rather soon, if he did not know it already, that he has a Senior Partner—government. More precisely, he has a committee of Senior Partners, composed of Federal, state, county, and, depending upon the locale, township and municipal authorities. These Partners may have thrown any number of obstacles in the way of his going into business in the first place; they may be in competition with him; they may have made low interest loans to his competitors or even granted them special privileges which he does not enjoy; they will rarely have invested anything in the business themselves. Yet once he opens his doors those Partners join the firm, so to speak, expecting him to perform special services for them for which they do not pay, having the first go at any profits that he makes, imposing their notions of how the business should be run, what wages he should pay, what prices he should charge, and what conditions should prevail in his place of business. Though they may be in competition with him they will expect numerous detailed reports about his undertaking. So that it be clear that these relationships are not simply a figment of the writer's imagination, some examples will be given.

In the first place, the Senior Partners require the businessman to be a tax collector. Though he has not been a candidate for the position, though it may be alien to his nature to do such things, though the citizenry have not elected him to the post, a tax collector he is most apt to be. If he is a storekeeper or otherwise sells to consumers, there are a variety of taxes he is supposed to collect. Both the state and local governments may impose sales taxes which he has to collect. (He may even be forbidden by law to pay them himself.) The Federal government imposes excise taxes which he has to collect on certain items. If he employs other people he has to deduct income taxes from their paycheck. Under most conditions, he must collect the worker's Social Security tax by way of payroll deductions. Some areas have employment taxes which he may have to collect.

In addition to the taxes which he collects from others, the

businessman has taxes to pay on his own account. He must
pay the fees connected with whatever licenses are required.
He has to pay income taxes, if he has sufficient income, to the
Federal government, and perhaps to other governmental divisions. He must charge enough for his merchandise or services to cover an array of hidden taxes, such as a manufacturer's tax, which has been passed on to him. One writer
points out that when "small businessmen are asked for their
own ideas on the best thing government can do for them, they
are likely to think first of reducing taxes. . . ." He notes that in
one survey where the following question was raised and businessmen were allowed to write in their own answers the most
frequent answer was very revealing:

"The best thing the federal government could do for
me . . ."

	All Dealers
Reduce taxes	41%
Enforce fair trade laws	13
Regulate big business	8

As this writer concludes, "The strong demand for lower tax
rates is common to most small businessmen and is the most
immediate help they want from the government."[13]

It is quite probable, though, that of near equal importance
would be relief from the great burden of recordkeeping which
tax collection and paying imposes. Records must be kept of
all taxes collected, of the gross income of the firm, of all
expenses of operation, and so on. This is particularly burdensome to the small enterpriser. He may have no training or
aptitude for such bookkeeping, though he may be an excellent
mechanic or display man. In any case, there is sure to be
much time and expense involved in keeping the records.
However small the business, it may be expedient to buy a cash
register. Though no secretary may be warranted by size, an

[13] John H. Bunzel, *The American Small Businessman* (New York: Alfred
A. Knopf, 1962), pp. 176-77.

accountant will usually have to be called in from time to time. Senator Proxmire of Wisconsin charges that the Internal Revenue Code places small businessmen at a disadvantage:

> Small businessmen have more difficulty than any other class of taxpayer in coping with the complexities and in- equities of our tax structure, both in terms of the Internal Revenue Code itself and also in its administration by the Internal Revenue Service.
>
> The revenue code is so complex, especially in those sec- tions which relate to business, that the average small busi- nessman cannot understand it. This places the small company at a disadvantage in preparing its returns, in tax planning, and in the audit of its returns by the Internal Revenue Service. . . .[14]

The Senior Partners are not particularly mollified by get- ting the first fruits from any income and having the business- man collect taxes in general from people. They take an active hand in deciding how the business shall be run. For one thing, some of the Senior Partners exert themselves strenuously on behalf of any workmen he may be able to employ. They will not let him simply take advantage of the labor market. It is not enough for them that the workers be willing to work at the price he offers and under the conditions he provides. In many instances, he must pay a minimum wage prescribed by the Federal government, and possibly a higher one dictated by the state. It does not matter much what the exigencies of his business are, he must pay time and a half if they work more than a specified number of hours in a day. If a union attempts to organize his employees against him, the Senior Partners will stand by unjudiciously stacking the deck against him.

Nor are the prices he pays to workmen the only ones which some of the Senior Partners may concern themselves with. In some instances, as in transportation, the rates he can charge may be prescribed by law. In others, in some states, he is

[14] Proxmire, *op. cit.*, p. 190.

subjected to "fair trade laws." These can be particularly burdensome to a trader new in the business. He may want to lure customers by advertising certain bargains for sale, only to find that he is guilty of "price-cutting" and "unfair competition." He may need to reduce prices drastically on some items he has stocked—remembering that he may be inexperienced in establishing an inventory of goods—in order to get them off his shelves. He may find that agreements into which he had to enter to buy goods in the first place prohibit him to do so. In short, all these prescribed prices reduce the flexibility which he needs so badly, particularly at the outset.

The Senior Partners often bestir themselves, also, to direct and control the manner and mode of the conduct of a business. This control may range from local ordinances prescribing hours and days in which a business may be open to intricate regulations of the operations of the concern. Truckers find themselves beset by state governments in the following ways:

> Truck operations on the Nation's highways are conducted under 49 differing sets of size and weight regulations which act to determine the length, height, and width of trucks as well as the loads they may carry. In addition there is a multitude of tax regulatory features affecting the movement of interstate truck traffic.[15]

The powers of the Federal Power Commission over producers and sellers of electric power show the extent to which the interference of a Senior Partner may go. It exercises the following powers:

> Prescribes and enforces a uniform system of accounts for privately owned public utilities engaged in the transmission, or sale or wholesale of electric energy in interstate commerce; determines the original cost and accrued depreciation of facilities for the generation and transmission of such energy; investigates and regulates the rates, charges and serv-

[15] Cornelius P. Cotter, *Government and Private Enterprise* (New York: Holt, Rinehart, and Winston, p. 1960), pp. 295-96.

ices for such energy; passes upon application of such utilities
for authority to issue securities, to dispose of, merge or consolidate facilities, to interconnect facilities, or to acquire
securities of other public utilities; passes upon applications
of persons seeking authority to hold interlocking positions;
evaluates applications for and, when in the public interest,
issues permits for the construction, operation, maintenance,
or connection of facilities at the borders of the United States
for the exportation or importation of electric energy; passes
upon applications for authority to export electric energy for
the United States.[16]

There is much more in the same vein, but the above may
serve to indicate the extent to which regulation may go. Not
all enterprises are regulated to the same degree of course; the
regulation of the pharmacist, say, may be much more
thorough than that of the operator of a newsstand.

The Senior Partners also concern themselves with the well
being of the customers of their junior partner, the businessman. At any rate, Federal and state governments have set up a
variety of bureaus and offices to oversee and establish standards or compel disclosures in the matter of selling and purveying foods, drugs, use of food additives, use of coloring
agencies, modes of advertising, descriptions of contents, advertising claims, interest charges, packaging, and so forth.
Probably, the aspect of all this which makes it most difficult
for the new enterpriser is the establishment of standards
which preclude new materials or may require extensive testing
or even court action before a product may be introduced on
the market, the bar to innovation, and the possibility of the
manipulation of these standards by established companies.
One probability seems ever and again to elude the awareness
of interventionists who favor and promote the establishment
of government standards and bureaus to enforce them, the
probability that these will come under the sway of or be influenced greatly by the large companies already in the field. Yet

[16] *Ibid.*, pp. 227-28.

it is not difficult to understand why it should work out this way. Professor Milton Friedman has explained it in connection with the recent government automobile safety standards. He points out that consumers will shortly "return to somnolence from which only an occasional scandal will reawaken them. The car manufacturers are in a very different position. They have billions at stake. . . . Sooner or later they will dominate the agency—as, despite well-publicized tiffs, railroads and truckers have dominated the ICC; radio and TV networks, the FCC . . . ," and so on. They are the ones most concerned, and they have the expertise. The effect: "Several small specialty-car manufacturers have already complained that compliance with the new safety requirements would put them out of business—the 1931 Ford that one company replicates has less glass in total in its windshields than the windshield wiper standards require the wipers to clear!"[17] However well meaning such government efforts, they result in making fields harder and harder to enter by small businesses, or for them to stay abreast with developments.

The Senior Partners of the businessmen have many favors to dispense. The Federal government is today the largest purchaser of goods and services in the country. When it is joined by states and local governments, the role of government as purchaser is an immense one indeed. Politicians have long expressed special concern that small businessmen get their share, or perhaps more than their share, of government contracts. Presidents have proclaimed that they would, and Congresses have exerted much effort to see that they did. Yet the record is somewhat discouraging. As Senator Proxmire points out, "Small business participation in this government spending has not been great. With 95 per cent of the firms and 40 per cent of the employment, the high point of small business participation in defense prime contract awards was 25.3 per

[17] Milton Friedman, "Auto-Safety Standards," *The Freeman* (August, 1967), p. 508.

cent in fiscal 1954. This percentage has declined each year until 1961, when it had fallen to 15.9 per cent."[18] The chances are that few government contracts go to really small firms, or to those new to the business. This is not due simply to favoritism, to the lobbyists maintained in Washington by large companies, to the employment by some concerns of retired generals and admirals, to the graft of 5 percenters, to gifts of deep freezes and vicuna coats, to well-placed government officials, or to any other malign influence. Even if all these things were put to nought, if they could be, there would still be in the nature of government-as-purchaser that which would make it difficult to give new or small firms much of the government trade. Government undertakings are usually large: they are usually on the order of a housing project, say, as opposed to a single building for much of private business. Governments are responsible to the citizenry for prudent expenditure. They should concern themselves with ability to perform. Ability to perform is something that established businesses have demonstrated but that newcomers to a field rarely have done. A man acting in his private capacity employing his own funds can take a chance, can rely upon his confidence in the ability of man which has not yet been demonstrated in the particular undertaking, can even favor a local builder, say, over the large contracter, can take the lowest bid and gamble on performance. These are options usually denied to governments, and quite rightly so. However much the Senior Partners may wish to aid their junior partners among small businessmen they are frequently enjoined from doing so by the public character of their undertakings and the rules surrounding them.

Even after a business is somewhat established—after the proprietor has learned to cope with his role as tax collector, is able to pay the ubiquitous taxes, has come to grips with the labor problem, has conformed to the standards and regulations, is charging the proper prices and advertising in a sedate

[18] Proxmire, *op. cit.*, p. 203.

manner—, the businessman is not done with obstacles from his Senior Partners. The Small Business Administration may provide low interest loans to his potential competitors. The rules of the game are subject to continued variations which he must learn and adapt to. If the business is a success and he becomes expansion-minded the owner will have to be wary of the antitrust laws. If he decides to go out of business, to sell to his competitors, they may be estopped from buying by anti-merger activity from the government. (Though much is usually made of the dangers of one business dominating an industry through merger, little if anything is ever said about the small business which is denied its purchaser.) Indeed, if the business is in that area referred to as public utilities, the owner may not be permitted to abandon services, and be allowed to go out of business only most reluctantly. If he is having labor trouble when he tries to close his firm, he may be the subject of court suits by the union. Finally, the government may suddenly drive him out of his place of business, if his establishment stands in the way of an Urban Renewal project.

The above account does not begin to exhaust the number of roadblocks to enterprise placed there by governments in contemporary American society. Virtually every businessman could no doubt add others to the inventory. Businessmen are not likely to disagree with the thesis in the least, though most of them may be disappointed that their particular pet gripe or difficulty has not been mentioned. Enough has been said, however, to demonstrate the hardships surrounding going into and operating an independent business today. (Indeed, in view of the role of the Senior Partners it is doubtful that there are any "independent" business.)

The attrition among small businesses is great. A large number of them die out each year. One writer notes that "a third of all [new] businesses . . . die out within the first year, and about half fail to reach the two-year operational mark." The share of discontinuances among very small businesses is greater than that for all businesses; "figures for 1948, for example, show that 86 per cent of all discontinuing firms employed fewer than four persons."[19]

There is no way of knowing how many of the discontinuing firms result from failures, inabilities, or frustrations in futile efforts to cope with the governmental roadblocks to enterprise. Surely, these must play a large role in the decision of many businessmen not to continue operation. Nor would the full impact of government intervention be measured if it were possible to calculate accurately the number who have discontinued operation primarily for this reason. The empty stores, the abandoned filling stations, the small factory no longer in operation, the fading signs on the premises which tell of the proud aspirations of the man or men who founded a business which once was, tell only part of the story. There are the hundreds of thousands of others who never accumulated enough savings because of inflation and progressive taxation, who backed out when they contemplated the expense of record keeping, who never got franchises, who found their fields preempted by government, whose innovations never got past the government bureaus, and so on. They are not in business, and we do not have their services. The Roadblocks to Enterprise were too much for them.

[19] Bunzel, *op. cit.*, pp. 40-41.

CHAPTER VII

Sacking the Cities

The building in which you now live is located in an area which has been taken by the Boston Redevelopment Authority according to law as part of the Government Center Project. The buildings will be demolished after the families have been relocated and the land will be sold to developers for public and commercial uses, according to the Land Assembly and Redevelopment Plan presently being prepared.[1]

"You have shoved out the poor to make homes for the rich. You may help the city's finances, but what happened meanwhile to the people who used to live on Oak Street?"[2]

But look what we built with the first several billions: Low-income projects that become worse centers of delinquency, vandalism and general social hopelessness than the slums they were supposed to replace. . . . Civic centers that are avoided by everyone but bums. . . . Commercial centers that are lackluster imitations. . . . Promenades that go from no place to nowhere and have no promenaders. Expressways that eviscerate great cities. This is not the rebuilding of cities. This is the sacking of cities.[3]

THE FARMER DRIVEN FROM THE FARM, THE WORKER DENIED A job, the would-be enterpriser stymied by the roadblocks to

---

[1] Notice quoted in Martin Anderson, *The Federal Bulldozer* (Cambridge, The M.I.T. Press, 1964), p. 1.

[2] Conversation quoted in William L. Miller, *The Fifteenth Ward and the Great Society* (Boston: Houghton Mifflin, 1966), p. 205.

[3] Jane Jacobs, *The Death and Life of Great American Cities* (New York: Random House, 1961), p. 4.

enterprise, have increasingly sought refuge and opportunity in the great cities of America in the twentieth century. It is not true, as history books are wont to say, that the end of the frontier occurred around 1890. It is true that around that date an increasing number of people saw the hope of a new start, or a start, not on the rural frontier but on the urban frontier. People have moved into the cities in a great stream from the late nineteenth century to the present, from the farm, from the small town or village, and from foreign lands. This movement has run from the great European migrations of the early twentieth century to the migration of southern Negroes into northern cities at the present day.

The war on the poor has been conducted on many fronts simultaneously, but there has also been a kind of chronological progression. The chronology of the campaigns is roughly indicated by the giving of Cabinet rank to departments dealing with the interest groups involved. The Department of Agriculture was raised to Cabinet rank in 1889, formalizing, as it were, the campaign against farmers. A Department of Commerce and Labor was established in 1903, signaling the institutionalization of campaigns against workers and business endeavors. This department was divided into two in 1913: the Department of Commerce and the Department of Labor. In 1965, a Department of Housing and Urban Development was set up, marking a more vigorous campaign against the city poor.

Federal aid to cities which is now in full bloom—as indicated by housing developments, Urban Renewal programs, subsidies to city transportation systems, and so on—is a strange reversal of direction in many ways. For years, it was farmers who were to be rescued, rural areas to be rebalanced against urban ones, and the rural poor who were supposed to be in need of help. Urban areas were taxed to aid rural areas. While all of this is still going on, there is today a new emphasis. The cities are now to be renewed, revived, renovated, by government activity. Turnabout may be Fair Play, but the more appropriate proverb may be that Every Dog has His

Day. At any rate, governments contributed much to the concentration of the poor in the central cities; they are now falling to the task of rooting them out.

The heart of the problem which these government programs are supposed to solve is what some refer to as the inner city and others as the central city. What follows here is a description of this inner or central city as it is to be found, presumably, in every great American city:

> The central city includes, typically, a business district; a railway and bus station; a university; Skid Row; a "hill," which, though it may be flat, has remained socially elevated amidst the surrounding decay, an island of gracious town houses for the sophisticated and well-to-do; a museum, housing a superb collection of pictures from every age and country except that in which the museum itself was built; and a park. Around these features, and extending far beyond them, miles of seedy tenements and row houses peel and flake, amiable or grim in their degenerate old age. . . . The metropolis, of which the central city is the heart, grows continually, but in the city itself there are sinister portents of decline. Department stores stand empty; buildings are pulled down and turned into parking lots, waiting for better times; offices follow their employees to the suburb.[4]

According to well established lore and considerable evidence, the inner city is either a breeding place or habitat of crime, disease, juvenile delinquency, a sense of futility, riots, and civil disorders. It is these things that many of the reformers wish to see changed. They do not think of themselves as besetting the poor, yet, as we shall see, that is perhaps the major impact of the programs.

Actually, of course, the concern of reformers and the promotion of government programs for city dwellers and slums did not suddenly emerge in the 1960's. As early as the 1890's some reformers were writing of conditions in tenements and

[4] Peter Marris, "A Report on Urban Renewal in the United States," *The Urban Condition*, Leonard J. Duhl, ed. (New York: Basic Books, 1963), p. 114.

slums, particularly in New York City, and urging that something be done about them. One of the first revelations of life in New York tenements to make any impact was a book by Jacob Riis, *How the Other Half Lives.* (1890). The following is an example of the evocative power of his descriptions:

> Enough of them everywhere. Suppose we look into one? No.—Cherry Street. Be a little careful please! The hall is dark and you might stumble over the children pitching pennies back there. Not that it would hurt them; kicks and cuffs are their daily diet. They have little else. Here where the hall turns and dives into utter darkness is a step, and another, another. A flight of stairs. You can feel your way, if you cannot see it. Close? Yes! What would you have? All the fresh air that ever enters these stairs comes from the hall-door that is forever slamming, and from the windows of dark bedrooms that in turn receive from the stairs their sole supply of the elements God meant to be free, but man deals out with such niggardly hand. . . . Here is a door. Listen! That short hacking cough, that tiny helpless wail—what do they mean? They mean that the soiled bow of white you saw on the door downstairs will have another story to tell—Oh! a sadly familiar story—before the day is at an end. The child is dying with measles. With half a chance it might have lived; but it had none. That dark bedroom killed it.[5]

His crusade, and that of others, bore fruit very shortly by the appointment of the Tenement House Committee of 1900. The work of these, in turn, resulted in the passage of new city building codes and other legislative provisions regarding tenement building and occupancy.

The thrust to do something about conditions in city slums melded into and became a part of the general reform movement of the early twentieth century which historians call the Progressive Movement. From this angle, the work of Jacob Riis was an early example of muckraking, to be joined by a steady stream of others in a decade or so, of such works as

[5] Jacob A. Riis, *How the Other Half Lives* (New York: Sagamore Press, 1957), pp. 33-34.

Robert Hunter's *Poverty,* John Spargo's *The Bitter Cry of the Children,* Edwin Markham's *Children in Bondage,* and Lincoln Steffen's *The Shame of the Cities.* So far as city slums were concerned, government action was undertaken at the state and municipal level. Other states joined New York in passing enabling legislation for cities or adopting general codes. An historian of the development says, New Jersey enacted a state-wide measure in 1904 "which followed the New York law in most respects. Connecticut's law of 1905 was adapted from the New York code also. . . . In Wisconsin a state law enacted in 1907 was declared unconstitutional, but was succeeded by another measure in 1909 which applied only to first-class cities (Milwaukee). In the same year Indiana . . . passed a housing code whose provisions were similar to the New York law."[6] Other states were soon to follow this lead: Kentucky (1910), Massachusetts (1912), Pennsylvania (1913), California (1917), Michigan (1917), and so on.[7]

The Federal government did not get into the urban housing situation until the 1930's. The Home Owners Loan Corporation was established in 1933 to aid home owners in refinancing mortgages. In 1934, Congress authorized the setting up of the Federal Housing Administration which provided government insurance for long term low interest mortgages. But it was the Housing Act of 1937 which got the Federal government into slum clearance and support of low cost housing directly. Slums were to be abolished by "local housing authorities set up by the cities, which would build good housing on the sites and let it to the slum dwellers at rents within their means. The federal government would provide the necessary annual subsidies."[8] The next major act along these lines was the Housing Act of 1949. It provided for further

[6] Roy Lubove, *The Progressives and the Slums* (Pittsburgh: Pittsburgh University Press, 1962), p. 145.

[7] *Ibid.*, pp. 145-46.

[8] Charles Abrams, *The City is the Frontier* (New York: Harper and Row, 1965), p. 21.

slum clearance and construction of public housing, but the emphasis under this law was to be upon construction by private enterprise where feasible. Another act was passed in 1954; this and the one that preceded it provided the heart of the program which became known as "urban renewal." In 1965, the Urban Renewal program, as well as so many other programs, got a new impetus from presidential and legislative activity.

The above, in sum, is a very truncated history of government effort in housing. Legislative history is complex; there is much overlapping of activity provided for and many twists and turns in policy. However, it may be useful to reduce the various phases of the war on the urban poor to three, and to keep in mind that these three have occurred roughly in the same chronological order as named. They have been: (1) the adoption of housing codes and zoning laws by municipalities under state direction, an effort which got under way around the 1890's and continued vigorously through the 1920's; (2) the Federal government's slum clearance and public housing program, from the late 1930's through the 1940's; (3) the Urban Renewal program, from 1949 to the present. The Urban Renewal program was joined by the interstate highway system in the 1950's. These two are the ones most deserving of the title, the Sacking of the Cities, but they are definitely related to the earlier interventions, as we shall see.

The reformers did not set out to sack the cities. Even today, as the Federal Bulldozer, as Martin Anderson has called it, is leveling city block after city block, those who favor such activities do not think of themselves as warring on the inhabitants of the cities. Some of them still speak in glowing terms of the City Beautiful that will emerge from the wreckage. The notion that they are engaged in people removal is foreign to them. True, some reformers do not appear to like cities; even more of them have a heady aversion to what they call slums, an aversion probably shared by now by most Americans. Much of this aversion has long since spilled over upon the inhabitants of the slums, and there are no doubt those who would like to get rid of even the inhabitants in some way. But that is no part of the conscious intent, at least, of most reformers. Let us assume, at this point anyhow, that those who have promoted, enacted, and administered the government programs have done so in the hope and with the aim of helping the poor.

It will be the burden of what follows to show that they have not done so. On the contrary, government programs have perpetuated slums, built slums, prevented people from improving them, and finally torn them down after driving the inhabitants out. They have failed because they have misunderstood the nature of the city, have misconstrued the needs of men, and ignored the claims of economy. They have sought to make over cities according to abstract notions of what a city should be like, notions that have little enough to do with the way any city is or ever has been. They have operated in clear violation of the wants and desires of people as they were expressing them in the most direct fashion. And they have set up codes and regulations which make it increasingly difficult for the poor to provide themselves with decent habitations. All these generalizations should gain meaningful content by an examination of what has happened.

First, however, it will be useful to make some observations about housing. The quality of housing which an adult has is a product of choice and economy in interaction. The first choice is the one of where to live. This makes a great deal of difference in the sort of accommodations which can be had in a given price range. If one chooses to live within the inner city of a great metropolis, for example, the range of choices of housing is limited by the high cost of land, by the demand for housing in the area, and by the many alternative uses for buildings and land. Within any location, however, there are many *potential* choices, at least. These choices are made in terms of or conditioned by the value system of the person making them. Strange as it may seem to some, not everyone

has the same order of priorities. There are people who prefer
owning a boat to a bathtub. There are people who, when
faced with the choice, prefer additional room to costly plumbing or heating facilities. There are those who would prefer an
automobile, or gambling at the racetrack, or large contribu-
tions to their church, or expensive toys for their grand-
children, or stockcar racing, or some considerable amount in
a savings account, to any but the most limited housing facilities. There are even those, to all appearances, who prefer a
certain amount of squalor to, say, antiseptic cleanliness and
rational order in their environs. They must certainly prefer it
to the exertion of the necessary energy of cleaning up, for
anyone but the bedridden or absolutely incapacitated can
have neatness in their immediate surroundings. The fact that
many people do not is a reflection of their order of priorities,
not of their lack of money or facilities.

On the other hand, there are—let it be said—those whose
incomes are so small that, as things stand, they can afford
only the most rudimentary shelter. This, too, is a conditional
statement. Except for the bedridden and the totally incapacitated—a tiny faction of the population in this day—,
government policies have contributed mightily to this condition. The restrictions upon farming, the erosion of the purchasing power of savings by inflation, compulsory school attendance and child labor laws, the enforced retirement of
older people, minimum and union wages with their con-
comitant unemployment, the difficulties of operating small
businesses, Social Security limitations on earnings, high taxes,
have made it difficult, if not impossible, for many to have and
maintain dwellings which contain many of the conveniences
which most of us desire.

In any case, dwellings have a price tag on them in the
inhospitable climes of the United States. Moreover, the higher
the quality and the greater the variety of conveniences and
appurtenances they contain, the better their location ("better," in the sense that there are more people with resources

who desire the location), the more costly they are. The point would appear to be so obvious as not to need making, but reformers have quite often managed to ignore the most obvious facts in pushing for their reforms. They have quite often advocated and caused to be passed regulations and restrictions which have made it increasingly difficult for the poor to afford any habitation, and then bemoaned the lot of the poor who were disfurnished without apparent awareness that their reforms had done much to produce the condition. This is well illustrated in what follows.

The first wave of assault upon the urban poor, a wave that has not diminished but been augmented over the years, was housing and building codes. Reformers in some big cities, notably New York at first, saw that the dwellings which many of the urban poor rented lacked many of the amenities which the reformer considered necessities. The solution that occurred to them would be to require that landlords provide the facilities; and the means by which they sought to accomplish this was by codes. The earliest concern focused upon the tenements—the apartment houses for the poor. New York's Tenement House Law of 1901 embodied many features that reformers had been seeking for some time in a code. Among the things it dealt with were these. Tenements had been built with air shafts—called dumb-bells—to provide air for interior apartments. The code required that in future tenements it be replaced by a court which would measure no less than four feet six inches. In future buildings, each apartment was to have its own water closet. The Law "limited the height of future nonfireproof tenements to five stories . . . , and re-enacted previous laws requiring the fireproofing of halls and stairs as well as the floor above the cellar in tenements five stories or more in height."[9] The code specified, also, where fire escapes were to be located and how they were to be constructed. In tenements already in existence, landlords had to provide a window in the wall of any windowless interior room and install water closets meeting certain standards. "Other

[9] Lubove, *op. cit.*, p. 134.

required improvements included the provision of satisfactory fire escapes, the lighting of dark hallways by substituting glass panels for wood in certain doors on each floor, and the waterproofing of cellar floors."[10]

In the abstract, the above codes have the look of being most humane requirements. Surely, it would be beneficial to tenement dwellers generally to have a window in each room, to have sanitary facilities in each apartment, to have fire escapes ready to hand, to have areas of greatest potential danger fireproofed, and so on. But these measures which were so humane from one point of view were not so humane when viewed from another. A whole train of unwanted consequences followed in their wake.

Everyone of these code requirements made it more expensive to build new tenements, for the simple reason that windows, sanitary facilities, glass panels, fireproofing, and other innovations are expensive. That these costs would be borne by landlords was more than anyone should have expected. Landlords neither would bear the costs nor, in most cases, could. They would be passed on to tenants. The tenants, faced with higher rents, frequently took the best option available to them, to crowd more people into a given apartment. Larger families would huddle into smaller apartments, rooms would be rented out, and the closeness of the apartments would be aggravated. Earlier in New York City, the Tenement House Committee of 1894 had recommended enforcing a statute which called for a minimum of 400 cubic feet of air for each adult. But, as the historian of this development points out, "It is apparent that if the Board of Health really enforced the laws against overcrowding, many immigrant families would have suffered a serious loss of income and been hard pressed to pay their rent." Moreover, people "who were driven onto the street had to find accommodations."[11]

Jacob Riis, who had advocated these reforms, advanced

[10] *Ibid.*, p. 135.
[11] *Ibid.*, pp. 96-97.

what he supposed would be the corrective for them. He said that the "state may have to bring down the rents that cause the crowding, by assuming the right to regulate them as it regulates the fares on the elevated roads."[12] Rent controls would only result in a housing shortage, which they have wherever they have been in effect for long, leading, presumably, to even greater overcrowding. Rent controls have a similar effect to that of raising standards for new dwellings to be erected, that is, of reducing the incentive to building.

Another adjustment to codes is evasion and non-enforcement. Early and late, it seems to have been characteristic of both tenants and landlords to evade the legal requirements, and for municipal officials to be lax in enforcement. Not all of this should be attributed to corruption, for it could well be that lurking behind noncompliance was the realization that somehow the poor had to have housing, and that rules and regulations made it ever harder for them to get it.

Over the years, building codes have become ever more minute in their prescriptions for new dwellings and have been extended to every sort of structure. They are no longer simply concerned that houses or apartments have a water closet but with how it is vented, with what materials are used in drains, how the whole is constructed, and the like. These restrictions add to the expense of the building, may be complicated or administered in such a way as to make it necessary to hire professionals, require blueprints prior to construction and permits from municipal authorities, limit the materials that may be employed, and quite often virtually prevent experimentation and innovation. The poor have increasing difficulty in the face of all this in providing themselves with dwellings. As small towns have turned to the adoption of such codes, many of the poor live outside the city limits, where they can still construct houses to satisfy their needs. In the great cities, of course, government has increasingly intervened to build housing to take the place of that which might have been built privately without the restrictions.

[12] Riis, *op. cit.*, p. 217.

Another major difficulty to city living for the poor is zoning. Zoning, as one writer defines it, "is the division of a community into districts or zones and the regulation within such districts of the use of land, and the use, height, and area of buildings. . . . A zoning ordinance properly gives legal effect to that portion of a comprehensive city plan which deals with private uses and development of privately owned land."[13] Zoning became popular in the 1920's in the United States; many states passed enabling legislation during that decade, and the Supreme Court found that comprehensive codes did not violate the United States Constitution.[14]

Zoning quite frequently makes building more expensive. For example, zoning restrictions may require that a building have a certain number of feet clearance on either side of the lot. This means that the cost for a particular projected house may be made more expensive by the larger lot that it requires. Restrictions as to height means limitations on the use of land so that less housing may be provided on a particular lot. Zoning restrictions may even prohibit certain types of dwellings. The borough in which I live prohibits house trailers or mobile homes as dwellings within its limits. Thus, one of the ways that technology has made the comforts and conveniences of home available to those of limited means has been eliminated from among the options of those who would live in this town.

The poor are harmed in many ways by zoning. Even slums come into being largely in consequence of zoning. But let that wait for a bit. Zoning laws are a major inhibition to small businesses. Businesses conducted in the homes are frequently prohibited in large areas of cities and suburbs. One of the homeliest victims of zoning has been the neighborhood grocery store, along with a great many other neighborhood businesses. Many have noted the decline of small stores and the rise of supermarkets and chains of stores. Now some, or

---

[13] Arthur W. Bromage, *Introduction to Municipal Government and Administration* (New York: Appleton-Century-Crofts, 1950, 2nd ed.), p. 412.
[14] *Ibid.*, p. 410.

even much, of this would have occurred in any case, we may believe. But zoning has kept many stores from coming into being, as it has driven others out. And, it has contributed to the development of large stores. It is not simply an interesting coincidence that chain stores and supermarkets became more ubiquitous in the 1920's as zoning became more widespread. Zoning encourages large concentrations of dwellings not intermingled with stores. It places stores and shopping areas at a considerable distance from almost everyone. The adjustment which has been made to this has been the development of shopping centers with huge supermarkets and stores equipped to handle large numbers of customers. Such stores require large capital investment, sophisticated merchandising techniques, and large volumes of sale. Small businesses find it most difficult to compete with them when they are denied the advantage of being located near their customers.

It is worth noting here, too, that zoning makes the automobile much more of a necessity, increases the number that are needed, and contributes to a much more extensive use of it. The separation of dwellings from stores and factories frequently makes these inaccessible except by motor transportation. The relative deconcentration of population makes frequent and convenient public transportation costly to provide. Husband and wife will both want automobiles in this case, and may use them extensively. The relation of this to the sacking of the cities and the war on the poor will be taken up in connection with the interstate highway program.

Zoning actually contributes to the deterioration of parts of cities, to the perpetuation or making of slums. This is the main historical lesson to be learned from a brilliant book by Jane Jacobs, *The Death and Life of Great American Cities*. Miss Jacobs does not single out zoning laws as the chief villains, but this is a logical deduction from her analysis. She has sought the answer to the question of why sections of cities become slums, why some areas begin to run down, why the streets are unsafe, why people begin to move out in large numbers, and so on. Conversely, she has looked for the sources of life and health on a street, in a district, in whole cities. Though there are many things which contribute to these, the one answer which predominates over the others to such a degree that it can be called the key is this: diversity of use or the lack of it. As she sees it, a healthy city street is one on whose sidewalks children may safely play, one that is continually under the surveillance of many eyes, one that is made interesting by its diversity. For a street to be this way it must have many uses during the day and into the night: it needs not only dwellings but also shops, purveyors of services, restaurants, perchance nearby factories, and, hopefully, public entertainment in the vicinity. The city, her work says, is an organic whole, and its pieces need to be knit together in a whole by being located where people may conveniently use them. There need to be all sorts of activities and services scattered throughout a city, not segregated from one another in airtight compartments. In short, there needs to be an integration of functions which, as I interpret it, zoning laws either prohibit or inhibit to the extent that it does not occur in many areas. This statement does not do justice to her thesis, but it does highlight an important aspect of it.

Besides building codes and zoning, the other major local deterrent to the provision of housing and its maintenance is the real estate or property tax. As one book indicates, "The Property tax has for many years been the mainstay of local government finances. In 1956 local governments collected $11.3 billion from property taxes in the United States, which constitutes 87 per cent of their total tax revenues."[15] The rate varies, of course, from state to state and locale to locale. In some, it is almost prohibitively high; in others, it is low enough that it probably has little effect on deterring new building and renovation. The general effect of the property tax is this: It penalizes the man who builds the more expensive

[15] John F. Due, *Government Finance* (Homewood, Ill.: Richard D. Irwin, 1959, rev. ed.), pp. 398-99.

house than the one he had, and it discourages the renovation of property. This latter effect is most important for the creation or perpetuation of slums, for those who improve their property significantly are often faced with higher taxes. If the neighborhood is upgraded so that it becomes attractive to buyers, the tax assessments may rise to take into account the higher price tag on property. It is of no consequence that for renters the tax bill goes to the landlord; if he is to continue to operate he must usually pass along any rise in taxes to the tenants.[16] If the rate of property taxes is lower in the suburbs than in the central city, this will contribute to a migration from the city.

According to the lore of reformers, there came a time when private enterprise could no longer provide housing for the poor. This has the same quality of truthfulness as the statement that a man with an anvil tied to his legs cannot run in a foot race. Private enterprise was severely handicapped in any effort to provide housing for anyone, and especially the poor, handicapped by building codes, by zoning restrictions, and by property taxes. The poor were deterred from providing for themselves by all those government impediments to enterprise which have already been examined. So, in the 1930's the Federal government entered the housing situation, presumably to help those who could not help themselves.

There followed what might be called the housing project era, overlapping with the suburban development era. The basic idea behind the housing project was twofold: one, to clear away and demolish city slum housing, and, two, to provide low rent modern housing for low income people. This aspect of the Federal housing effort was supplemented by subsidized loans to private home builders through the FHA. Together, these programs were efforts, in the minds of some, at rehabilitating cities, perhaps "remaking" is a better term, and

---

[16] The moral of this is not necessarily that property taxes are unfair or that the tax money should be raised from other sources. Any taxation of consequence is likely to have unwanted effects. A more appropriate solution would be to keep taxes in general low.

providing "standard" housing for those who could not afford it under the conditions that prevailed. There was hope, I suppose, that the massive intrusion of money from the Federal government would upgrade neighborhoods in the vicinities in which projects were constructed, along with the environmentalist notion that the inhabitants would be redeemed by better, or standard housing.

Whatever the purpose of the housing projects may have been, they have surely failed to achieve it. They failed to transform cities into wholesome livable places, failed generally to upgrade neighborhoods, failed to alter significantly the habits of their tenants, and failed to provide attractive housing. The only person I have ever encountered who was enthusiastic about the achievements of housing projects was a "guide" on a tour of New York City. According to his spiel, almost all of the private housing which he pointed out in the city consisted of slums. By contrast, he could wax almost poetic on the marvels and wonders of the projects. The chances are good, however, that his spiel was memorized, possibly taken initially from some pamphlet issued by the City. At any rate, most of those who have studied the projects seriously appear to agree that they have failed.

The following are some comments taken from those who have in some way surveyed the subject. One book describes a project in New Haven, Connecticut, one called by the attractive name Elm Haven. It was completed around 1940, and was then "new, shiny, functional, and presented as an appealing example of the better life that was coming at last for New Haven Negroes. . . . By now . . . , Elm Haven had come to have a negative meaning to many New Haven citizens. . . . A proposed hundred-unit project for a nearby town could be criticized because 'you are building another Elm Haven.' "[17] The writer goes on to generalize: "The projects have too often been miniature cities of poverty and social disorganization cut off from the surrounding neighborhoods, multiplying

[17] Miller, *op. cit.*, p. 86.

difficulties by collecting them in one spot, and by providing an unappealing institutional setting."[18] Another writer notes that the "usual product . . . has a sameness of look which labels it as 'the project.' Irrespective of an architect's genius or his passion for originality, he could not create either a private or an individual appearance. Towering and prophylactic, these structures often overwhelm the mortals who live in them."[19]

Perhaps the most telling indication of the failure of the projects is that those for whom they were meant frequently shun them. Jane Jacobs declares, "Nowadays, relatively few people enter low-income projects by free choice; rather, they have been thrown out of their previous neighborhoods to make way for 'urban renewal' or highways and especially if they are colored and therefore subject to housing discrimination, had had no other choice."[20] Another writer, speaking of families to have been relocated by public authorities, indicates the judgment of the poor on public housing in one city:

> In San Francisco, a third of both white and Negro families have been estimated to be still living in slums because they refused public housing. There seems, then, to be a widespread prejudice against public housing among the families relocated.[21]

As for the assault on crime and the transformation of cities into peaceful and safe places with housing projects, Miss Jacobs makes some disturbing observations.

> "Street gangs" do their "street fighting" predominately in parks and playgrounds. When the New York Times in September 1959 summed up the worst adolescent gang outbreaks of the past decade in the city, each and every one was designated as having occurred in a park. Moreover, more and more frequently, not only in New York but in other cities

---

[18] Ibid., p. 87.
[19] Abrams, op. cit., p. 30.
[20] Jacobs, op. cit., p. 400.
[21] Marris, op. cit., p. 121.

too, children engaged in such horrors turn out to be from super-block projects, where their everyday play has successfully been removed from the streets. . . . The highest delinquency belt in New York's Lower East Side, where the gang war described above occurred, is precisely the parklike belt of public housing projects. The two most formidable gangs in Brooklyn are rooted in two of the oldest projects.[22]

Nor did the vast government guarantee of loans to house buyers result in the salvation of cities. On the contrary, it made it possible for an increasing number of people to leave the inner city and build in suburbs, depopulating inner cities and contributing a vast amount of traffic to the other troubles of those cities. Indeed, government programs of slum clearance have contributed to the blacklisting of whole districts of cities by those with money to lend. The FHA has been a major source of the subsidization of suburban building.

The tendency of these programs was to make life increasingly difficult for the poor in the city. Building codes made habitations more expensive and zoning restrictions often confined them to ever narrower areas. Real estate taxes pressed upon them. The housing projects built for them, however well meaning their builders, became so intolerable as living places so quickly that the poor often avoided them when they could. It was as if the governments were saying to the poor: We do not want you in the cities. Your houses are an affront to decent people. Your small businesses are eyesores. You live in such circumstances that we wish we could somehow be rid of you. True, government officials have not used such language, for it suggests that the people are to blame. They have, however, described the habitations and their environs in very harsh terms, and they have made it difficult for the poor to remain.

Even so, the poor clung to the inner cities. The more efforts that were made to do something about them, the more they fastened themselves on the heart of the city, living in crowded

[22] Jacobs, *op. cit.*, p. 76.

quarters, inhabiting places where crime was rampant, persisting in their habits, and remaining as a reproach to those on the outside. Their lives might be beset by building inspectors, by welfare workers, by eviction notices, and by assortments of would-be redeemers of them. Still, the city was their refuge, perhaps their last refuge from a government whose language, and apparent intent, was benevolent, but whose programs quite often intensified suffering.

There may have been those all along who saw as the solution to the city slums the driving of the inhabitants out. Rexford G. Tugwell, of New Deal fame, is quoted as saying the following in those days: "My idea is to go just outside centers of populations, pick up cheap land, build a whole community and entice people into it. Then go back into the cities and tear down whole slums and make parks of them."[23] At any rate, around 1950 a shift in action began to take place. The Federal government has not abandoned housing projects, but it has intensified the assaults on the slums. It has undertaken people removal on a vastly expanded scale. Two programs account for most of this: Urban Renewal and the interstate highway program. The poor are being hunted down, as it were, and booted out of their homes (though they apparently remain in the city somehow).

The interstate highway system and the Urban Renewal program constitute a two-pronged assault upon the urban poor. That is, they have resulted in a vast amount of demolition of city property formerly owned or occupied by the poor. These two programs may be considered jointly because they were begun on a considerable scale at about the same time and have had many of the same effects.[24]

Much more that is critical has been written about Urban Renewal programs in this respect than has been said about the interstate highway system. Not much attention has been paid

---

[23] *Ibid.*, p. 310.
[24] The first major appropriation for the interstate system was made by Congress in 1956.

to the interstate highway system development in relation to cities. Yet there is something very strange about it. In state after state and locale after locale interstate highways converge upon and thrust through the heart of large cities. The Rand McNally *Road Atlas* for 1967 tells this story graphically state by state. Interstate highways are projected for Alabama to go through the center of Birmingham, Montgomery, and Mobile; for Arizona (either projected or completed) through the centers of Phoenix and Tucson; for New Mexico through Albuquerque; for Arkansas through Little Rock; for Louisiana through New Orleans, Shreveport, and Baton Rouge; for Mississippi through Jackson; for California through San Francisco, Oakland, Sacramento, San Jose, Fresno, San Diego, and Los Angeles; for Colorado through Denver and Colorado Springs; for Connecticut through Hartford; for Massachusetts through Boston, Springfield, and Worcester; for Rhode Island through Providence, for Maryland through Baltimore; for Virginia through Newport News, Norfolk, and Richmond; for Florida through Miami, Jacksonville, Tampa, and St. Petersburg; for Georgia through Atlanta; for Illinois through Chicago and Peoria; for Indiana through Indianapolis; for Iowa through Des Moines; for Kansas through Topeka and Kansas City; for Kentucky through Louisville; for Tennessee through Memphis, Nashville, Knoxville, and Chattanooga; for Michigan through Detroit, Grand Rapids, and Flint; for Minnesota through Duluth, Minneapolis and St. Paul; for Missouri through St. Louis and Kansas City; for Montana through Butte; for Nebraska through Omaha; for Nevada through Las Vegas; for Utah through Salt Lake City; for New Jersey through Trenton and Newark; for New York through Rochester, Syracuse, Albany, Schenectady, New York City, and Niagara Falls; for North Carolina through Winston Salem; for South Carolina through Charleston; for Ohio through Akron, Cleveland, Columbus, Toledo, Canton, Dayton, and Cincinnati; for Oklahoma through Oklahoma City and Tulsa; for Oregon through Portland; for Pennsylvania through Scranton, Pittsburgh, and Philadelphia; for Texas through Dallas, Houston, Fort Worth, San Antonio, El Paso, Austin, and Beaumont; for Washington through Seattle and Spokane; for Wisconsin through Millwaukee.

It does not make sense in an *interstate* system for the main highways, in most instances, to go plowing right through the center of cities. It would be much more convenient for the interstate travelers if the highways skirted the cities, as the Pennsylvania and Ohio Turnpikes, as well as the New York Thruway, did. More, it is fantastically expensive to build multi-lane limited access highways through cities. This complicates the traffic problems of those within the city, for they must compete on the interstates with long distance travelers, as well as for those just passing through. (Much smaller and more readily useable limited access highways could be built within cities, if they are wanted.) Politically, what happened makes somewhat more sense. The concentrations of population (voters, that is), are in the cities, and the program was early turned to uses which planners for cities wanted. But there is more to it than that.

An example may help to show what has been done. In Nashville, Tennessee, the state capitol was once ringed around with what are usually called slums. It had the outward appearance of what is sometimes denominated as the rotting inner core of a city. These buildings have been demolished now, and the capital is nearly surrounded by a grid of bypasses and interstate highways built or abuilding. In short, the system has been used for the demolition of dwellings, places of business, churches, and so forth that were not deemed desirable by someone.

Generally speaking, the homes and businesses of the poor are the ones destroyed in the wake of highway building as well as Urban Renewal. Floating amidst the myths that all of us imbibe is the notion that Urban Renewal is a part of the War on Poverty, that the poor are somehow the beneficiaries of this. It does not work that way. Clearly, it is *their* property or dwellings that are confiscated and demolished, but it is by no means clear that something is generally built for the poor instead of what was destroyed. On the contrary, little is done along these lines. Professor Martin Anderson examined the figures for new construction begun under the Urban Renewal program through March of 1961. He found that 56 per cent of the new construction was of private residential housing. Since this is apt to be very expensive, he says that "we can reasonably conclude that virtually all of this new, privately owned construction is destined for a completely different group of people than those who originally lived in the urban renewal area." By contrast, "Six per cent of the total construction started was devoted to publicly subsidized housing." This housing, because of subsidies, could be rented *eventually*, perhaps, by some of those displaced. "The remaining 38 percent of the construction was devoted to nonhousing uses." As to the character of this very considerable portion of new construction, he says: "Approximately 24 per cent of the total was devoted to public works, such as parks, schools, libraries, roads, sewerage systems, and other public facilities."[24] This character of what was happening began to be apparent as early as 1954. It is revealed in the following colloquy between Senator Paul Douglas of Illinois and a Mr. Follin, Commissioner of Urban Renewal:

> SENATOR DOUGLAS: . . . Have any of the slum clearance or urban redevelopment sites been made available for public housing?
> MR. FOLLIN: In a few instances.
> SENATOR DOUGLAS: How many instances?
> MR. FOLLIN: Probably 3 or 4.
> SENATOR DOUGLAS: Out of how many?
> MR. FOLLIN: How many out of how many projects?
> SENATOR DOUGLAS: Yes.
> MR. FOLLIN: There are 52 projects that are under contract.

[24] Anderson, *op. cit.*, pp. 93-94.

SENATOR DOUGLAS: Almost all the projects have been cleared
and they have been used either for business or for residences
for upper income groups, but the people who were displaced
from these areas are not rehoused in the areas themselves?
MR. FOLLIN: Only to some extent.
SENATOR DOUGLAS: To a very slight extent.
MR. FOLLIN: Yes, sir.[25]

This pattern has continued. The homes and businesses of
the poor are torn down and in their stead are built public
buildings, highways, shopping centers, high rise apartments,
and dwellings many of which are too expensive for most of
the poor. In view of the failure of the earlier housing projects,
it would not appear that even when these are constructed any
boon to the poor results. In any case, the impact of all this
upon the poor makes clearer than any of the material studied
thus far that this is a war on the poor.

Let us examine now the fate of those whose houses and
businesses are condemned, acquired by some government
authority, razed or demolished, and the barren land turned
over to or sold to those who will put them to approved uses.
First, let us look at the fate of the small businesses, and occasionally large businesses, that have been displaced by Urban
Renewal and interstate highways. There have been thousands
upon thousands of these in cities, and many in small towns
will soon join them. Miss Jacobs tells what happened in the
one area of East Harlem. "More than 1,300 businesses which
had the misfortune to occupy sites marked for housing
were wiped away, and an estimated four-fifths of their pro-
prietors ruined. More than 500 noncommercial 'store front'
establishments were also wiped away."[26]

In the first place, these and other businessmen were not
fully compensated for their establishments. Government
seized their property by the exercise of the power of eminent
domain. This procedure, itself, makes it very difficult, if not

[25] Quoted in Abrams, *op. cit.*, p. 83.
[26] Quoted in Jacobs, *op. cit.*, p. 312.

impossible, to determine what "just compensation" would be. Ordinarily, the price of anything is what someone will take for it. Under condemnation proceedings, however, a man is not permitted to hold out for his price; he must take what someone decides to pay him. But businesses taken under Urban Renewal frequently are not paid anything in the vicinity of a reasonably just compensation. According to a New York City management expert the government only pays for what it acquires, not for what the businessman may lose—in setting, in good will, and so forth. The following is given as an example:

> A druggist purchased a drug store for more than $40,000. A few years later, the building in which his store was located was taken in condemnation. The total sum which he eventually received was an award of $3,000 for fixtures and that sum had to be paid over to the chattel mortgagee. Thus his total investment was completely wiped out.[27]

Here is another case of a businessman, in Philadelphia this time; his name is Edward Litman, a taproom operator paralyzed from his waist down:

> "In the last four years the Litmans rejected offers of $150,000 for their properties. . . .
> "The redevelopment authority . . . set its price: $41,500 for both buildings, 28 percent of what Litman turned down previously.
> " 'This is my livelihood,' Litman said. 'I need a fulltime man to look after me. I've spent all my cash trying to stay alive. . . .
> " 'With what I'm offered, I wouldn't even be able to reopen, much less survive.' "[28]

Small wonder, then, that another survey revealed that many of those who had had their businesses taken in condemnation proceedings said that they had not received a fair price. "The

[27] Jacobs, *op. cit.*, p. 312.
[28] Bryton and Ella Barton, comp., *The Inhumanity of Urban Renewal* (Arlington, Va.: Crestwood Books, 1965), pp. 46-47.

major complaint, expressed by nearly half of the nonsurvivors
[those whose businesses did not survive the dislocation] who
felt that they had not received a fair price, was that they
should have been compensated for the 'value of the business,' and not just for the value of the building (and land)
occupied."[29] Miss Jacobs concludes that businessmen are
"subsidizing these schemes, not with a fraction of their tax
money, but with their livelihoods, with their children's college
money, with years of their past put into hopes for the future—
with nearly everything they have."[30]

Even if businessmen were amply compensated for all the
tangible and intangible losses connected with their dislocation, it would still be a great blow to them. Many have simply
gone out of business when they have had to give up their old
location rather than attempting to start anew. This is quite
understandable in view of the difficulties many of them have
encountered in trying to go into business elsewhere. A business is quite often integrally a part of the neighborhood in
which it is situated. Businessmen have often built up a clien-
tele over a period of years. They may serve some group, such
as an ethnic group, which, once it has been dispersed will not
be likely to re-assemble. They would hardly be likely to wait
around until an Urban Renewal project was complete to rent
or buy in the old vicinity. Not only would many of their
customers be likely to be gone, but they would have a long
period of inactivity. At any rate, many of those who are dis-
located simply go out of business. Professor Anderson indicates below the results of his study of this.

> The "death rate" experience of 21 urban renewal projects
> in 14 cities covered by this study reveals that 756 of the
> 2,948 firms involved either went out of business or disap-
> peared. On the basis of this study one could conclude that it
> is likely that one out of every four firms, that gets involved in
> an urban renewal program will cease operations.[31]

[29] Basil G. Zimmer, *Rebuilding Cities* (Chicago: Quadrangle Books, 1964),
pp. 58-59.
[30] Jacobs, *op. cit.*, p. 312.
[31] Anderson, *op. cit.*, p. 69.

The attrition may be greater than this, however, for businesses that have moved frequently have difficulties, either in getting a suitable location or maintaining their operation there. Some types of businesses are hard put to it to find places where they are permitted. Junk dealers experience particular difficulty in finding a new location. One man who had once had an income of $1400 per month was trying to re-enter the business but could find no location zoned to permit his operation. "This man shared with others the opinion that junk yards are needed and they can be attractively camouflaged so as not to be a blight on an area. He bitterly resents the fact that there is a strong resistance to zoning for this type of function. He is very dissatisfied with how he had been handled and claims that no one tried to help him find a new location. According to him the only concern on the part of the state was to get him out of the area."[32] Many had trouble getting licenses in new areas. There has been widespread complaint that rents were higher in new locations than the old. One man moved his business to the suburbs but found himself encountering problems. "His rent is higher than at the old location, and he is doing less business. He also reports that he does not see any reason to expect business to increase as long as he stays at the present location. . . . The old location was much preferred because it was centrally located and more accessible to his customers who came from the whole . . . area."[33]

The smallest businesses are the ones that have been hardest hit by having to get out of an area. Professor Zimmer's study shows this clearly. He notes that among "those who went out of business following displacement, one-third were owner-operated units with no employees. . . ." Moreover, "When non-survival rates are computed by size, the proportion going out of business range from 10 per cent among those with ten or more employees to 40 per cent of those with no employees. Thus, it seems quite evident that displacement works a partic-

[32] Zimmer, *op. cit.*, pp. 65-66.
[33] *Ibid.*, p. 92.

ular hardship on the smaller business establishments."[34] He also shows that non-survivors were *highest* among those with low incomes from their businesses, among those with the least formal education, among those on their own, and among those who had learned the business while working for someone else.[35]

What of those who have had their homes taken from them and demolished? "Be it ever so humble," go the words of an old song, "There is no place like home." But if it is "ever so humble," it may not be *home* for long, for interstate builders and urban renewers have a penchant for humble dwellings. "A man's home is his castle," is a familiar refrain of Anglo-Saxon jurisprudence and lore. *Only* if it is a castle, or mansion, is it likely to be so secure any longer. Urban Renewal marks a new phase in the assault upon property; the courts have ruled that the power of eminent domain may be used to take private property which may then be sold for use to other private individuals or corporations.[36] Homes that have been taken thus far by urban renewal have been those of the poor. Professor Anderson says that between "1950 and 1960, the program was responsible for the destruction of approximately 126,000 housing units. . . . All of the 126,000 homes that were destroyed were located in older sections of cities, and almost all were low-rent units."[37] The humble have been driven from their homes.

There have been many consequences thus far of this development, in all their variety probably as many as there have been people displaced. Neighborhoods have been disrupted or destroyed. The fabric of the lives of many has been rent by dislocation. There have been the difficulties of finding another place to live, of moving, of getting to work from new locations, of making friends, and so on.

[34] *Ibid.*, pp. 50-51.
[35] *Ibid.*, pp. 71-74.
[36] For discussion, see Martin Anderson, "The Fiasco of Urban Renewal," *The Freeman* (March, 1966), pp. 53-54.
[37] *Ibid.*, p. 49.

An immediate problem, mundane but no less pressing, for the displaced poor is to find comparable housing at comparable prices. Generally, they have to pay higher rent, regardless of the quality of the housing. One study indicates how this worked out in some cities. "Chicago found for all families relocated in 1953 and 1954 that gross rents in off-site shelters rose $30 monthly. . . . For Philadelphia . . . , the documentation . . . indicates a less extreme leap. Forty-five cooperatively relocated families sustained only a $3 average monthly increase in rents; 100 self-relocated families, a $5.25 average monthly increase."[38] A study of 100 families relocated in New Haven "showed that they paid 16.8 per cent of their income for rent before relocation, 20.3 per cent afterward."[39] This is as should have been expected. Urban renewal (and interstate highways) destroys housing a great deal faster than it replaces it; in many cases, it has not even scheduled housing to replace that destroyed; even when it has, it is rarely low rental property. In short, there are more people wanting houses, and less housing of the quality wanted. Prices ineluctably rise in such a situation.

Far from relieving the totality of slum districts or of slum areas, Urban Renewal frequently shifts them or spreads them out. The experience in Southwest Washington, D.C. illustrates this well. "About a third of those displaced were given units in public housing. . . . But concedely about one-fourth 'slipped back into bad housing,' according to the local director of the program, and most of those chose the slum next to their old slum. 'Admittedly, Southwest Washington was cleared only at the price of creating the need for additional clearance in parts of Northwest Washington and a spread of blight in a segment of the Northeast.' "[40] Even the rats moved from the demolished areas to surrounding settlements. Miss Jacobs says, "Unless they are exterminated . . . , the rats

[38] Quoted in Anderson, *The Federal Bulldozer*, p. 62.
[39] Miller, *op. cit.*, p. 206.
[40] Abrams, *op. cit.*, p. 141.

simply move into the next inhabited area. One of the severe problems in the Lower East Side of New York . . . is the influx of rats and other vermin from the demolished buildings on the site of a huge new cooperative project, Seward Houses."[41]

The case of the aged who are forced to move is often particularly pitiful. As one writer points out, "Because many of these people live in old housing, they are also among the first victims of demolition through urban renewal, public works, or code enforcement. What should be the cocktail hour of life becomes their bitter evening."[42] The following story was told at a public hearing in Washington, D. C.:

> "Mrs. A, age 67—university graduate retired minister— member of distinguished Boston family—had a fine old brick home on Virginia Avenue S. W., facing the Mall and Freer Art Gallery. Her main source of income came from rental of rooms in her home which gave her an income of $195.00 a month. Tenants were ordered out by R.L.A. as soon as the house was taken instead of being left until owner moved which made it necessary to take her only child, a daughter, out of college. The daughter aged 26 suffered a nervous breakdown from shock and worry over the loss of their small security. The condition appears to be permanent and her mother says she cannot earn enough to support both of them. No suitable home was found for them by R.L.A. and just before they were due to be evicted the mother took the only place she could find, a house in a bad neighborhood on 7th Street, N. E. The rent was $100 a month unheated plus $60.00 a month for fuel in cold weather, but one of her tenants had agreed to share the house with her and pay half of the rent. The house was in bad condition but the owner through her agent promised to make all necessary repairs. Mrs. A. moved in but most of the repairs were not made, heat did not reach the upper floors and the electric wiring was so inadequate that appliances could not be used so the young lady who had promised to share the house did not come. Mrs. A. had $1,000 in cash above the mortgages

[41] Jacobs, op. cit., p. 334.
[42] Abrams, op. cit., p. 46.

when her old home was disposed of but that went for medical and other expenses for her daughter and for part of each month's rent as the $42.00 a week she earned in a book store could not nearly cover her expenses. When that sum was gone she fell behind with her rent and was evicted. She took a two-room and kitchenette apartment at $71.00 a month which she thought would be large enough, as her daughter was in St. Elizabeth's Hospital at the time but soon after that her daughter was sent home from St. Elizabeth's not cured and without having received any treatment. The apartment is too small for both of them and too expensive. We have tried to find a better paying position for the mother but so far without success. She is a gentlewoman of courage but grows more frail from week to week. After her first move she was brutally attacked by a man with a knife (and assaulted) late at night and robbed of all the money she had in the world. That was a few doors from the house to which she had moved and there was later on a murder in the next house and a knifing in the one beyond. All this greatly increased her daughter's fears and made her condition much worse."[43]

Many people interviewed were deeply grieved by having had to leave their old neighborhoods and friends. A researcher elicited such comments as the following:

"I felt as though I had lost everything."

"I felt like my heart was taken out of me."

"I felt like taking the gaspipe."

"I lost all the friends I knew."

"I always felt I had to go home to the West End even now I feel like crying when I pass by."

"Something of me went with the West End."

"I felt cheated."

"What's the use of thinking about it."

"I threw up a lot."

"I had a nervous breakdown."[44]

[43] Bartons, op. cit., pp. 7-8.
[44] Mark Fried, "Grieving for a Lost Home," The Urban Conditions, op. cit., pp. 151-52.

In general, "Among 250 women . . . , 26 per cent report that they still feel sad or depressed two years later, and another 20 per cent report a long period (six months to two years) of sadness or depression. Altogether, therefore, at least 46 per cent give evidence of a fairly severe grief reaction or worse."[45]

Housing codes made it increasingly expensive for the poor to find adequate shelter. Zoning pressed severely upon small businessmen and added to the costs of house building for those seeking improved dwellings. Real estate taxes have penalized renovation and discouraged new building. Government housing projects failed to provide attractive housing for the poor but have themselves, in many instances, been centers of vice and crime. All these made life in the city expensive or perilous, or both, but still the poor clung to the inner city, apparently seeing no hope elsewhere. Since World War II, a massive demolition of the inner city has gotten underway, by way of Urban Renewal and interstate highways. Vast areas have been leveled, homes and businesses destroyed, and the people moved out. The sack of the cities has left many homeless, disenchanted, without businesses, grieving over lost communities, but the war upon them goes on.

[45] *Ibid.*, p. 152.

CHAPTER VIII

The Battle in the Streets: A Civil War

THE WAR ON THE POOR WAS IN MOST RESPECTS METAPHORICAL until the mid-1960's. It took on a full fledged warlike character, then, as some of the poor moved into the streets to do open battle. Here is an account of one of the skirmishes at Watts in Los Angeles in the summer of 1965:

> On Imperial Highway, Los Angeles County deputy sheriffs who went to the assistance of police that night, along with Highway Patrolmen, fought off a mob which had overturned a Volkswagen driven by a pretty young woman. The deputies remember that particular incident because the young woman was French and newly arrived in this country. "They'd already pulled her from the little car and struck her. God knows what would have happened if we hadn't been able to force them back," said one young sheriff's officer. . . .
>
> There was little reason the mob should have spared the young Frenchwoman. No car bearing a white motorist was spared. Whenever one entered the neighborhood, word spread like wildfire: "Here comes Whitey—get him." While

their elders watched in the background, urging them on, young men and women rushed the cars.

"Kill! Kill!" bystanders chanted. It was a miracle no one died that night. Some were saved by the intercession of ministers. . . .

In one instance when a mob jumped two white men and felled them, several ministers rushed to the beaten Caucasians. One had an eyeball hanging from its socket. The ministers carried both white men into a nearby apartment building and called an ambulance. . . .

Another Negro clergyman . . . saw a mob set upon a car occupied by a terrified teenage couple. . . . "The crowd threw bricks through the car's windows. They dragged the young man into the street and began beating him. They threw bricks and stones at the girl . . . ."[1]

One participant described the outbreak at Watts in this way: "You hear people say it wasn't a race riot. Let them. The average person out there in the streets knew what it was and he considered it a war. A civil revolt. That's what it was—a civil revolt. . . ."[2]

There have been many other such battles—or revolts—in the last several years: Harlem-Rochester-Cambridge, Maryland-Hough-Newark-Detroit-Philadelphia-Memphis-Washington-Pittsburgh-Cincinnati-Dayton, and many others. Associated with them are such things and events as molotov cocktails, looting, overturned cars, burning buildings, policemen in helmets, national guards, paratroopers, sniping, dead, wounded, imprisoned, and hundreds of millions in property damage. These outbreaks have been described as Riots, Rebellions, Civil Revolts, Insurrections, Revolutions, and the Negro Revolution. They might better be linked together under one rubric—Civil War.

On March 16, 1964, President Johnson declared War on Poverty in a message to Congress. In the summer of 1964, within about three months, the outbreaks of the kind and

---

[1] Jerry Cohen and William S. Murphy, *Burn, Baby, Burn* (New York: Dutton, 1966), pp. 95-96.
[2] *Ibid.*, p. 102.

order referred to above began to occur. They have since assumed a regular pattern, though the intensity of them has picked up and havoc wrought appears to increase rather than diminish. The following are a part of the generic pattern that has emerged. They take place in the summer, usually in the midst of a heat wave. There is usually an incident—a Negro arrested, youths halted in a car, someone killed—at the outset which becomes the ostensible cause of the outbreak. Stores are broken into, looted, and burned. The authorities—police, firemen, national guard—are beset by the rioters, stoned, harassed, and even shot at. There is usually a vast amount of destruction of property; stores, houses, buildings, and the like. It is almost invariably in Negro sections and otherwise in some of the areas of the city occupied by the poorest of the inhabitants. Those who are most obviously hurt are the poor —Negroes in this case. The stores that serve them are destroyed, the houses in which some of them live are burned or wrecked, and services to their communities disrupted. Their areas take on the aspect of a battleground with the dangers, disorders, disruption, and destruction that the phrase no-man's-land connotes. These things are fresh enough in our memories not to need documentation or even illustrative examples.

To say that many, perhaps most, Americans are baffled by all this is to understate the case. As the War on Poverty has mounted so has the discontent it was supposed to allay. Nor were President Johnson's words simply empty rhetoric, unbacked by legislative action. On the contrary, rather quickly in 1964 Congress began to act on Johnson's proposals. He was able to sign a Civil Rights Bill on July 2, 1964. "The most sweeping civil rights act in American history, the new law enlarged *federal* power to protect voting rights, to provide open access for all races to public facilities, to sue to speed up lagging school desegregation, to insure job opportunities in businesses and unions with more than 25 persons."[3] Congress

[3] Richard Hofstadter, *et. al., The United States* (Englewood Cliffs, New Jersey: Prentice Hall, 1967, 2nd ed.), p. 857.

continued to follow the President's lead in August of 1964 when it appropriated nearly a billion dollars "for ten separate anti-poverty programs to be supervised by the Office of Economic opportunity set up by the bill. Key features included a Job Corps to train under-privileged youths for the labor market; a work-training program to employ them; an adult education program; and a 'domestic peace corps' to enlist the privileged on behalf of the poor."[4]

This was but a prelude to the action taken in 1965, when the President and Congress plunged into legislation on a scale not experienced since the famous Hundred Days of the New Deal in 1933, itself a unique occurrence theretofore. In addition to providing nearly four billion dollars in Federal aid to education, Congress took the following major actions, as summarized by one book:

> Antipoverty funds were doubled.
> The minimum wage was again raised.
> Agricultural workers and more than 8,000,000 other employees came under minimum wage coverage.
> National foundations in the arts and in the humanities were established.
> Basic hospital care under social security for those over 65 (Medicare) was provided, supplemented by a voluntary insurance program for paying laboratory and doctor fees.
> A Voting Rights Act outlawed poll taxes and literacy tests and permitted federal registrars to be used in a state if less than half the potential voters were registered.[5]

The flood of legislation did not cool the fires of rebellion; instead, it seemed to feed them. As Congress and the President appeared more and more sympathetic and willing to open the national purse to the poor, particularly Negroes, the resistance picked up momentum. Some Negro leaders began to talk of Black Power, to become more militant in their

---

[4] *Ibid.*

[5] Harry J. Carman, Harold C. Syrett and Bernard W. Wishy, *A History of the American People* (New York: Alfred A. Knopf, 1967, 3rd ed.), p. 797.

rhetoric, and the battles in the streets spread. These militants were not following the script. According to the prevailing view, the poor should have been mollified, grateful to the nation, and quiescent. They were not. At least, some of the Negro poor were not.

Even after four summers of violence, after Newark and Cincinnati and Tampa and Minneapolis and Milwaukee and, even, Detroit, many had drawn no helpful conclusions; they were still repeating the same old tired cliches. They were still calling for more government programs and larger expenditures —even trying to make a significant issue of rat control legislation. In the wake of the outbreaks of 1967, Whitney Young of the Urban League called for a Marshall Plan to wipe out poverty in America. He said that "we've got to give the war on poverty the same priority we have given the railroad strike, the war in Viet Nam, the supersonic plane and the space program." To implement these suggestions, he called for the expenditure of $10 billion a year over the next ten years.[6]

There is still no widespread recognition, if there is any at all to speak of, that the War on Poverty is the continuation of a long term war on the poor, a civil war which has finally exceeded the bounds of a semblance of peacefulness and erupted in the streets. There are aspects of the battle in the streets which this work does not purport to describe or explain, such as the role of the agitators, the revolutionary content of the agitation most notably by Stokely Carmichael and Rap Brown, the part that hoodlums have played in it, the racial character of it, and the history of the Federal government's encouragement to sit-ins, lie-ins, walk-ons, "civil disobedience," non-violent resistance, and the like. It should be clear, too, that the explanation which follows does not condone the violence, or free individuals from responsibility for crimes they have committed or wrongs they have done. But this work does offer an explanation for the crucial economic aspects of what is behind the Battle in the Streets.

[6] Washington *Evening Star* (July 22, 1967), A-4.

The war on the poor is, and has been, a covert civil war: that is the conclusion that follows from the evidence of this work. It can be likened to a civil war because it musters some of the people against others. It musters those farmers who benefit from government programs against those who are driven out. It privileges unions to organize against workers, denying jobs to those who are willing to work. It raises the minimum wage, thus throwing men out of work. The employed are pitted against the unemployed. The protective tariff has for a very long time arrayed manufacturers against farmers. Government has warred upon enterprisers by closing the avenues of opportunities; and even when it has aided some it has done so to the disadvantage of others. It has beset the urban poor, demolished their dwellings, made it increasingly difficult for them to find suitable homes, and turned the lands they occupied over to others.

The government—the Federal government, sometimes preceded, joined, or followed by state and local governments—has engineered this conflict. It has arrayed group against group; they have preyed upon each other to victimize the poor. This is the more strange because the United States government, as well as the other governments, is supposed to represent the people, all the people.

It may appear to anyone who has read thus far that the writer has portrayed our governments as alien forces, has referred to them as if those who govern were not elected, as if they were foisted upon America by some conquering army. This latter has not been the case, of course; those who govern have been, generally, freely chosen by the electorate. That is what makes the whole business so strange.

There is an explanation for this dividing of the country by government and fostering of covert war. It is an explanation which takes us again into reformist lore and mythology. Reformers—presently described for the most part as liberals—have generally advanced the notion that there are elements in the country who cannot stand on their own. They have proposed that government should come to the aid of these—of farmers, of wage workers, of labor unions, of small business, and of the urban poor. They have fostered government action supposedly in behalf of these groups or classes of the population. We have seen that these programs, far from benefiting those who stood most in need of help, have harmed them. Nonetheless, these ideas went into the political rhetoric and became a powerful mythology to which politicians could appeal. Politicians became adept at forging these groups into majorities for electoral victories. They would say that they were for the farmer, for the worker, for the small businessman, for the labor union, and for the urban poor. They pointed with pride to the legislation they had promoted and passed which was supposed to aid these elements. No matter that the victims were strewn about over the country in great number, they did not know what they were the victims of and, in any case, were largely inarticulate and, most likely, helplessly dependent on government. In so far as government has promoted the interest of some at the expense of others, it has become a force alien to the general welfare. But my point is that this has been covered up by an aura of sentimental concern for the poor as well as exorbitant claims of the benefits to those who were in fact harmed.

These programs have not only pitted group against group for benefits, pitted those within one category against others of the same category, pitted coalitions of groups against the population as a whole, but they have also pitted each man against himself. In economic terms, they have arrayed one portion of a man's interest against another. This is best seen in connection with the War on the Consumer. The war on the consumer is a part of the attacks discussed in earlier chapters, but it is sufficiently different to warrant a separate discussion. In the first place, while the war on the consumer does afflict the poor, it is not the poor alone who are hurt: everyone is. Secondly, all the developments discussed thus far are parts of the war on the consumer. And, thirdly, it is in its character of a war on the consumer which makes the war on the poor essentially a civil war. Some little discussion of this side of the matter is in order.

To see how government intervention results in a war on the consumer, it will be helpful to explore both the mystique and reality of what and who a consumer is. One of the ideas which interventionists kick about from time to time is that consumers need representation in government agencies. Indeed, they go farther than merely mulling over and advocating the idea. Sometimes they go so far as to try to implement it, as they would say, by appointing "representatives" of the consumer on arbitration boards, government commissions, and investigation committees. It is quite probable that we shall shortly be treated to a vigorous pressing of the proposal that a department of consumers be created and raised forthwith to cabinet rank to join such other departments as Agriculture, Labor, Commerce, Housing and Urban Affairs, and Transportation.

Now if consumers could be represented, a case could certainly be made that they ought to be. Those who claim that consumers are frequently injured and in need of protection within government and government-sponsored agencies and organizations are right. When big labor confronts big business, when regulatory commissions meet to decide upon gas or transportation or electricity prices, when farmers vote on acreage controls to get crop subsidies, it would be most helpful if consumers could somehow be represented. The assortment of government programs that have been examined do have as a major consequence the short-changing of the consumer, of making war on the consumer, as we shall see. But no one seriously maintains that consumers are represented in government agencies, and no one has ever explained how they could be (despite the stabs at doing it that have been made). There is a very good reason for this which will emerge from an examination into the nature of what is involved, an examination which will also show why the programs in effect are harmful to the consumer.

The notion that consumers can be represented is derived from the extension of an idea that has been much acted upon in America. This is the idea noted above, that the people are divided into various interest groups to which politicians can appeal and in the interest of which they can act. Some of these interest groups have been given official status by having a Secretary in the President's Cabinet. It is possible, of course, to divide people into many categories; economically, they may be divided into such classifications as farmers, wage earners, and businessmen; sexually, there are men and women; ethnically, there are those of European descent, African descent, Asian descent, and so on; by religious denomination, there are Methodists, Baptists, Presbyterians, Catholics, Jews, and so on. That any of these categories encompasses all that a man is, is doubtful in the extreme. Each of us is different from and much more than any single classification that can be devised. As I have pointed out elsewhere, "A man may be not only a worker in a factory but also a husband, a son, a deacon in his church, a Mason, a golfer, a property owner, a debtor, a creditor, a consumer, a seller, a hunter, an army veteran, plus all those tangibles and intangibles which make him the unique individual he is."[7] There is great difficulty, in any case then, in a man's having his interests represented by anyone other than himself. Still, the imaginary man described above is a wage worker in a factory, and this does distinguish him and his interests in this regard from those who are farmers or shopkeepers. It is conceivable, at least, that someone else might represent him to others in the matter of this peculiar interest.

But there is no special interest group made up of consumers. No one may act as a representative of consumers in a government agency, any more than any one could be the especial representative of mankind on a committee. The truth is that *we are all consumers.* The labor union leader is a consumer; the housewife is a consumer; and the child is a

[7] Clarence B. Carson, "Divide and Conquer," *The Freeman* (July, 1966), pp. 48-49.

consumer. Whatever is in the interest of the consumer is, ipso facto, in the interest of all of us. If there is a general welfare and there is, in economic affairs it is to be found at that one point of common kinship that makes each of us a consumer.

Since the interests of consumers are co-extensive with those of mankind, they stand in the same need of government protection. That is, consumers need protection from fraud and violence, and a system of courts for the administration of justice to settle disputes which may arise among them. This is the office of government itself. No special department for consumers could perform it, and none is needed.

Under the conditions of peace that would prevail if government performed its proper offices, every consumer is a king, of sorts. All those who have anything to sell court his favor; each vies with the other to give greater quantity and higher quality at lower cost. The legend that the customer is always right might well be rendered the consumer is always right, for the great cater to his whims, and the mighty are brought low by his adverse decisions. There is daily evidence of this in our lives in America. The daily mail brings its catalogs or circulars describing a vast variety of merchandise available at my command; the merchants have stocked their shelves in anticipation of my wishes; the salesmen may even beset me with persuasive arguments, so eager are they to satisfy my desires and have my custom. Indeed, advertisers wax poetic in the description of their wares thinking by some means to lure my trade their way. The business which does not serve the desires of its customers will lose out and fail, no matter how great the name of its founder, how far flung its establishments, or how numerous its salesmen. If men may not use fraud and violence, the consumer is king.

But each of us is not only a consumer; many of us are also producers or servers. We are both of these during the course of most of our lives. It is this that enables government to divide each of us against himself as well as to pit one group against another, or against all the rest of the population. No doubt, it is better to give then to receive—to serve than be served—as Jesus said, but most of us are not in the State of Grace that enables us to perceive, accept, and act upon this constantly. On the contrary, we prefer to be served rather than to serve, to receive than to give. In our Fallen State we find the idea of being served without returning service in kind most appealing. The benefits of economy appeal from that angle of our view as consumers; the discipline of economy weighs upon us heavily in our capacity as producers. As producers, we can see the great advantage to ourselves of being relieved of the burden of discipline, of being relieved of the necessity of serving, of being served without serving. This is the appeal of the government programs of intervention.

The attraction of the protective tariff is that it frees the domestic producer from competition with foreign producers for the home market, that it relieves him of part of the necessity of making a better product, of serving more expeditiously, of watching costs, and of maintaining the highest quality. Franchises and limited licensing free those who hold them from the necessity of serving as effectively as they otherwise would in order to get and keep their customers. Crop controls and subsidies enable some farmers to make a living without attending carefully to economy. Workers who can compel a wage will not serve their employers as readily or compete with other workers as vigorously under equalized pay scales—and thus serve consumers—as they would without minimum wages and union organizations. In short, men have been drawn into support of these programs because of the extent to which they believed that they would be relieved of the need to serve others in order to prosper.

The consumer benefits from an abundant supply of goods and services. The government programs are devoted to making these scarce and hard to obtain. The most dramatic instance of government planned and authorized scarcity occurred in 1933 when farmers were paid to plow up crops and to kill animals. This was the sort of thing that caught the eye, but it was different from a host of other programs only in that it dealt more with actualities than potentialities. If government programs work so as to inhibit or prevent the availability of goods and services that are potentially available, no one may ever see the goods and services. Yet the one is as destructive of plenty as is the other. The difference is this. In 1933, the government reduced production by paying for cotton to be plowed up. After that, it operated to discourage the planting of the cotton in the first place. Both are scarcity-making operations.

The general tenor of a great variety of the government programs has been to make goods and services more scarce than they would otherwise be. The protective tariff is an attempt to reduce the goods available on the domestic market. The crop controls are attempts to reduce production and bring about artificial scarcity of farm products. Labor unions try to make workers scarcer to employers and generally operate in ways to reduce production. Franchises, licenses, special restrictions upon entry to a field, all have the effect of limiting those who would provide goods and services.

The consumer wants goods and services at the *lowest* prices he can obtain them. The government programs have been devoted, generally, to trying to *raise* prices. This followed from the analysis which reformers made of the situation. According to them, farmers needed higher prices, workers higher wages, the small businessmen higher prices, and so forth. Thus, government attempted to accommodate these and others by inducing scarcity and raising prices; scarcity was not the goal but rather the means employed; higher prices were the object. Artificial scarcities of farm products, produced mainly by controls and subsidies, presumably raised the price of these. Artificially induced labor scarcity, induced by labor unions, by prohibitions against child labor, by fostering early retirement, by exemptions from the armed services during college attendance, and so on, were to raise the wages of workers and, of course, the prices of what they produced or provided to consumers. Roadblocks to enterprise inhibit competition and keep goods and services off the market where consumers might obtain them.

An example of how government intervention thwarts the aims of the consumer may make the matter clear. Pennsylvania has a Milk Control Commission dating all the way back to the 1930's. According to the lore about it, this Commission was supposed to be for the protection of consumers, to see that the price of milk was held down. It has not worked out that way (as, in fact, numerous other regulatory bodies have not worked out that way). Milk is more expensive in Pennsylvania than in surrounding states without such a commission. Moreover, sellers of milk are hamstrung by restrictions. The Commission has been under fire in recent years. Those who claim to speak for the consumers say that milk is too expensive; farmers claim that the price they get for raw milk is too low. Despite the apparent contradiction, both of these claims may be correct.

Some enterprisers have attempted to correct the situation by selling milk at lower prices, and, in one instance at least, paying farmers more for it. The most recent instance is a most imaginative effort at getting around the controls. Six dairy farmers have opened the C and D Budget Dairy in the West End of Pittsburgh. The "C and D" stands for cats and dogs, and the store is ostensibly a pet store. According to a newspaper, "The C and D Dairy . . . is selling milk at 29 cents a gallon below the price established by the State Milk Control Commission. Although the product is being sold with explanations that it is for pets, customers are told that the milk is pasteurized and meets all requirements for human consumption."[8] The store has been doing a land office business during the brief period it has been open, and there is no doubt that much of the milk is being bought for human consumption.

[8] " 'Pet' Milk Sellers on County Carpet," Pittsburgh *Press* (August 23, 1967), section A, pp. 1 and 4.

The authorities are in a flurry over the whole business. "Six dairy farmers . . . were to appear today," the newspaper said, "at a County Health Dept. hearing to show cause why they should be allowed to continue selling milk at bargain rates for cats and dogs."[9] It seems that they had neglected to get a permit from the State Department of Agriculture and that the Health Department was concerned about the "jugging" process used which could lead to contamination. If these ploys fail to stop the store from selling milk cheaper than the established price, other forces of the state will probably be brought into play. The chances are that the authorities are employing what may turn out to be delaying tactics until they have hit upon the best method for stopping it.

One of the cries that has been raised about the milk control mess is that consumers need to be better represented on the Commission. The consumers are looking after their interests very well at the C and D Budget Dairy, but they cannot be represented on the Milk Control Commission. Every member of the Commission *is* a consumer: anyone taken off it or added to it will also be a consumer. There is nothing distinctive about any person that can make him any more a consumer than anyone else or better suited to represent consumers in general. Obviously, the Milk Control Commission in question does represent certain "interests." It represents milk companies, labor unions composed of those who deliver milk to the homes, and, possibly, the dairy farmers. It also represents Pennsylvania "milk interests" as opposed to those, of say, Ohio, New Jersey, Delaware, and Maryland. Ice cream makers want, and get, cheaper milk than the individual consumer. Farmers want higher prices for their milk. Milk companies want to buy milk at lower prices and sell it at higher ones. Supermarkets want to sell milk much cheaper than those who deliver it at home. Deliverymen want a narrow spread between store prices and delivered prices. Each of these interests is ranged against the other, and every one of

[9] *Ibid.*, p. 1.

them is divided against itself. The farmer may want a higher price for his milk, but he must also want inexpensive ice cream. (These are not equally weighted desires, of course, for inexpensive ice cream is likely to be much less important to him than a higher price for milk. This is illustrative only; it would be necessary to see the higher price of milk ranged against higher prices for all that he consumes to see that in principle he is divided against himself in what he seeks.) The deliveryman wants higher prices for supermarket milk, but his wife and family would like to pay less.

No consumer or "consumer representative" can mediate these differences, for the simple reason that the aims of each of these interests are opposed to the aims of the consumer. If "consumers" were sufficiently well "represented" on the Commission they would simply negate every proposal put before it, unless the unlikely should happen and there should be a proposal that it adjourn *sine die*. This is so because anything the Commission might do would be harmful to all of us as consumers of milk and milk products. If it "helped" the farmer by raising the price of milk it would hurt all of us. Even if it lowered the price of milk below what the free market price would be, that would be harmful to consumers. Those engaged in providing milk to consumers would be driven out of business, and there would be shortages, something hardly calculated to help the consuming public.

The point is that government interventions are harmful to consumers, and all of us are consumers. Let us examine some expert testimony to this effect in some of the interventions already studied. Regarding the tariff, F. W. Taussig noted that its principle was set forth in a party platform in 1908: "In all protective legislation the true principle of protection is best maintained by the imposition of such duties as will equal the difference between the cost of production at home and abroad, together with a reasonable profit to American industries." He goes on to point out how this would logically work out in practice:

Anything in the world can be made within a country if the producer is assured of "cost of production together with reasonable profits." In a familiar passage of the *Wealth of Nations*, Adam Smith remarked that "by means of glasses, hotbeds, and hot walls, very good grapes can be raised in Scotland, and very good wine can be made of them at about thirty times the expense for which at least equally good can be bought from foreign countries." In the same vein, it may be said that very good pineapples can be grown in Maine, if only a duty be imposed sufficient to equalize cost of production between the growers in Maine and those in more favored climes. Tea, coffee, cocoa, raw silk, and hemp,—any quantity of things that are now imported can be grown in the United States provided only that a duty high enough be imposed.[10]

Obviously tariffs have not usually been so prohibitive. Nonetheless, this shows that the one who bears the ultimate expense of such interventions is the consumer—that is, all of us. Lest it be thought that tariffs are a dead issue, it should be pointed out that to the extent they have been abandoned or reduced to inconsequence, they have often today been replaced by quotas and international agreements which quite often soak the consumer by causing him to pay a higher price than he would otherwise have to do, sometimes in order to benefit the foreign producer rather than the domestic one.

The Agriculture Department has been highly successful in virtually pricing some farm products off the market. Cotton is a notorious example. In 1958 the New England Governor's Textile Committee reported that acreage controls had so reduced the production of cotton that the price had risen to the point that American cotton goods were losing out in competition. They said, regarding the reduction of acreage and cotton production, that

> This inevitably has raised the price of finished goods, with a resultant reduction of purchases. . . . American manufac-

[10] Taussig, *op. cit.*, pp. 363-64.

turers are quite properly aroused over the shortages of good cotton at reasonable prices for 1958. A considerably larger crop is required in 1958-59 if prices are to stabilize.[11]

The raising of wages by labor unions and government edict is another aspect of the war on the consumer. An economist says "that the more fundamental clash of interest in any particular labor dispute is between labor and consumer of the product involved, and not between labor and the businessman or corporation who employs it."[12] Another says: "The contest of strength, insofar as the most powerful unions are concerned (viz., those dominating the big . . . industries such as steel, autos, rubber, glass) is with the public, the firms in question acting chiefly as intermediaries. It is the public the unions are really battling and impoverishing, not the managements with whom they are ostensibly contending."[13] He suggests that where a whole industry is unionized that collective bargaining "then moves increasingly toward a syndicalism in which unions and employers collaborate to fix wages, prices, and output to mulct the ultimate consumers."[14] It would be more precise to say that the initial impact of unions is upon other workers but that if they succeed in raising wages above the market level that the consumer pays for it in one way or another. In any case, union wages and minimum wages are a part of the war on the consumer.

The ways that the poor—as consumers—are harmed by government programs are not only so numerous that no one may be certain he has enumerated all of them, but also so subtle and remote as to almost defy detection. Here is an example of subtle and remote ways. A recent book was written with a thesis expressed in the title, *The Poor Pay More*. More specifically, the book deals with the urban poor and

[11] Peterson, *op. cit.*, p. 179.
[12] Edward H. Chamberlin, "The Monopoly Power of Labor," *The Impact of the Union*, David M. Wright, ed. (New York: Kelley and Millman, 1956), p. 182.
[13] Boarman, *op. cit.*, p. 91.
[14] *Ibid.*, p. 165.

how they pay higher prices for many items, get inferior products, and pay higher carrying charges than do the generality
of Americans. A couple of particular instances will illustrate.
The first is an account given by a Negro housewife:

> In 1955 a salesman came to the door selling wrist
> watches. I had promised my daughter I would get her one.
> We were both home and my daughter pleaded with me to
> buy the watch. So I agreed to buy it for $60. I gave him $3
> down and I got a payment book in the mail. *About a month
> later I had the watch appraised in a 125th Street store and I
> found it was worth only* $6.50. I called up the company and
> said *I wouldn't pay for it and they should come and get it.
> They told me I had to pay or they'd take me to court. And I
> said, "fine, take me to court and I'll have the watch there."*
> Next thing I know about this, I get a court notice of Judg-
> ment by Default from Brooklyn Municipal Court for $69
> balance, $3 interest, $5 "costs by statute," $14 court costs.
> *The total cost of the watch was* $91.[15]

Another case concerns a Negro couple who bought furniture
priced at $450 on an installment plan. They missed two pay-
ments and the company pressed for payment in full. When
they could not do so, the husband's wages were garnisheed.
According to the woman, *"We were cheated because
we'd already paid* $250, *but on the garnishee we're pay-
ing* $490, *although the furniture was originally valued at*
$450."[16]

There is much evidence, both in such charges as the above
and by more direct investigation, that the poor do indeed pay
more frequently. But what has this to do with government
action? The connection is remote, as I have said, but nonetheless real. The poor pay more, when they do, because they
do not shop around for the best price. They do not benefit
from cost shopping because they buy on credit. They are not

[15] David Caplovitz, *The Poor Pay More* (New York: Free Press of Glencoe,
1963) p. 160.
[16] *Ibid.*, p. 157.

good credit risks (those involved in this judgment), and buy where they can get credit, though prices are frequently much higher at such places. The author of the study suggests that "the most desirable change in their shopping patterns would be to get them to buy for cash instead of credit. The findings have shown that 'easy credit' plans are frequently hard, not easy, and in any case, are very expensive. Yet this educational goal is also apt to meet with only limited success."[17] In the main, he thinks this would be so because the habit of installment buying is deeply ingrained in Americans of almost all income levels.

Buying on credit and paying in installments has some good arguments in its favor, in any case. In the case of durable goods, one may enjoy them while paying for them. This reason is offset, however, by the fact that one pays more for them that way and could thus have more goods or better quality goods by saving and paying cash, particularly when the interest on savings is taken into consideration. The claim that one will not save in this manner is not an argument for installment buying; it involves only a question of individual values. What tips the scales in favor of installment buying is government action. Mainly, it is inflation. Inflation reduces the value of money saved; even with interest it may be worth less at the end of the saving period than it was at the beginning. Installment buying became widespread in the 1920's, and has become a fixed habit of many Americans during the inflationary binge from the 1930's to the present. The government adds further inducement to buying on credit by allowing deductions for interest paid out on income tax reports, but by taxing interest received. In short, government action promotes buying on credit which in turn leads many of the poor to pay more for their goods than does the general populace. The poor may not know the rational arguments which would support this line of conduct, but they are following patterns set by those who do.

[17] *Ibid.*, p. 183.

Government roadblocks to enterprise are another subtle aspect of the war on the consumer. They result in higher prices, as, for example, of haircuts, taxi fares, transportation costs, and of goods in general. Service may be much poorer also. The man who is getting soaked waiting in the rain for a taxi may not think to lay part of the blame on state or municipal regulations, but the chances are good that there is where much of it should lie. If the number of taxi drivers were not limited, it is most likely that part time vehicles would appear in great numbers on the streets in inclement weather, and at rush periods. Of course, none of us knows how many helpful innovations are not available because of the difficulties governments put in the way of their being introduced and provided.

Much of the intervention in the housing situation is directly a war on the consumer. Building Codes and regulations make housing for the consumer much more expensive. Taxes discourage house building and renovation. The destruction of dwellings and the appropriation of land by government reduce the supply of houses, making those that remain more expensive, and make land at suitable locations harder to obtain. Government building or fostering of building increases demand for builders and raises costs again.

Nor should it be forgotten, finally, that taxes are a part of that war. Taxes have mounted over the years to pay for an increasing variety of government programs—programs that go as far as the subsidizing of luxurious airports to accommodate prestigious passengers, the paying for buildings and land in inner cities to turn over to private developers to build high rise apartments, the providing of low interest long term loans for people to build split-level houses in the suburbs, and so on. Except for *personal* income taxes and a few other minor ones, all taxes are paid either directly by the consumer or indirectly in the price of the product.

Generally speaking, the taxes that great corporations as well as small businesses pay are passed on to the consumer (why would the business do otherwise—even if it could?) in the price of the goods or services. This fact is pointed up by the researches of the Tax Foundation, Inc. They took one product in 1967 and reckoned taxes hidden in its price paid by consumers:

Choosing a loaf of bread made and sold in Indianapolis, they limited the counting to the federal and state taxes paid by the grocer, the baker, the companies making ingredients that went into the bread, and the railroads and vehicles that hauled the ingredients.

The sleuths found the grocer paid four federal taxes— individual income tax, telephone tax, transportation tax . . . , and safe deposit box tax.

The baker, a national company owning its own trucks, paid seven federal taxes—corporation income tax, stamp taxes on its security transfers, telephone tax, transportation tax for its salesmen, transportation tax for its product, and safe deposit tax, and the social security tax.

The grocer and baker also paid 15 state taxes, the researchers learned, with the bakery paying most of them because it was a corporation and because of the gasoline and motor vehicle taxes on its trucks.

Included in the state taxes paid by the baker were four corporation taxes paid in Delaware, where the company is chartered. Both the grocer and baker paid an Indiana gross income tax.

That's not all, the tax foundation said. A Kansas City flour mill which supplied the baker paid seven federal taxes and eight Missouri state taxes. And the railroad that brought the flour to Indianapolis paid five taxes to the federal government and an assortment of taxes to Missouri, Illinois, and Indiana.

The sugar that went into the bread came from a New Orleans refining company that paid eight federal taxes and six Lousiana taxes. Then there were taxes paid by the railroad that hauled the sugar to Indianapolis, the salt warehouse in Chicago from which the salt came, the salt company in Chicago, the shortening manufacturer in Cincinnati, the milk solids and the yeast companies in Chicago, and the railroads that carried these ingredients.

"Assuming that all these outfits passed along part of their tax burden in prices, there were at least 151 taxes on the single loaf of bread," the foundation report said. "No wonder the price of bread has doubled in 20 years or so."[18]

Politicians often speak as if they were soaking the rich when they levy taxes on corporations, but rich and poor pay the levy alike when they buy a loaf of bread.

The war on the consumer has not been confined to the United States. No more has the war on the poor which it entails. American restrictions on foreign trade, on the one hand, and American foreign aid, on the other, constitute a war on the foreign and domestic poor. In so far as foreigners only are concerned, these results are tangential to this work. But there are two reasons for taking the matter up briefly. The first is that they provide further illustrations of how government intervention is harmful to the poor. Secondly, programs have been undertaken for foreigners that are a burden on Americans.

That there is much hardship and suffering in the world, no one should doubt. That poverty is widespread and well nigh universal is true beyond doubt. Barbara Ward has said that "If you fix the level of wealth of 'wealthy' communities at a per-capita income of about $500 a year, then eighty per cent of mankind lives below it." Again, she says that in "some countries—one thinks particularly of India—per-capita income may be as low as $60. Yet between 400 and 500 million people live in India—something like two-fifths of all the poor people in the uncommitted world."[19] Another writer reports of another part of the world: "In considering Latin America, one soon recognizes the problem of survival; more than half of its population is undernourished. While more advanced

[18] "Sliced Bread Exposes 151 Hidden Taxes," Chicago *Tribune* (March 11, 1967), section 1, p. 3.

[19] Barbara Ward, *The Rich Nations and the Poor Nations* (New York: Norton, 1962), p. 38.

countries consume 2,750 to 3,280 calories daily per person, in Brazil the average is 2,350 and in Honduras, 2,030."[20]

The market has a way of ameliorating and improving such circumstances. The methods by which it works are capital investment flowing from richer countries to poorer, introduction of new techniques from technologically more advanced to other countries, by trade, and by population movements. Charity may be important in emergencies, but the market is probably much more helpful in ordinary circumstances.

But the ameliorative work of the market has been mightily hampered in this century. Protective tariffs and international agreements have made prices of American exports higher than they would otherwise have been, if not prohibitive. Thus, foreign countries have harmed their own peoples. Moreover, American policies of planned scarcity—crop restrictions, subsidies, production controls—have made it difficult if not impossible for foreigners to buy our goods. Doctrinaire socialists around the world have clamored against international capital investment and described its results as exploitation and fastened upon certain of its practices as being associated with the despised colonialism. As socialism has spread with its property restriction and confiscation, it has become increasingly perilous for Americans to invest abroad. Immigration restriction in the United States, as well as in other countries, has restricted population movement. Hence, the free market way of dealing with hunger has not been permitted to work its beneficent results. Governments, both of the United States and foreign countries, which have followed these policies have warred upon their own and the citizens of other lands.

The hampered and mutilated market is the proper context from which to view the American foreign aid program. Since World War II, the United States has launched a massive foreign aid undertaking, the cost of which has now gone far

---

[20] Luis Alberto de Souza, "Affluence and Poverty in Latin America," *Wealth and Want in One World*, Muriel S. Webb, ed. (New York: Friendship Press, 1966), p. 63.

beyond one hundred billion dollars. The associated programs have been government intervention by one nation into other nations to attempt to do the work that otherwise would be done by trade, investment, and population movement. Since most of the countries involved have been more or less social-istic (or interventionist), these programs have been a sub-sidization of socialism. To put it another way, the govern-ments of most of these countries, probably all of them, were already making war on their own poor in a similar fashion to that of the United States as well as in ways unique to each of them, and the United States government has come to their aid to enable them to do so more effectively.

Some examples of the malfeasance of these programs are in order. The aid to Laos is a particularly poignant story. Mil-lions of American dollars have been poured into that interest-ing country. With these interesting results, as one reporter tells it. "Sleek Cadillacs, Buicks and Fords have been im-ported by the dozen, although the principal highways still are hardly more than jungle trails."[21] These and other such items are hardly for the delectation of the poor. More,

> There is a lush building boom going on. Leading traders and government officials (often the same people) are hud-dling with architects and contractors for lavish new resi-dences or flashy additions to formerly modest homes. Both the Laovieng Bank and the Bank of Indochina are preparing to move into sleek new glass brick and concrete structures. The Finance Ministry is constructing an ultra-modern build-ing right next door to the newly completed Ministry of Plans.

The reporter says that it is "generally agreed that some two or three hundred leading families in Laos (population: 3,000,-000) are getting most of the benefit from the massive import program." As to the rest of the population, "the rank and file of the Laotians . . . live much as they have always lived, oblivious of the U.S. help. Their flimsy shacks are built on

[21] Igor Oganesoff, "Living It Up in Laos," *United States Foreign Aid*, Devere E. Pentony, ed. (San Francisco: Howard Chandler, 1960), p. 131.

stilts to protect them from snakes and flooding during the rainy season. They farm rice and a few vegetables and raise chickens. In the torrid climate only the scantiest cotton clothing is needed and hardly anyone wears shoes."[22]

Here are two examples of programs in Peru. The first was an irrigation project known by the name of Pampas de Noco. The United States spent $125,000 on it, though the engineer's report indicated that the undertaking was not feasible. When the money was spent and the project completed it was useless, useless for the simple reason that there was not enough water to fill the works.[23]

Much more distressing was the mismanagement of a drought relief program. In 1956 a fifty-day drought occurred in a region of Peru. The United States sent 106,000 tons of grain as a gift. The auditor who eventually investigated found "that only 5,028 tons, or 5.7 per cent of the shipment, were actually distributed free to hungry people in the drought area." The rest was sold, and "more than 60 per cent of the sales proceeds were spent for purposes that violated the intent of the agreement. One of the glaring examples of misuse was the construction of eight houses which were sold below cost on the installment plant to prominent persons in the town of Puno." A third of the grain was eventually sold to millers who disposed of it in the normal trade channels, and "28,000 of these 35,000 tons were sold to a single mill that was outside the drought area."[24]

The foreign aid war on the poor took on a more open and ominous character in Indonesia. As two reporters tell the story "that with one hand Sukarno had been accepting our predominantly 'economic' assistance. With the other he had been bleeding the economy to build up a war machine. By late 1963 he was more than a billion dollars in debt to the

---

[22] *Ibid.*, p. 135.

[23] Andrew Tully and Milton Britten, *Where Did Your Money Go?* (New York: Simon and Schuster, 1964), p. 21.

[24] *Ibid.*, pp. 22-23.

Soviet Union for military hardware."[25] Not only did he spend lavishly for military hardware but also for foreign luxury materials. Senator William Proxmire said, "The nation is bankrupt, yet Sukarno purchased some 7,000 midget sport cars from Japan for luxury purposes."[26] What had happened to the poor Indonesians in the meanwhile?

> . . . Indonesia, once a major rice-producing area and exporter of rice, was forced to import a million tons a year. Once the world's major rubber supplier, she had fallen behind Malaya. Once a major producer of tin, her production had dropped about two-thirds over a period of fifteen years. Sugar production also fell. Retail prices rose—almost eight times in eight years. In 1962 the price of rice, a staple in the Indonesian diet, had climbed 17 per cent, eggs were up 139 per cent and sugar was up 239 per cent.[27]

That the United States is fostering and subsidizing socialism abroad could be demonstrated by numerous instances. One example will suffice. The International Cooperation Administration, one of the organizations to dispense foreign aid, reported that "India's Five Year Plans encompass almost every phase of agricultural, industrial and commercial life and also set goals for progress in education, health and social welfare." This is a fair enough description of a socialist undertaking. They also say, "U.S. assistance, on authorization basis, amounted to about $330 million as of June 30, 1956."[28] That should be enough said.

Those who report the malfeasances that occur in the foreign aid programs frequently allege that these are only abuses resulting from corruption that could be straightened out with better administration. They hold out the hope that the poor can still somehow be aided—*if* the United States administers the program more prudently, *if* corruption in recipient coun-

[25] *Ibid.*, p. 83.
[26] Quoted in *ibid.*, p. 85.
[27] *Ibid.*
[28] "Aid and the Indian Experiment," Pentony, *op. cit.*, p. 139.

tries is rooted out, *if* better projects are chosen, *if* Soviet practices are imitated, *if* pressures are brought to bear on recipient countries to straighten out their affairs, and so on. Unfortunately, there is no reason to suppose that such contingencies will ever be satisfied. It is probably true that better contrived programs honestly administered would provide fewer dramatic instances of wastefulness. But if angels could be found to administer the programs they would still be wasteful, because they are not economic. Economy involves selling to the highest bidder; these programs entail the dumping of goods. Economy requires buying from the lowest seller; these programs attempt to remove price as a consideration, and in so doing remove the means of determining what is most wanted.

Of course, no angels have been found to administer the programs. All known human frailties are fully in play, so far as can be determined. Moreover, these are *not* economic programs at all. They are *political* programs. As such—and this is their nature regardless of the motives of those who advance them—, they provide means for politicians to extend their power as well as benefit materially. Not only do they demonstrably work in this way, but when they do so they are only fulfilling the nature of the programs. The foreign poor suffer because they labor under the restrictions of interventionist programs, because they must not only continue to support themselves but their swollen governments as well, because they continue to pay high prices for the goods they buy, and because little if anything is done to increase markets available to them.

American intervention in foreign trade and by foreign aid has harmed the American consumer as well. In the first place, Americans have been harmed by the interventions which hampered trade and population movement. They have been denied goods and services of a quality and at a price which they might have had. Secondly, American taxpayers have had to pay for foreign aid. The poor have again been hard hit. They are the ones most in need of bargain prices for goods and services. Moreover, they can least afford to pay taxes to make gifts for others. And, the American poor *do* pay taxes which support such programs. At the least, they pay sales taxes, excise taxes, hidden taxes, and so on.

A war is likely to have its victors and its vanquished. The vanquished in this conflict are the conquered poor. They are the ones whose cause appears to have been lost, who often appear hopeless and helpless. They are officially recognized in America today as being defeated, and spokesmen rush forth to proclaim their helplessness in our society. After nearly a century, of what is now dubbed a War on Poverty, a war that has picked up intensity and become much more pervasive in the last 35 years, we are stuck with poverty which is described as great as or greater than it ever was. Official spokesmen are given to hyperbole, but let us attend to some descriptions by Vice President Humphrey:

> This is the revealing and paradoxical story of today's America—a country of unprecedented wealth and prosperity that harbors in its midst 35 million people without sufficient food, shelter, and clothing. It is the story of one out of five Americans who live in poverty, shame, misery, and degradation. . . .
>
> Four years ago, during the presidential primary in West Virginia, I visited a town whose sole source of income—a coal mine—had been closed. The houses and stores in the town were dilapidated, the people wandered about aimlessly.
>
> I was having breakfast with some of the townspeople, discussing their problems and trying to inject a note of optimism into the conversation, when a tall, spare, shabbily-dressed man whose face had turned red from the cold walked in the door and came up to me. I shook his hand and said, "I'm Hubert Humphrey. I'd appreciate your vote in the election."
>
> The man looked me in the eye—I shall never forget that look—and said, "Yes, I know, Senator, I need a job, any kind of job. I've got three kids and they're hungry. Is there something you can do about that?"

That spring in West Virginia I met thousands of men looking desperately for work, each man's face reflecting bewilderment and need. And every time—every single time—it hurt.[29]

We may doubt, of course, that there are very many men whose children are hungry in America today, or who have been in recent decades. Moreover, the present writer has steered clear of any precise definition of poverty that would serve to determine how many are living in this condition. Such calculations are for political purposes; however exacting the statistician has been in making his count, his figure is not an objective one. This is so because poverty is a relative classification. It could only be absolute if it were used to describe absolute deprivation, where the person had nothing. The relativity of poverty is pointed out by the following newspaper account of the reactions of a foreign visitor to Washington D.C.:

> A visit to the slums of Washington astonished Helen Hui, of Hong Kong—but not in the way you might expect.
> "What you call slums here would be a haven in heaven for many people in Hong Kong," Miss Hui, a senior in sociology at Smith College, said. . . .
> "It is your definition of poverty which surprises me most," Miss Hui explained. "Poverty, you see, is relative."
> In Washington she visited people living in crowded two-story houses yesterday. Many of the people she met complained that the schools weren't good enough and that they weren't integrated.
> "At home people live in cardboard houses, sometimes without roofs, and there is no compulsory education at all. Even the government schools require tuition," she said.[30]

When I say that the poor are conquered, then, I do not mean that they are without material goods, that they are nec-

---

[29] Hubert H. Humphrey, *War on Poverty* (New York: McGraw-Hill, 1964), pp. 9-10.
[30] "Poverty is Relative," Washington *Post* (March 15, 1967), section A, p. 13.

essarily, or even likely to be hungry, that they do not have shelter and clothing of sorts, or that they are suffering from material deprivation. On the contrary, the poor, whoever and how many of them there may be, are looked after by a great variety of government programs. There are Social Security payments, Welfare checks for the aged, Aid to Dependent Children, Public Housing projects, rent subsidies, school lunches, food stamps for surplus food, Unemployment Compensation, scholarships to attend college, Veteran's Pensions, payments for allowing land to lie idle, job retraining programs, and so on, almost *ad infinitum.*

Indeed, so numerous and bountiful are the government favors available that an outfit called the National Counseling Service has thought it worthwhile to put out a book listing them. The book is appropriately called, *Encyclopedia of U. S. Government Benefits.* According to its full page advertisement in a prestigious national magazine, the book contains over 1,000 pages and lists more than 10,000 benefits. There is a money-back guarantee on the book that if the buyer is not able to get at least $500 in cash or services within the year the book may be returned without cost. One of the pitches for the book reads this way:

> Under *The Great Society* a staggering amount of Government money is available for every American to use for every imaginable way of enriching the lives of all his family. Government experts are plainly alarmed. Last year alone Government agencies had to turn back millions of dollars to the Treasury that had been earmarked for rich benefits that weren't applied for. People like yourself just weren't using the money. *They didn't know it was available for them. Or how to go about getting it.*
>
> Now this handy, fact-filled volume tells you how to get the equal of 21 per cent increase in your salary, and much MORE! Tells exactly how our Government will help SEND YOUR CHILD THROUGH COLLEGE . . . Help you START A SUCCESSFUL BUSINESS . . . Provide needed

cash to CLEAN UP OLD DEBTS . . . Get HOME IM-
PROVEMENT MONEY . . . BUILD SWIMMING or
FISHING POND, STOCK IT WITH FREE RAINBOW
TROUT . . . AND MUCH MORE.[31]

Even allowing for hyperbole, the story unfolded in the advertisement must be essentially true.

So bountiful are the government favors that many have lost
sympathy for the poor today because they are being supported
in idleness by those who work. It appears that there are even
great advantages to being "deprived," for then one may not
have to work for his daily bread. There may be those for
whom this is true, but it does not change the fact that they too
have been conquered.

The poor are not conquered in the sense that they are materially deprived; in that respect, they probably live better than
the poor have in any age anywhere. They are conquered because they have lost their independence, or never gained it.
They are conquered because they have become *dependent
upon government*. They have had the door of opportunity
slammed in their faces. Those who are lazy and unambitious
have had the salutary necessity of providing for themselves
taken away. But mainly, opportunities for maintaining independence have been taken away. The poor have been
driven from the farm by a century of government intervention, had their entry to factories blocked by labor unions,
been priced off the market by wages and hours legislation,
blocked from going into business by the obstacles thrown in
the way by government, had their houses and businesses taken
away by government appropriation, and found it increasingly
difficult to find legal housing to satisfy their needs.

They have become dependent upon government, dependent for food, for clothing, for shelter, and, in many instances, for such jobs as they have. One more example may
show how government has rendered so many impotent and
dependent. One of the deep desires of man is to provide a

[31] *Saturday Evening Post* (June 15, 1968), p. 17.

modicum of security for himself and his family. Many wish to provide for themselves in their old age, for themselves and their families should they become incapacitated before old age, for their survivors should they die before their time. The inflationary policies of government make this increasingly difficult to do. Money that is saved may lose value through inflation. Insurance will become increasingly inadequate as prices rise. The knowledgeable know that common stocks may provide a hedge against the ravages of inflation, but this is not much of an option for the poor. They are not likely to wish to risk their hard earned savings in such fashion, even if they have the know-how to play the stock market, which is unlikely. Social Security does appear to provide for them, minimally at least. That is, the political powers may find it expedient, as they have thus far, to increase payments to compensate for inflation. Those who rely upon this have become dependent upon government, are hostage to the whims of a Congress which mediates among the various interest groups which play upon it.

As they have become dependent upon government, the poor have had their dignity and much of the meaning of life stripped away. There is a deeper dimension to life than that which immediately meets the eye. Paradoxical as it may seem, it *is* better to give than to receive, to serve than be served. If this formulation is unacceptable, then it should at least be granted that in human terms it is equally good to give as to receive, to serve as to be served. To put it another way, work is a necessary and rewarding experience for man. The chances are good that the West Virginian was exaggerating when he told the then Senator Humphrey that his children were hungry. It is much more likely that the hunger was his, the inner hunger to work, to do something useful, to provide for his family, to rejoin the society of men in mutual help and exchange.

Whiting Williams, a lively and energetic nonagenarian, spent much time with workers of all sorts. His conclusions point for him to one central fact: Men do not work simply to be paid; jobs do not simply mean a livelihood; there is more to it than that. He says, regarding his experience with many men under many circumstances,

> Every blessed one of all these was giving one identical testimony:
> "*My job proves I'm important!* I belong! I count! The world needs me! Sure, it puts money in my pocket and bread in my stomach. But it also lets me look every other son-of-a-gun right square in the eye!"
> To make a long story short, every day of my experience as a worker-listener made plainer and plainer this conviction.
> *Even the hardest pressed of my companions was seeking in his work, along with even the most sorely needed cash, his utmost right to believe in his personal worth and dignity. Furthermore, he was seeking this in his work. AS NO-WHERE ELSE! The rungs of the job-ladder were furnishing him the most reliable of all imaginable yardsticks.*
> *For a one-word explanation of the wage-earner's soul-deep fear of no job and his unquenchable hope for a better one, the "Pay-check" theory, so universally taken for granted, falls far, far, short. Infinitely better, is the single word PRIDE.*[32]

This is not so difficult to understand. Man is a social being, so philosophers have told us through the ages. He realizes this aspect of his being through work, through the recognition of others of his contribution, through the use of his powers to serve, through an integrity of his being that he finds in an identity with what he produces, to an integration with society in the desirability it has for others and its contribution to the well being of people in general.

It is in the assault upon human dignity, upon human integrity, upon the lineaments of society that the full meaning and import of the war on the poor is revealed. It is in the alienation of man from man and the disintegration of society

[32] Whiting Williams, *America's Mainspring and the Great Society* (New York: Frederick Fell, 1967), pp. 57-58.

that the greatest havoc is wrought. When the novelist, Ernest Hemingway, wished to portray the withdrawal of his hero from society in A *Farewell to Arms,* he sent him to Switzerland, that epitome of neutrality. More pointedly, the hero did not work there; instead, he lived off money sent from America. Had he worked, he would have been ending his withdrawal from society by intertwining his efforts with others, by serving others, by his produce becoming bone of their bone and flesh of their flesh. It is by such exchange that society is knit together in a meaningful whole.

The humblest resident of Harlem, of Hough, or of Watts may know in his heart of hearts (that is, feel) the emptiness and futility of the government's pathetic efforts at decreeing racial integration. The government has gone much too far in producing disintegration to achieve any kind of integration by its methods. It has pitted farmers against urban dwellers and all consumers; it has set tenants against landlords, migrant workers against their employers, labor union members against other workers, bureaucrat against enterpriser; and it has fostered conflict between a host of special interest groups and the general welfare. It has completed the process of alienation and disintegration by supplying the wherewithal to exist as government favor to those for whom it has denied access to independent means and a useful existence.

The alienated abound in America today. They are known by many names and euphemisms: the poor, the unemployed, the juvenile delinquent, the "hippy," the Negro, the unskilled, the culturally deprived, and the senior citizen, among others. Their lack of integration with the rest of society is not because of race, color, or previous condition of servitude. They are, after all, members of the several races, of many hues, and have a varied historical background. Their lot has not been much affected by Supreme Court decisions, Fair Employment Practices Commissions or Civil Rights Commissions, nor is it likely that it will be. For all their differences, they have one thing in common. They are not productively employed. They live largely off government favors, or the fallout from them. They have been put out to pasture, so to speak. If they are young, they may be forced to attend school from which they get nothing of value to them, denied employment by law or governmentally imposed conditions, left to seek meaning in a round of thrills. If they are old, and they have been retired, left to try to find meaning in a truncated existence, often in "segregated" neighborhoods where the existence of all is equally meaningless. In short, they are alienated because they are not fruitful and useful members of society. Not all of this is due to government interference, but much of it is.

We all suffer today from the disintegration of society. Those who produce resent the fact that part of the fruits of their labor are taken away to provide subsistence to those who do not produce. But that resentment thus far is as nothing compared to the resentment of many of the recipients of government favors. One writer, describing the attitudes of slum dwellers whom he refers to as members of a "subculture," says that they divide "the world into 'we' and 'they.' 'They' are all the agents of the dominant culture, official or unofficial, benevolent or persecutory police, government, schools, social workers, and indeed anyone who carries the stigmata of the successful middle class. All these are held to discriminate against the people of the subculture, and to exploit them: even the apparently benevolent must be getting something out of it, a personal advantage which is concealed by the hypocrisy of their avowed intentions."[33] The supposed beneficiaries are here seen as resenting, fearing, and rejecting their supposed benefactors.

There is, then, an explanation for the Battle in the Streets, to which we may now return. The civil war has moved partially out into the open. Some of the poor are now engaging the representatives of authority—the firemen, the police, the army—in guerilla warfare. But there is an apparent contraction here. Those most obviously harmed quite often by the

[33] Marris, *op. cit.*, p. 125.

Battle in the Streets are the poor themselves. One analyst goes so far as to declare that "the worst enemy that the Negro has had . . . has been the Negro himself." He goes on to show why he believes this to be so, with examples taken from the Cleveland disturbance:

> The destruction of the Playmor Auditorium removed a facility for wholesome recreation from the Negro community. Dry-cleaning stores in Hough that were looted, wrecked and closed were stocked full of clothing from the Negro community. When a supermarket located at East 89th and Superior was burned out in June 1966, as a prelude to the major riot, Negro employees were put out of work and Negro residents were forced to walk extra blocks for food, as it was the only market between East 71st and East 105th Streets on Superior. Similarly, the burning out of the lone pharmacy on Hough Avenue between East 55th and 105th, merely because it was operated by Jewish brothers . . . , also created a hardship for the Negro sick in the district. The gutting of a Goodwill Store at the corner of Crawford Road and Hough put additional people out of work. The firing of small grocery stores, despite unproven charges of poor quality meat and high prices again hurt the Negro, for often as not these same shops were the only ones to extend credit to Negroes between employment or relief checks. As Negro Councilman Leo Jackson indicated in the *Plain Dealer* for July 26, 1966: "This in my opinion is not an attempt to get 'Whitey.' You don't get Whitey in a predominantly Negro area. It is not Whitey who is being killed. It's the Negro who's being killed."[34]

All this is quite correct, but, also largely irrelevant. It would be much more to the point if the Battle in the Streets were a rational phenomena. It is not. It is an irrational reaction to irrational programs.

The Battle in the Streets is an omen, a sign, a portent, and it must be interpreted as such. It is a dramatic presentation for

[34] Saul S. Friedman, "Riots, Violence, and Civil Rights," *National Review* (August 22, 1967), p. 904.

all of us to see of what is wrong with the programs the government has employed. The rioters are following the lesson plan learned from the government; they have learned the lesson well and are now applying it. For decades, government has made war on the poor with programs that were supposed to benefit them. It has sanctioned the use of force to achieve what would otherwise be economic ends. It has penalized production of farm products, fostered union organization and tactics, taken by force from those who produce to give to those who do not. The government, by example, has taught that the way to prosperity is to avoid the requirements of economy, to spend rather than save, to destroy rather than to produce. It has taught, by its actions, that those who save, invest, build, produce, provide jobs, offer services are dangerous antagonists, if not outright enemies, of society. On the other hand, it has taught that those who do nothing worthwhile, who roam the streets and parks, who malinger or plan demonstrations to force concessions, are objects for special consideration and solicitude. Government has said, by way of its programs, that the way to improve life in the cities is to demolish the buildings and make the earth bare.

The Battle in the Streets is a paradigmatic imitation of all this. The rioters demolish buildings with molotov cocktails and fire, leaving structures scarred ruins, driving out small businessmen and inhabitants. They loot the stores, taking from those who produce for those who do not. The enemy is clearly made up of those who have saved, invested, built, produced, provided jobs, offered services, and so on. The work of years is undone in short order by the rioters. All this is clearly diseconomic, but then government had shown the way. These rioters should have been producing prosperity, according to the new economics, for they were destroying buildings that might be rebuilt, gutting stores of goods that might be replaced, even making jobs by creating new "needs" that would be met. (The new economics has taught for years that the basic problem in America is to stimulate demand.) The force and violence employed in the Battle in the Streets was an imitation of that which government has been employing for years in its war on the poor.

For years, reformers have proclaimed that their programs fell short of attaining their ends only because they were too timid, were not carried out in a sufficiently thorough fashion. The Battle in the Streets tests that hypothesis. There are no half-way measures there. Rioters do not wait for bulldozers to level buildings. They do not wait for property to be acquired by the way of the exercise of the power of eminent domain. They simply take it over for destruction. They do not wait for goods to be taken by taxation and given to the poor. They simply confiscate them by looting. If prosperity can be achieved by force, it should be more readily attained by massive and direct force. Many of the reformers do not appear to misunderstand the import of all this; they stand by today calling for the appropriation of tens of billions of dollars for spending in these areas demolished by rioters, and other areas of like character.

Even the assaults upon firemen, police, and the armed forces brought into the field of combat are not hard to understand. There are overtones in this of the expression of hatred for authority, a hatred that may contain in it glimmers of understanding of how deeply government has failed the poor by making war on them. More directly, though, the police, particularly, are the representatives of traditional authority, charged with the task of protecting life and *property*. This is an assault upon property, and police must not be permitted to exercise their assigned duties. In this circumscription of the power of the police, the rioters are imitating in a more direct fashion what the Federal courts have been doing for some time now.

It is true that the Battlers in the Streets are making war on themselves. In this, too, they are following the pattern set by the government. The government has set citizen against citizen and group against group. It has also turned one aspect of a man against his other aspects, as in the case of the war on the consumer. Those who have taken to the streets demonstrate this same behavior. It is quite likely that sometimes a man may have thrown a molotov cocktail which set fire to a dry cleaning establishment where some of his own clothes were.

This interpretation is not at odds with the fact that the Battle in the Streets has been spurred by agitators, that various and sundry radicals have fomented it. Instead, these agitators share much common ground with the reformers who have promoted the government programs. Both have wished to transform society by force; the reformers would do so by using formal government; the agitators pursue their course more directly. Of course, those in control of government cannot and do not condone rioting and insurrection, but so far as they reward it by government appropriations into the ruined areas, as they did at Watts, they show a remarkable affinity with the aims of the rioters.

It may be appropriate to complete the answer here of a question partly answered earlier. Who are the victors in this civil war that results from the war on the poor? This is not the story of the victors, so the question will not be dwelt upon here. But there are many who have benefited and do presently benefit from the government intervention. Many have a vested interest in the continuation of the government programs. It will only be necessary to allude to some of them.

Among the victors, thus far, have been the politicians. These range from Presidents of the United States to the local favor dispensers. Many politicians have become accustomed over a good many years now to getting elected to office by promising favors to various interest groups, to farmers, to labor unions, to the aged, to the young, and so on. In effect, they have become used to buying their way into office by promising benefits bought with the tax money of all of us. For those who desire power, there seems to be no better way to attain it than to cater to one of the basest of human desires, the desire to get something for nothing. It does not seem to matter that the bulk of the population does not and cannot benefit from such practices.

The beneficiaries are numerous even so, but let it suffice that they simply be named: the bureaucrats who dispense the favors and wield the power, the labor union leaders who enjoy both munificent salaries and prestigious positions, the corporations that get government contracts, the builders who get inexpensive land in strategic locations by way of urban renewal, established businesses that benefit from the blocking of potential competitors by government restrictions, the holders of franchises, monopolies, and licenses, the farmers who are growing wealthy by way of government subsidies,[35] the members of labor unions who are able to keep their jobs at higher wages, the intellectuals who provide grist for the programmatic mills, and all the others who have good incomes or prestigious positions in consequence of the interven-

[35] While the following quoted letter written to the editor of the New York *Times* (December 28, 1966) in confirmation of a column by James Reston may overstate the case and contain some class bias, it does point up how the well-to-do frequently benefit from government programs:

> James Reston's December 7 column "Washington: The Fat Cat Subsidies" was a provocative piece in the best Restonian tradition. Unfortunately, he underestimates the extent to which the government benefits the "fat cats."
>
> He spoke of large farm operators receiving irrigation subsidies. But he made no mention of the fact that the farm price control program also works to their advantage rather than serving the needs of the marginal small farmer.
>
> He underlined the subsidy that taxpayers are making to the owners of private and business planes but he overlooked the much more gigantic urban renewal program, which subsidizes corporations to build stores, office buildings, factories and high-rise high-rent apartment dwelling facilities that will be patronized by, or worked in, or lived in by the relatively "fat cats."
>
> He indicated that Congress was opposed to eliminating the subsidy to the school milk programs that included middle class children, but he failed to note that the Federal Government has for some time been subsidizing the purchase of homes by middle class families. Likewise he was critical of the federal government's aid to public schools in . . . impacted areas, but he said nothing about the fact that the overwhelming share of Federal funds for scientific research goes to a relatively few of the largest and richest universities in the nation. . . .

tion. When all these are joined with the millions upon millions who are now dependent upon government for subsistence (all those receiving welfare payments, farm payments, subsidies, Social Security, unemployment compensation, and so forth), who believe themselves helpless without the government aid (and have been made nearly so by the intervention), their number is probably sufficient to form electoral majorities.

This is not to imply that the victors are necessarily conscious that they are victors over the poor. There is every reason to believe that many of the politicians (and those who succor them) really wish to help the poor. In any case, charity demands that we give them the benefit of any doubt and believe that even now many of them do not know how badly awry their programs have gone. When Vice President Humphrey declared that it hurt him to hear a man pleading for a job, it is greatly to be doubted that he understood, or understands, how his own efforts may have contributed to the plight of the man in West Virginia. Mr. Humphrey has long been a vigorous supporter of organized labor and has benefited at the polls from their support of him. Yet it was the labor unions which demanded so much pay that coal was largely priced off the market for many uses. To put it another way, these men were disemployed by their demands, or the demands of their leaders. Mr. Humphrey would surely feel much worse than he does if he ever accepted the evidence for the consequences of the programs he has fostered.

The War on Poverty, then, has not resulted in the conquest of poverty. It has, instead, resulted in the conquest of the poor. Government has divided the populace into contending factions, has empowered portions of the people against others, has lent its force to the cause of some and turned its back upon others. The incipient civil war that is an inevitable result of such policies has finally broke out in the streets. Strictly speaking there are not yet victors, for the war is not over: there are only those who have been advantaged by the conflict. Even so, it is surely time for the work of pacification.

Those who have been contending are not natural enemies. Farmers are not at odds with urban dwellers by nature, capital with labor, government with the poor. The Battle in the Streets is not even a logical consequence of or response to poverty. On the contrary, the various peoples in a country complement one another; specialization of function requires and begets cooperation; the appropriate response to poverty is not destruction, but economy. The work of reconciliation proceeds from this understanding.

CHAPTER IX

Reconstruction—The Hope for the Poor

Aт THE END OF A WAR WHICH HAS BEEN A CIVIL CONFLICT comes the time for reconstruction. It is surely time for the war on the poor to end. With that, it is time, too, for reconstruction to begin. But what has been described in what has gone before is both more subtle and more complex than war and peace as they are ordinarily conceived. Nor is the reconstruction which could follow simply a matter of physical rebuilding. It involves a reconstruing of reality, for it is misconstructions at this level that led to the ill begotten war. Some basic instruments for man's use have been misused and abused. To get to reconstruction it is necessary to reconsider these instruments.

An instrument can only be effectively and constructively used in the sort of operations that are appropriate to its nature. A hammer, for example, is an excellent instrument for driving nails into wood. But it is ill-suited, for instance, to the work of a hairdresser, being worse than useless for inserting hairpins in a woman's hair. Nor would it be of much use in putting water under pressure, the material being inappropriate to its method of exerting force. All instruments, from the simplest to the most complex, have their appropriate uses and their inherent limitations.

One of the instruments that has been misused in the war on the poor is government. Government is an excellent instrument. No substitute has been found for it as a means of keeping the peace and settling disputes, nor is there likely to be. Indeed, so necessary is government to our well-being and so determined are men to have one that if the established government fails to perform its duties another, or others, will rise to take its place. But government, too, is limited in what can be done effectively with it. It provides an essential framework for production and trade, but it is ill-suited to the producing of goods or to the delicate fabric of trade. It can cause men to cease and desist from injuring one another, but it cannot make them love one another.

Just so, economics is an excellent instrument. There is no replacing it as a guide to the means of producing the most goods of the highest quality at the lowest price, or for the least expenditure of materials and energy. Those who would prosper must needs follow its dictates. It, too, however, is a limited instrument. The principles of economics are excellent guides to men in their individual and private capacities for the production of wealth. But if government tries to use these principles by intervening in private affairs, it negates their beneficent effects. Expert chemists cannot mix oil and water. No more can a Council of Economic Advisers mix positive government action to produce economy. The nature of the instruments makes this so.

John Dewey, the Father of Progressive Education in America, dubbed his variation of pragmatism *instrumentalism*. The basic insight was that all sorts of things are instruments meant to serve men. It is a valuable insight. Unfortunately, in the hands of Dewey and his disciples it was a flawed insight. It was flawed because it was abstracted from the relationship to reality which is essential to its usefulness. Ideas are instruments, Dewey said, but he neglected to explain that they are only legitimate instruments when they express relationships that inhere in reality. On the contrary, Dewey used words cut loose from their moorings, without taking care to follow conventional usage. In the same manner, government is an instrument for human use, but it is only appropriate when it is used in accord with its nature.

Government is that instrument which maintains itself by and is *authorized to use force*. It is not the only body that may use force. Parents may use force upon their children, and anyone may use force in self-defense, subject to legal restrictions. But government is the only body that is characterized by the reliance upon the use of force, and it alone may use force generally throughout a society within its jurisdiction. In this latter sense, government has a monopoly of the use of force. When a government—or, more precisely, some agent of it—acts without the threat or use of force, it is not performing a distinctly governmental function. For example, if the President of the United States were to admonish parents not to spare the rod and spoil the child, if this admonition were accompanied by no penalties to apply to violators, he would not be performing an act peculiar to government. Anyone of us might utter the same admonition, and, depending upon our influence and prestige, achieve the same salutary results. In short, the *sine qua non* of government is its inherent power and authority to use force.

This is a fearsome and potentially destructive power. The use of force is a thing to be shunned rather than sought. For that reason, it is good if men stand in awe of government, if they fear to challenge it in its domain, if they bow to its edicts without resistance. The more readily government can accomplish its ends by inspiring awe, the less it will have to resort to brute force. For that reason also, government should be strictly limited (all government, not *just* the Federal government) in the functions it performs, lest all of life be permeated by force and its destructive possibilities. Moreover, that awe which is essential to the smooth functioning of government will not likely survive encounters with it becoming too common. Government, then, should perform only those functions appropriate to it.

What functions are appropriate to it? One way into an answer is to say that government may only be appropriately used where force can be properly employed. To what ends may force be properly exercised? The Founders of these United States made a general summation of these when they set forth the purposes for founding the Republic: to "establish justice, insure domestic tranquillity, provide for the common defense, promote the general welfare, and secure the blessing of liberty to ourselves and our posterity. . . ." It should be granted that there are many who can give assent to these general aims without seeing in them any limitations on government. This occurs, I suspect, because they do not generally think of them as intertwined but rather as separate and distinct functions. At any rate, let us examine a little closer into the proper functions of government.

The basic task of government is to keep the peace. Most of its functions are closely related to this task. Keeping the peace involves, most fundamentally, protecting peaceful men from attacks upon them by aggressors. Aggressors, or trespassers, may be individuals or groups, domestic or foreign. In any case, a government is providing for the common defense and insuring domestic tranquillity when it holds these at bay. Keeping the peace also involves dealing with those who have committed offenses, and settling disputes that arise between individuals and groups. In this fashion, then, government can properly act to establish justice. It can be seen, too, that these are objects to which force is appropriate. Force can be used to defend against aggressors and to compel acceptance of the verdict of the court.

The statement that government should promote the general welfare appears to us to raise questions rather than to answer them. This is so because we have been taught to misconstrue the phrase. We have been taught to believe that government may act to advance the well-being of some portion of the population, perhaps at the expense of another, and that this is somehow for the general welfare. But that cannot be: The general welfare is the *general* welfare, not the welfare of some part. The general welfare is the welfare of all, a welfare which no man or group of men can have more interest in, or less, than all others. To maintain peace in a society promotes the general welfare—hence, to establish justice, to insure domestic tranquillity, and to provide for the common defense. But, it may be objected, there are those who would disturb the peace. Just so, that is why we have government in the first place. But is the maintenance of peace in their interest? Of course it is.

There is another order of services that a government may provide that can be said to be for the general welfare. They are those services of general use and benefit whose costs cannot readily or equitably be divided among individual users. Many types of roads, such as city streets, may fall in this category, but the maintenance of means for fighting fires in towns and cities is an even better example. Fires are a danger to all the inhabitants of a town. It is, therefore, for the general welfare that some means for dealing with them be maintained at public expense. It is proper, though it may not always be necessary, that force be used to collect taxes so that the cost of this will be equitably divided. There are, of course, other activities which need to be maintained for the general welfare.

It is proper, also, that government and its instruments of force and for administering justice be supported with tax money. The keeping of the peace being for the general welfare, it must follow that all those with means should contribute to it, whether they will or not.

Government is the right instrument, also, to secure the blessings of liberty to a people. It may see to it that peaceful men are not detained and that all such are permitted to exercise their faculties without restraint, so long as they do not injure others and that they exercise them on their own facilities or on those of others who have hired or invited them or in public places and at times appointed to the particular uses. Force, defensive force, can be employed so as to prevent the strong from oppressing the weak or anyone from interfering with the liberty of another.

The crucial question for this work has to do with the appropriate relationship between government—force, organized and under control—and economy—the thrifty employment of capital, labor, and materials for the production of goods and provision of services. That there is a necessary and fruitful relationship between government and economy everyone will admit who accepts the necessity for both these instruments. Economy depends upon government for the maintenance of peace, for defense from foreign and domestic aggressors, for the protection of property, for the protection of traders at home and abroad, and for the enforcement of contracts. Government lies under a similar necessity of economy in its operations that the rest of us do if it would be effective in providing services to the citizenry.

These are not at issue in this work. They have only been stated to make it clear to all and sundry that there are necessary and fruitful relationships between government and economy. What is at issue is government *intervention* in the *private* efforts at *economy* by individuals and voluntary groups. The issue may be put in two ways. *Can* government intervene so as to improve the lot of people generally, and particularly of the poor? And, *should* government intervene in order to improve the lot of people generally, and particularly that of the poor? The first is a question phrased in expedient terms, the second in ethical ones. The answers to these questions have a great deal to do with what the poor may do to improve their own lot, as we shall see.

This work has attempted, mainly, to provide an answer for the expedient question. It has brought the weight of historical evidence to bear on the question to show that government interventions cannot help the poor; that, on the contrary, the poor have been the victims of many of them. Now, if government intervention cannot help the poor, that should make the ethical question moot. It can hardly be argued that though government cannot help the poor in this wise that it should nevertheless try to do so. This would amount to an ethical imperative to harm the poor.

The matter has not, however, been that completely settled by the appeal to the historical record. At best, the record of the past can only show that the poor have not been helped but harmed. If there are interventions yet untried, or those for which experience is too limited, there would remain the possibility that programs might yet be devised, or have recently been conceived, that would have the desired effect. The historical record cannot be consulted for the effects of things that have not been done, though it may well shed light on the probabilities of their success, if they are similar in kind to what has been done. This work has not been executed in an historical vacuum, however. It has proceeded from the analysis of the nature of things. By such analysis, it is quite often possible to predict what the consequences of a particular line of action will be before it has been tried. It is this approach that gives ultimate support to the conclusion that government intervention cannot help the poor generally, that force is the wrong instrument to produce economy. Before going into this farther, however, it will be helpful to look into the ethical question.

The ethical question may be restated to give it as much vitality as possible. Should government intervene in the economy if by so doing it could help the poor? To answer this question, we need to have in mind in what way the proper function of government may be ethical. The Founders of these United States declared, in effect, that it is the function of government to establish justice. Since reformers have usually advanced their programs by claiming that they were to bring about social justice, it will be sufficient to explore the ethical question by way of government and justice in relation to economy.

The most obvious thing we know about justice is that it is blind. Representations of justice show it blindfolded, and it is a matter of long-standing prescription that it should be. Justice—that ideal of it that has guided men in Western Civilization—cannot see. It cannot see whether those who come before it are black or white, rich or poor, farmers or industrial workers, old or young, men whose hearts have generally been pure or are as black as the Ace of Spades. Justice is concerned with but one thing: *To give each man his due.* To put it in economic terms, justice is concerned with seeing that each man gets what is his. To this end, justice must attend to the character (or nature) of acts and transactions, ignoring all else.

What is a man's due, or what is his? A man is due what has been promised him, and that is his which he has made for himself or has acquired from others by purchase or gift. In determining any question of ownership, justice has been done when it has been decided who made the object in question and whose it is, otherwise, by transfer from the original owner, and restitution has been made. There can be, properly speaking, no question of race, color, previous condition of servitude, class, or other features which distinguish one man or group from another. These are irrelevant. (This is not to say that in some places at certain times positive law may not establish such distinctions. I speak of justice here, not of law.)

Justice holds, roughly speaking, that he who does not work shall starve. He who does not earn his keep shall be deprived. Justice will not allow the excuse that a man was hungry, that his family was hungry, that he had been ill, or that for any other reason he may appropriate the property of another. The rules are firm and inflexible. A people who attempt to establish justice have undertaken a formidable task.

Justice is blind; Mercy can see. Mercy can see the helplessness of children, the plight of the aged, the ravages of disease, the suffering from deprivation, the discrimination because of color, the hard work that has not been rewarded with produce, the hard luck with which some are afflicted, the lame, the halt, and the blind. Mercy can distinguish between the deserving and undeserving of pity and of charity. Justice knows no such categories.

The dispensing of justice and mercy are incompatible functions when exercised by the same person or body at the same time. The question of whether justice or mercy shall be extended is an either-or proposition in every particular instance. If government does justice, it must deny mercy; if it is merciful, it will at the same time work injustice. This is so for government because force may be properly used to do justice, but mercy must be freely—not forcibly—offered else there will be injustice. Specifically, it is proper to use force to see that a man gets what is his. But mercy involves conveying upon a man that which is not his by right, that which he has not earned, that which is not his due, but which someone out of pity or charity wills that he shall have. For government to extend mercy in this manner means that it must take from someone who has and give to someone who had it not In short, when government extends mercy it produces injustice.[1]

Governments make a stab in America today at performing both functions of establishing justice and extending mercy. To attempt to do both, a strange reversal has been made. Justice has had the blinders removed, and Mercy has been blindfolded. To state the matter bluntly, courts have long since taken to admitting all sorts of evidence about the environment, social conditions, economic backgrounds, and so forth

---

[1] There is, of course, a very limited and precise variety of mercy which those who govern can, and traditionally have dispensed without working injustice. When a Governor exercises it, it is known as the prerogative of mercy. He exercises this privilege when he commutes the sentence of a convicted criminal and, perchance, restores his civil rights. This is a restoration to a man of what was once his, and does not involve taking something from someone else.

of defendants before them. Such evidence when compiled is known as a "social brief," and its successful introduction in American jurisprudence is credited to Louis D. Brandeis. In this manner, the blinders have been removed from Justice. On the other hand, social welfare advocates have worked to remove "means tests" from the determination of who receives welfare payments. Indeed, some of those in the city government of Newburgh, New York found themselves pilloried in national publications some years ago when they proposed that all able-bodied recipients of welfare should be put to work by the city. The tendency of these things is to blindfold Mercy, to extend it without discriminating between the deserving and undeserving. There is a kind of perverse logic in this. Welfarists do not call what they do mercy or charity; they prefer the rubric social justice. They attempt to merge Justice and Mercy by dissolving them in sentimental goo. Mercy is blinded by the goo, and Justice can see. In consequence, injustice becomes pervasive, and merciless government preys upon the citizenry in the name of Justice.

We have already examined the consequences of this confusion in this work. Programs that were supposed to aid the poor have harmed them instead. Justice with eyes wide open has discriminated among the citizenry, has selected farmers for special ministrations, has looked with favor upon labor unions, has bestowed privileges upon some businesses, has gone with its bag of goodies into the hearts of the cities. Mercy blinded has taken from the poor to give to the rich, has taxed the generality of people to pay subsidies to wealthy farmers, has driven workers away from the gates, has priced the poor, the unskilled, the disabled, out of the labor market, has driven small businesses to the wall, and has forced the urban poor from their habitations to make room for multilane highways and high-rise apartments.

Cruelest and most deceptive of all, government has raised false hopes and expectations of the good which it claims can be done by its methods. The employment of force was supposed to benefit the poor; Mercy could take up guns, so the program implied. Some of the poor have taken the message to heart. They have taken up weapons to improve their own well-being. The Battle in the Streets is the dramatic result. In consequence, the poor are poorer; they have only preyed upon one another.

What was inexpedient turned out to be also unethical. To turn it around, and get first things first, the unethical is also inexpedient. It is unjust to take from the poor to give to the rich. It is equally unjust to take from the rich to give to the poor. But even if it were just to take from the rich to give to the poor, governments do not operate in that fashion. They take from all producers, rich and poor alike, to give to non-producers, at best. Nor can it be otherwise. The resources of the wealthy would soon be exhausted, if some devices could be found to appropriate these alone. In that case, we should all be impoverished, however, for the distributed wealth would be used to vie for the decreasing supply of goods that would result from the decline of investment.

There is no hope for the poor from government intervention. The reason is that government is not the right instrument for increasing wealth. The results of the massive governmental programs thus far illustrate the fallacy. Large numbers of the poor have been made perpetually unproductive, dependent upon government, and perennially poor. To pay for this, the productive have been reduced to servility to government by way of taxation and regulation, and those who would rise by their own efforts have had the way made harder.

Nor is this failure due simply to corruption, malfeasance, or even the tendency of men to pervert the programs to their own ends (the latter being not only a possibility but a virtual certainty). This work has generally steered clear of tales of corruption. Readers might have been titillated by accounts of the doings of Billy Sol Estes, Jimmy Hoffa, or Bobby Baker, to name a few. Sargent Shriver provides an all-too-human goat for the doings of the Office of Economic Opportunity.

The political shenanigans of petty local politicians grasping for War on Poverty funds would no doubt make interesting reading. But to focus on these would be to suggest that the programs have failed because of incidental corruption. It would leave the way open to hope that with better administration and some improvements the programs would work. There is no reason to suppose that this is the case.

The programs have failed because they misconstrue the nature of government and economy. They have attempted to employ force to produce economic results. Men cannot be forced to be economical; yet when left to their own devices, men *will* be economical. Economy results from *willing* effort, from *willing* innovation, from *willing* exchange, from *free* decisions, and from *voluntary* combinations. Government action tends to produce rigidity, to keep things the way they are, to make it much more difficult for the poor to improve their lot. It raises costs, raises prices, produces surpluses—goods that will not be bought at the prices it decrees—, causes unemployment, reduces competition, removes opportunities, and results in shortages, depending upon how it is employed. The poor cannot benefit from all this because they need economy.

The war upon the poor will be ended when the numerous interventions are ended. This is of a piece with what is needed for the reconstruction. Governments must be restricted to their proper sphere in order that the poor, as well as everyone else, may be freed to improve their own condition, if that is their desire. To suppose that the poor would be clever enough and have the perseverance to manipulate government to their advantage is to suppose something contrary to what has ever been or is every likely to be, in any case. If the poor were that clever and persistent they would not remain poor for long in any conditions. Government intervention has ever been a device to give additional advantages to those who already have power and wealth. It was an illusion that it could be otherwise. The fact that wealthy men predominate as national political figures today and advance these strange welfarist notions—such figures as the Kennedys, the Roosevelts, the Rockefellers, and so on—should have alerted us to the power quest that is involved.

The hope of the poor lies with freedom. The politics of expansive government is not for the poor. Politics is the arena of influence peddlers, of batteries of lawyers, of five-per-centers, of special tax exemptions for oil millionaires, of cost-plus contracts, of those who have the inside track, of demagogues who feather their nests at public expense, of the powers that be. The poor have neither the resources, the background and education, nor the time to spend on such quests. They cannot compete in this arena; at best, they will only get some of the crumbs that fall from the table; at worst, they will have television sets with which to view the political spectacles put on with their money.

The hope of the poor lies with restricted and limited government. It is indeed a work of reconstruction to regain this condition. Limited government and free men was once the great promise of American life. The Founders of these United States constructed a government of separated and balanced powers so that hungry politicians might vie for power against one another rather than the populace. They limited governments and specified their powers so that men might compete in an arena of freedom rather than contest for political spoils, so that industrious men might have the fruits of their labor, and so that the indolent might be spurred to labor by their needs. And they perceived that it was better for all that charity proceed from those who were concerned than that the poor receive government favors exacted from the industrious by power-seeking politicians.

The Jacksonians, in the mid-nineteenth century, demonstrated this insight at the height of its fulfillment. Andrew Jackson was a most successful politician, and many of those who labored in his shadow were also. Jackson had great appeal for the poor farmer and the city worker. He attacked privilege and vested power, but he did not offer special favors to his followers. In a typical pronouncement, he said:

> ... In the full enjoyment of the gifts of heaven and the fruits of superior industry, economy, and virtue, every man is equally entitled to protection by law; but when the laws undertake to add to these natural and just advantages artificial distinctions, to grant titles, gratuities, and exclusive privileges, to make the rich richer, and the potent more powerful, the humble members of society ... who have neither the time nor the means of securing like favors to themselves, have a right to complain of the injustice of their Government.[2]

Martin Van Buren, the man whom Jackson picked to succeed him in the Presidency, had this to say when he was being pressed to propose some interference with the economy:

> All communities are apt to look to government for too much. . . . The framers of our excellent Constitution and the people who approved it with calm and sagacious deliberation acted at the time on sounder principle. They wisely judged that the less government interferes with private pursuits the better for the general prosperity. It is not its legitimate object to make men rich or to repair by direct grants of money or legislation in favor of particular pursuits, losses not incurred in the public service. This would be substantially to use the property of some for the benefit of others. But its real duty—that duty the performance of which makes a good government the most precious of human blessings—is to enact and enforce a system of general laws, commensurate with, but not exceeding, the objects of its establishment, and to leave every citizen and every interest to reap under its benign protection the rewards of virtue, industry, and prudence.[3]

William Leggett, a more obscure Jacksonian, makes a similar point:

[2] Quoted in Robert J. Harris, *The Quest for Equality* (Baton Rouge: Louisiana University Press, 1960), p. 17.

[3] Henry S. Commager, ed., *Living Ideas in America* (New York: Harper, 1951), pp. 323-24.

As a general rule, the prosperity of rational men depends upon themselves. Their talents and their virtues shape their fortunes. They are therefore the best judges of their own affairs and should be permitted to seek their own happiness in their own way, untrammeled by the capricious interference of legislative bungling, so long as they do not violate the equal rights of others nor transgress the general laws for the security of person and property.[4]

The Jacksonians are chosen as particularly appropriate spokesmen for these views because they made much of their appeal to the poor. They were saying that the hope for the poor lies in not being beset by government, in its observing its appropriate limitations, and in their using their liberty for their own ends.

Reconstruction which will be beneficial for the poor, then, depends upon restoring to government that limited role for which it is suited by nature to perform, and for men in their private capacities to practice economy. The hope for the poor, especially, lies in the exercise of economy, in becoming more productive, in helping themselves.

This is not new advice, of course. In the nineteenth century this view was widely held. Samuel Smiles, a nineteenth century Englishman and practical philosopher, reduced the doctrine of self-help to a number of homilies, which he buttressed with numerous references to men's lives. Though his examples are out of date, his maxims are as appropriate today as when they were first written.

> We often hear the cry raised, "Will nobody help us?" It is a spiritless, hopeless cry. It is sometimes a cry of revolting meanness, especially when it issues from those who, with a little self-denial, sobriety, and thrift, might easily help themselves.
> . . . The mob orators, who gather "the millions" about them, are very wide of the mark, when, instead of seeking to train their crowds of hearers to habits of frugality, temper-

---

[4] Joseph L. Blau, ed., *Social Theories of Jacksonian Democracy* (New York: Liberal Arts Press, 1954), p. 76.

ance, and self-culture, they encourage them to keep up the cry, "Will nobody help us?"

The cry sickens the soul. It shows gross ignorance of the first elements of personal welfare. Help is in men themselves. They were born to help and elevate themselves. They must work out their own salvation. The poorest men have done it; why should not every man do it?[5]

Smiles continues in the same vein elsewhere:

"Heaven helps those who help themselves" is a well tried maxim, embodying in a small compass the results of vast human experience. The spirit of self-help is the root of all genuine growth in the individual; and, exhibited in the lives of many, it constitutes the true source of national vigor and strength. Help from without is often enfeebling in its effects, but help from within invariably invigorates. Whatever is done *for* men or classes, to a certain extent takes away the stimulus and necessity of doing for themselves; and where men are subjected to over-guidance and over-government, the inevitable tendency is to render them comparatively helpless.

Even the best institutions can give a man no active help. Perhaps the most they can do is, to leave him free to develop himself and improve his individual condition. But in all times men have been prone to believe that their happiness and well-being were to be secured by means of institutions rather than by their own conduct. Hence the value of legislation as an agent in human advancement has usually been much overestimated. . . . Moreover, it is every day becoming more clearly understood, that the function of Government is negative and restrictive, rather than positive and active; being resolvable principally into protection—protection of life, liberty, and property. Laws, wisely administered, will secure men in the enjoyment of the fruits of their labor, whether of mind or body, at a comparatively small personal sacrifice; but no laws, however stringent, can make the idle industrious, the shiftless provident, or the drunken sober. Such reforms can only be effected by means of individual

[5] Samuel Smiles, *Thrift* (Chicago: Bedfords, Clarke, and Co., 1879), pp. 34-35.

action, economy, and self-denial; by better habits, rather than by greater rights.[6]

Smiles was, of course, an advocate of economy:

> To secure independence, the practice of economy is all that is necessary. Economy requires neither superior courage nor eminent virtue; it is satisfied with ordinary energy, and the capacity of average minds. Economy, at bottom, is but the spirit of order applied in the administration of domestic affairs: it means management, regularity, prudence, and the avoidance of waste. . . .
>
> Economy also means the power of resisting present gratification for the purpose of securing a future good, and in this light it represents the ascendancy of reason over the animal instincts. . . . Economy may be styled the daughter of Prudence, the sister of Temperance, and the mother of Liberty. It is evidently conservative—conservative of character, of domestic happiness, and social well-being. It is, in short, the exhibition of self-help in one of its best forms.[7]

But can the poor help themselves? Can they by the practice of economy raise themselves from the condition of poverty? The answer would appear to be in the affirmative. History is studded with examples of men who have risen from the most abject poverty even to riches. Andrew Carnegie started out his working career as a bobbin boy at $1.25 a week. Of course, not every poor boy is going to equal such a feat as his. But the number is legion who have been able through their efforts to achieve a modest competence. Any man who does not live in surroundings of abject poverty may discover examples by inquiring a little into the background of his neighbors.

Before accepting the question as answered, however, let us peer once again into the dismal world of the mind of the

[6] Samuel Smiles, *Self-Help* (New York: Allison, no date, rev. ed.), pp. 21-22.
[7] *Ibid.*, p. 327.

reformer. Interventionists have not generally questioned that there was once a time when the poor might by their own efforts improve their condition. On the contrary, they are given to saying that the nineteenth century was such a time. When Samuel Smiles wrote, his words may have contained some truth, so they are apt to hold. But things have changed since then, they say. The era of opportunity, at least so far as the bulk of the poor are concerned, has long since ended. Historian Arthur Link describes in the following passage the attitude of Franklin D. Roosevelt and those around him toward the opportunities for men to help themselves. He says:

> . . . To begin with, Roosevelt and his advisers accepted the then popular view that the American economy had reached a stage of full maturity, that the closing of the agricultural frontier, the restriction of immigration, and the sharp decline in the birth rate had removed the self-generating mechanisms from the economy. The age of expansion and confidence, when businessmen invested in the future and expanded the nation's economic frontiers, was allegedly over.[8]

The touchstone of this view was the notion that when the lands of the West had been taken up—the End of the Frontier thesis—the era of opportunity had ended. This thesis was joined with the one that large trusts had formed monopolies, and that there was little chance for newcomers in the field. The hope of the poor lay with collective action, fostered by the government, according to this view.

It is difficult to cope with nonsense seriously. And that is what this view is—nonsense—, regardless of how widely it is or has been held. Neither the so-called end of the agricultural frontier nor the development of corporations foreclosed opportunities in general, nor is there evidence or reason to suppose that it became more difficult for the poor to get ahead because of either of them. Indeed, the chances are probably

[8] Link, *op. cit.*, p. 388.

immensely greater that one will succeed by working for a great corporation in the twentieth century than that his counterpart could have done so by claiming Western lands in the nineteenth century. Opportunity has to do with circumstances, it is true, but only in the sense that the areas of opportunity change from generation to generation. Opportunity is a matter of seeing some human need or want and finding ways to fill it effectively. The only way to end it is to end human wants or forbid the satisfaction of them.

Even freshmen in college are often able to see the fallacy in the notion of the end of opportunity with the end of the frontier. I have sometimes thought to pose the question to a class of whether they think opportunities for their succeeding today are better than they were in an earlier America, or worse—whether it will be easier for them or harder. Those who have expressed themselves have invariably done so to the effect that it is easier today.

This is opinion only, but there is some rather impressive evidence available to show that men can start poor and become wealthy today, just as they could in the nineteenth century. *Time* magazine made an interesting survey of the millionaire situation in America recently, and included in it some profiles of men who had risen to wealth in the years just past. They noted that the "number of U. S. millionaires . . . has swelled from 40,000 in 1958 to nearly 100,000 at present."[9] The stories of some of these men parallel the rags-to-riches tales of the nineteenth century. For example, "Arthur Julius Decio started in the garage behind his childhood home in Elkhart [Indiana], which is next to—and on the wrong side of—the New York Central Railroad tracks. His father, an Italian immigrant grocer sank some savings into mobile homes in 1951, but did poorly and begged son Art to try either to rescue or liquidate the small company. Decio, then a steel salesman, put in $3,200 of his own, recruited three friends and started to work." At the age of 35 in 1965, Decio

[9] "Millionaires," *Time* (December 3, 1965), p. 88.

was president of Skyline Homes "the industry's biggest producer," and "is worth just over $5,000,000." Another interesting example is a man named Charles Bludhorn who came to Manhattan from Europe at the age of 16. (This was during World War II.) He "went to work as a $15-a-week clerk in a cotton brokerage house. . . . At 23, he invested $3,000 and started his own export-import business in a small Manhattan office." At 39, Bludhorn was chairman of Gulf and Western Industries, and was "worth more than $15 million."[10] Other examples could be adduced, but these should show the possibilities that still exist.

That there are opportunities at the more mundane level for those who will work is illustrated daily in the Want Ad sections of city newspapers. The following are a few selected advertisements taken from the Want Ad section of such a paper on a weekday.

> Men (10) —Full and part time watchman work. . . . Uniforms furnished; $70 weekly. . . .
> Telephone contact work in fiberglass company. Experience not necessary. If you have a good telephone voice we will train you to contact customers by telephone. Hrs., 12:30-9:00 p.m. Salary, $80 per wk. to start, $110 after 6 wks. . . .
> MAIL CLERK. No experience necessary. High school grad. Large downtown co. Opportunity for advancement. Salary $300. . . .
> Plumber-Plumbers helpers and plumbers apprentice. Must be able to drive truck. . . .[11]

There are many, many other such advertisements in that paper for one day, though they frequently do require skill and experience.

The hope of the poor, I have said, lies with economy. If they would prosper, they will find it in working, in saving, in prudent investment, in innovation, in seeking out oppor-

[10] *Ibid.*, p. 89.
[11] Pittsburgh *Press* (August 30, 1967), p. 76.

tunities, in applying their energies to their own betterment. That there are opportunities for those who are willing to work in America today is clear from the evidence.

But the situation is as nothing compared to what it might be. Those who speak of the diminution of opportunities in America in the twentieth century are right, in a sense. But this diminution had little, if anything, to do with the End of the Frontier or the Rise of Corporations. It has been the product of government intervention, of farming made unprofitable by free land and restrictions, of work made more difficult to obtain by labor union activities and government proscription, of almost innumerable obstacles thrown in the way of those who would go into business on their own, of houses not built and goods not produced and urban dwellers buffeted by government involvement and regulation. Untold opportunities *have* been foreclosed by government intervention, and the way of the poor has been made much harder than it would have been.

American ingenuity has done much to overcome the baneful effects of intervention. Enterprisers have sought out areas for development and means of development that were not yet denied to them. Innovators have supplied the technology which would enable many men to be employed even at high union rates or wages required by law. But the intervention has been too great and overbearing at some times and in certain areas to have been overcome. For most of the 1930's, government action came fast and was too pervasive to be counteracted sufficiently well to restore a semblance of prosperity. The intervention in agriculture and affecting agriculture has been so massive that there have been millions of farm victims. The unskilled, the inexperienced, the young, the aged, the Negroes, the farm workers, do not find nearly so much opportunity as they might. American ingenuity has not yet found satisfactory ways to ameliorate the condition of many of the poor in the large cities by offsetting the vast assortment of government interferences. The poor are, as has been abundantly shown, the ones least able to cope with the situation created by the interference.

The hope of the poor lies not only in their own efforts, then, but in the removal of the impediments to enterprise and prosperity. No one should have to struggle against such odds as the government programs put in the way of material success. Surely, the poor should not. Their hope lies in lower prices, in higher *real* wages, in freedom of enterprise to innovate and build, in loosing the ingenuity of private enterprise (so much of which is now devoted to circumventing government programs) to meet their needs and wants. In short, if government would get off the backs of the poor, there would be every reason to suppose that many, or most, of those who desire to improve their lot could and would do so. Millions of jobs would open up; thousands of companies of all sizes would come into being, bringing new products and services for the benefit of all; "pockets of poverty" would be apt to get so much new industry that before long real wages there would approximate those elsewhere; juvenile delinquents would, in many instances, become productive workers; the tasks of law enforcement would be greatly diminished; an integrated society would emerge, integrated because its members would be serving one another, not organized against one another.

Let us recapitulate some of the essential points about poverty. The restriction of government to its proper sphere, or even a reasonable facsimile thereof, would do much to enable men to help themselves. It would not produce utopia; no system can or will. There would be great disparity of incomes, of course, depending upon the productivity and service involved, and the fickle tastes of the public. Poverty would not be likely to disappear. There are those who, in the best of circumstances, will not earn enough to make them affluent. There are those absolutely incapacitated to produce; there would remain the sick, the lame, the halt. There would no doubt be those who would prefer considerable leisure to strenuous work; these would be likely to remain poor. Others, due to failure of some enterprise would be at least temporarily poor.

It is not the purpose of this writer to make moral judgments about the condition of poverty. He does not view it either as a reproach to the society in which it exists or a sign of moral inferiority for those in that estate. Great teachers of the past have been by no means united in abhoring poverty or in praising wealth. If they are free to do so, men may choose where to exert their energies; if they do so to improve their material lot, whatever the rewards or punishments for that may be, they should surely receive them.

Men of good will may agree, however, that those who cannot help themselves are the proper objects of concern of those who can. It is the part of pity, charity, mercy, to render aid to such in their need. However, it does not follow that government is the proper instrument to provide such aid. On the contrary, government action is flawed for this purpose because it is accomplished by force rather than by free will. Those who administer it are actuated by the demands of political expediency rather than out of concern for those in need. (If a man gives of what is his, that is sufficient evidence of concern so far as men may judge. If he gives what is taken from others, his motives are necessarily suspect.) And, government aid is derived from taxes, some portion of which must inevitably be levied upon the poor who need help as badly or almost as badly as those to be aided. Mercy is properly the prerogative of moral individuals, many of whom have ever shown themselves willing to help those in need when they have been left free to do so. The wealthy exert great energy to keep what is theirs where taxes are involved. They have sometimes exerted as much or greater energy in works of charity when they have been left free to do so.

The most pressing problem, however, is to remove the government restraints, restrictions, interferences, regulations, proscriptions, obstacles, and impediments which make it so difficult for those who otherwise could to help themselves. The poor will be with us always, but their lot should not be made harder by making war on them. Life is a struggle at best, but there is no reason why those for whom this is especially true should have to struggle against their government. Offenses must needs come, Jesus said, but woe to him from whom they come. For a whole people to give offense to the weak and struggling is a thing unpleasant to contemplate. This writer believes, in charity, that Americans have not understood—that if they had, they would not have willed it so. To do wrong unknowingly is forgivable; to conspire in evil revealed is a perilous thing. Thomas Jefferson said, regarding the existence of slavery in his time:

> Indeed I tremble for my country when I reflect that God is just, that His justice cannot sleep forever. . . .

The war on the poor is equally reprehensible. We, as Americans, may well tremble before a just God for what we are doing.

But the last words of this work should not be despair but hope. There is hope for the poor. There is hope for them in the restoration of liberty and their return to useful service, to bringing forth crops from the soil, to making and purveying goods, to providing much needed services. When the disaffected poor learn again to serve rather than to bribe, their labors will result in providing healing ministrations to society.

Let this work show, too, that it is not only interventionists who are concerned with the poor. Certainly, those who entertain grave doubts about the beneficence of government programs may at the same time be deeply concerned about the poor. That parent who does everything for his child does not love more than others; he is only more indulgent. He is actually denying the child experiences that would lead to much needed progress toward being able to look after himself. Love not only gives generously when the occasion warrants but also withholds wisely for the good of another. The greatest gift that America can bestow upon the poor is that liberty by which they may receive the fruits of their toil. The promise of American life, as Thomas Jefferson put it in 1801, is "a wise and frugal Government, which . . . shall not take from the mouth of labor the bread it has earned."